TURNING
THE TIDE

TURNING
THE TIDE

The University of Alabama in the 1960s

EARL H. TILFORD

THE UNIVERSITY OF ALABAMA PRESS
Tuscaloosa

The University of Alabama Press
Tuscaloosa, Alabama 35487-0380
uapress.ua.edu

Hardcover edition published 2014.
Paperback edition published 2016.
eBook edition published 2014.

Inquiries about reproducing material from this work should be addressed to the University of Alabama Press.

Typeface: Caslon, Trajan, and Helvetica

Manufactured in the United States of America
Cover photograph: Silent antiwar vigil on steps of Alabama Union held for fifteen minutes each Friday at noon starting in March 1968; courtesy of the W. S. Hoole Special Collections, University of Alabama Libraries
Cover design: Gary Gore

∞
The paper on which this book is printed meets the minimum requirements of American National Standard for Information Science–Permanence of Paper for Printed Library Materials, ANSI Z39.48-1984.

Paperback ISBN: 978-0-8173-5858-7

A previous edition of this book has been catalogued by the Library of Congress as follows:

Library of Congress Cataloging-in-Publication Data

Tilford, Earl H.
   Turning the tide : the University of Alabama in the 1960s / Earl H. Tilford.
      pages cm
   Summary: "Turning the Tide is an institutional and cultural history of a dramatic decade of change at the University of Alabama set against the backdrop of desegregation, the continuing civil rights struggle, and the growing antiwar movement"— Provided by publisher.
   Includes bibliographical references and index.
   ISBN 978-0-8173-1814-7 (trade cloth) — ISBN 978-0-8173-8725-9 (e book)
   1. University of Alabama—History—20th century. 2. College integration—Alabama—History 20th century. 3. Civil rights movements—Alabama—History—20th century. 4. African Americans—Civil rights—Alabama—History—20th century. I. Title.
   LD73.T55 2014
   378.009761—dc23
                                                                    2013026912

In Memory of Tom Hall, Class of 1968

Tom rolled with the tide.

Contents

Photographs follow pages 69 and 120.

Foreword

Earl Tilford's carefully researched book leads me easily to the conclusion that 1963–70 is the most important period in the University of Alabama's history. True, the years immediately following the Civil War were challenging, even at times seemingly hopeless to the university that, with two buildings, a small armory, and the President's Mansion excepted, was burned to the ground. The World War II years, and those immediately following, were also difficult to manage. During the war, male students were hard to find. Then there was an onslaught of them. Nothing, however, compares to the June 1963 desegregation of the university and the enormous cultural changes resulting from the Vietnam War.

I was a student at the university from September 1963 until I graduated law school in May 1969. My experiences at the university in many ways mirrored those of my classmates. Neither of my parents were high school graduates. After the Second World War, my father used the GI Bill to complete the machinists apprentice program at Pensacola Naval Air Station. Following an apprenticeship, he returned to my parents' home in Jefferson County where he worked first at US Pipe and then at the American Cast Iron and Pipe Company. I grew up in the working-class neighborhood of Gardendale.

I was one of the few high school graduates in my family to attend college. When I departed home for the University of Alabama, I did so with all that I possessed in two cardboard boxes and a suitcase. My college years were not only great fun but exposed me to the world in ways I had not imagined.

I still recall several seminal events and activities. I heard Katherine Ann Porter lecture at Morgan Hall and was shocked that she dressed in a full-length evening gown and that Professor Thomas Roundtree, who introduced her, wore a tuxedo. I don't remember a thing she said. I was in Morgan Auditorium to hear Eudora Welty read, first, her acceptance speech at the National

Book Awards luncheon earlier that year, and then one of her best-known short stories. Unlike Katherine Ann Porter, I remember much of what Welty said. I can still hear her magnificent reading voice.

I also recall the conference on Vietnam described in chapter 2. Prior to the three senators' speeches, I sat at the dinner table next to Senator Frank Church and across from Senator Ernest Gruening. I also saw "Waiting for Godot," as described in this book. I marveled at the acting skills of Bob Penny, who remains a friend to this day.

As a member of the university's debate team, I traveled over much of the United States. My debate partner, Boots Gale, and I came very close to winning a national championship, finishing third at the National Debate Tournament.

My story is like that of thousands of other working-class kids who experienced their college years at the University of Alabama . . . except mine is also different. In 1963, I was a senior at Phillips High School in Birmingham, Alabama. I experienced first hand the civil rights struggles of that year. My experience was not unlike that of African Americans at my age, except I did not go to jail. I was simply frightened by what was happening around me. Most of us white residents of Birmingham were not Klansmen or even inclined toward violence. But we were scared.

In the late winter of 1965, during my sophomore year, I watched events in Selma unfold on television and read about them in the newspapers. I was not scared. Rather, I was embarrassed and angry. By 1967, I had seen and read enough about the Vietnam War to conclude that it was a disastrous mistake. In 1968, while in my second year of law school, I was called for a preinduction physical. Despite being blind in one eye, I was found eligible for military service. That decision was reversed on appeal and I was reclassified as 4-F. By then I had become an antiwar activist and over the next year attended several national meetings of students opposed to the war.

In May 1969, I graduated from the Alabama School of Law. The following day, I married Carol Self. I went to work for the Selma Inter-Religious Project, a civil rights organization sponsored chiefly by the Episcopal Church in the United States. By May 1970, I was working as the project's staff counselor.

Reading Tilford's description of events during this seven-year period prompted an epiphany, albeit minor compared to some epiphanies in history. I realized that it was foolish of me to continue to hold, even espouse, views I formed while a student over forty years ago. I want to revisit some of those views.

President Frank A. Rose and I had a contentious relationship. I viewed him as too slick, too eager to compromise, too concerned about the political reaction to events on campus, and condescending in private meetings. After reading *Turning the Tide*, I now realize that Frank Rose was unquestionably the greatest president in the history of the University of Alabama. Tilford's casting of him is extraordinary. True, the years after the Civil War must have been daunting to all involved with rebuilding the university, but the truth is that there was not much to be replaced. Alabama was a small military school serving the rich sons of plantation owners who brought their personal slaves with them to Tuscaloosa. Frank Rose did not rebuild the university after its destruction—but rebuild it he did.

It was George "Mike" Denny who brought the University of Alabama into the twentieth century, but only the early part of the century. He did not desegregate the place; the idea probably never crossed his mind. Frank Rose did and he did it with style and grace, and most importantly, without getting anyone hurt. Furthermore, he changed the perception in Alabama of what a university president looked and talked like. He was not a scholar called from the library stacks. Rather, he was young, smart, good looking, and, above all, tough.

Frank Rose had the good sense to surround himself with like-minded people like J. Jefferson Bennett and to listen to people like Dean of Men John L. Blackburn and Dean of Women Sarah M. Healy. They were already on board when Rose took the helm in 1958 and they were no-nonsense, tough talking, and decisive. Blackburn was my mentor, giving me two jobs to get through law school and protecting me during difficult times in 1969.

I did not know Jeff Bennett at the time, but after he retired as vice-chancellor of the University of the South (Sewanee), he returned to Tuscaloosa for a few years. During that time, he joined a State Bar Task Force I chaired and we rode together to meetings in Montgomery several times. We became friends and discovered that we had much in common politically and, as active Episcopalians, religiously. Jeff is due much of the credit for Rose's success. Jeff always had Rose's back, and he not only did the heavy lifting, but more costly to him personally, he delivered a lot of unwanted messages to powerful people. As depicted in the following pages, those people took their revenge.

I was pleased to read Tilford's descriptions of speeches and statements made by Ralph Knowles. His portrayal of Ralph correctly reflects his courage and integrity; traits he still has in abundance today.

Finally, I have rethought my conclusions about F. David Mathews, Rose's successor. I did not know, until I read *Turning the Tide*, that Mathews had been a student at Alabama in February 1956 during the first attempt at desegregation that almost resulted in the lynching of Autherine Lucy. I understand better his concern for safety on campus in May 1970, the events that form the culmination point of this book. In 1956, Mathews had witnessed, or heard about, Robert "Dynamite Bob" Chambliss and other Klansmen beating Reverend Emmet Gribbin. He also witnessed, or heard about, the mob that attacked Sarah Healy, Jeff Bennett, and Autherine Lucy.

Understanding, however, is not agreement. I still believe Mathews overreacted in May 1970. At that time he was dealing not with Dynamite Bob and the Ku Klux Klan. Rather, he was dealing with a bunch of idealistic nineteen- and twenty-year-olds who did not harm the person of anyone and did no violence to property, with the exception of Charlie Grimm, as covered in chapter 9 of this volume. I believe Mathews acted as he did because of what was happening—or had happened—on other campuses. The killing of four students at Kent State must have been a shock to him and all university presidents. That said, I believe that his decision to bring in the Alabama State Troopers resulted in violence by the Tuscaloosa Police Department (TPD) and led to the arrests of more than two hundred students, not one of whom was ever convicted of any crime associated with those "Days of Rage" in May 1970.

A parting word is in order concerning the behavior of the TPD during those events. The TPD at that time was, for the most part, an unprofessional, poorly trained, and poorly managed police force. Tilford refers to the phony charges of "FOPO" or failure to obey a police officer. Ralph Knowles and I later discovered that the TPD routinely charged people with "FOPO" or "D&S," the latter meaning "dangerous and suspicious." Neither charge was an offense under either the Alabama Criminal Code or the Tuscaloosa City Code. These were fictional or "made-up" charges that allowed officers to haul people off to jail for long enough to become, in the minds of the police, less dangerous, less suspicious, and, above all, more willing to obey.

The most disturbing thing about the May 1970 attack by the TPD on unarmed students—and quite often uninvolved bystanders—was that it was clearly planned. It was no coincidence that fifty police officers left their department without name tags and with black tape over their badge numbers. At a minimum, the shift commander was in on it. The chief had to have been involved as well. At the time, Tuscaloosa had a commission form of governance involving three men, one being the commissioner of public safety with exclusive supervisory authority over the police and fire departments. It is inconceivable to me that this commissioner did not know of the planned attacks in advance.

Turning the Tide is a must read for anyone who attended the University of Alabama from the early 1960s through the mid-1970s. Students from 1975 to the present inherited an institution that is—in large part—a product of the "turning" detailed in the following pages. In fact, anyone who ever attended the University of Alabama should be proud to read the way their school, and its students, handled the enormous challenges of this extraordinarily dynamic period.

Jack Drake

Preface

On June 11, 1963, the enrollment of Vivian J. Malone and James A. Hood ended 132 years of segregation at the University of Alabama, the state's first public university. In September 1964, I enrolled as a freshman. A large billboard greeted my parents and me as we drove into town. It read, "Welcome to Tuscaloosa: Home of the Ku Klux Klan." The billboard featured a Klansman holding a fiery cross, sitting atop a rearing horse.

When I entered the university it was best known for winning football teams. Under legendary coach Paul W. Bryant, the Crimson Tide won the national championship in 1961, a feat it repeated during my freshman and sophomore years. The university also possessed a well-deserved reputation as one of the South's leading party schools.

Turning the Tide is about change. During the turbulent 1960s, when campuses erupted into confrontations between student dissidents and administrations unable or unwilling to deal with them effectively, a handful of student activists at the University of Alabama formed an alliance with President Frank A. Rose, his staff, and a small group of liberal professors. They were allied in a struggle with Governor George C. Wallace and a state legislature reflecting the worst aspects of racism in a state where the passage of federal civil rights laws in 1964 and 1965 did little to reduce segregation and a lot to inflame the fears and passions of many white Alabamians. That alliance held until the end of Frank Rose's presidency in 1969 when, for a variety of reasons, student dissent went in a more radical direction.

Even then, dissent at Alabama failed to attain the intensity extant on other campuses, even some in the Deep South. Alabama was unique in that dissent originated within the traditional student power structure formed by the top fraternities and manifested in the "Machine," a group that shaped and dominated not only campus politics but also the state's business, legal, and political communities. The "revolution" at the University of Alabama, like the French Revolution or the Russian Revolution, was conceived by the privileged and then, like those revolutions, degenerated into a wider and more radical manifestation.

The University of Alabama was unique in other ways. From its origins in 1831 it served the sons of Alabama's "bourbon" planter class. In 1860, in an effort to instill discipline into this class of unruly young men, the university became a military school, which it remained until the early twentieth century, a decade after admitting its first female students. In 1900, the student body numbered fewer than five hundred.

During the twentieth century the university benefited from extraordinary leadership, especially during the presidencies of George Hutcheson "Mike" Denny (1912 to 1936) and Frank A. Rose (1958 to 1969). President Denny increased enrollment from five hundred to almost five thousand. During the Great Depression, when many universities abandoned football, Denny used the sport to gain national attention. He also recruited students from outside Alabama, which proved financially lucrative.

Frank Rose built on the foundation laid by Mike Denny. Rose worked against extreme odds in a state where segregation's hold had only started to loosen by the end of his tenure in 1969. For some, especially the more idealistic faculty and the small cadre of student dissidents, the tide turned too slowly. Frank Rose, however, turned the tide despite winds that often buffeted his efforts. Of necessity he moved cautiously and picked his causes carefully, leading many to see him as "facile." Some dubbed him "Slick Tony." But in the end, amid turmoil and the constant threat of violence, Frank Rose charted a course away from the university's party school reputation and academically mediocre past. Rose urged students to "pursue excellence." While that pursuit often seemed more like an ambling stroll amid the campus's stately oaks and magnolias, the transition was filled with conflict that jeopardized its success.

This book was conceived during my days as an undergraduate. I nurtured the concept through four decades. In July 2008, thirty-nine years after leaving Tuscaloosa with a master's degree in history, I returned to explore and then write about the changes that went on while I was a student unable to understand or appreciate the sociocultural turmoil I sensed but did not fully grasp.

What I failed to see as a student, but what I have discovered in researching and writing this book, is the sense of "in loco familia" that pervaded the campus. This went beyond the concept that a college or university became substitute parents during the four years students spent between adolescence and adulthood. Frank Rose, and administrators like Jefferson Bennett, John Blackburn, and Sarah Healy, who were in place when he became president, along with men and women he brought on board, people like David Mathews, Joab Thomas, and E. Roger Sayers, worked with students who challenged the system, even when this was frustrating, to guide them and nurture their sense that change was needed without letting them get into the kind of trouble from which they might not recover. Consequently, student "dissidents" not only helped to turn the tide at the Capstone, many went on to build a new, different, and better South.

This book also remembers the vast majority of students who, while learning, did not try to change anything beyond enhancing their chances to lead successful and happy lives. The University of Alabama provided that opportunity and many students benefited from the determination of administrators to keep the university in its role of serving the people of Alabama by educating the next generation of citizens. At Alabama, the tide turned without upsetting the boat, even if on occasion the waters became troubled.

I owe much to F. David Mathews, President Rose's successor, who truly epitomized what a university president should be: a teacher, mentor, as well as a visionary. I also must thank professors whose names appear throughout this volume, most of them gone, but their influence invigorated a generation that changed Alabama and did much to change America. Any success I had as a teacher, I owe to mentors like John Ramsey, David McElroy, Hugh Ragsdale, and Sarah "Belle" Wiggins.

David Mathews opened his personal papers kept at the Kettering Foundation, where, since leaving the presidency at Alabama in 1981, he served as chief executive officer and president. I also want to thank University of Alabama president Robert E. Witt whose tenure ran from 2003 to 2012, for granting access to the papers of Frank Rose and other administrators.

Clark Center, director of the Hoole Special Collections at the University of Alabama, and his staff deserve a large measure of credit for facilitating my research and for lending their own perspectives to a past we share. Jessica Lacher-Feldman, Tom Land, Kevin Ray, Donnelly Walton, Marina Klaric, and Allyson Holiday typify excellence in research service. I also am indebted to Dr. Frank M. Donnini, an Alabama alumnus, and Tina Horner, director of publications at Clarion University of Pennsylvania, who offered detailed critiques of the manuscript at each stage of its development. Dr. John David Briley of Eastern Tennessee State University, author of *Career in Crisis*, a look at Alabama football during the late 1960s, also provided suggestions and encouragement at critical points in the process. A special thanks goes out to Dan Ross who read the original manuscript and whose incisive comments facilitated the reduction of those 534 pages to a manageable—and publishable—number. I am particularly grateful to Dan Waterman of the University of Alabama Press for his patience and suggestions on tightening and strengthening the text. I also thank Susan Harris for her expert editing of the entire manuscript.

Former students, people I knew of but did not know when I was enrolled at the Capstone, also proved very helpful. Carol Ann Self, the Bama cheerleader who "went rogue" to become a founding member of the Tuscaloosa Women's Movement, read every version of the manuscript. Jack Drake, the campus's leading dissident of the 1960s, Don Siegelman, perhaps the most effective president Alabama's student body had during that era, and Redding Pitt were among the campus leaders who went on to serve the people of Alabama by bringing about real and positive changes that would have seemed impossible during our student days. Fletcher Thornton, president of the Inter-Fraternity Council May 1970 provided his insights into those events. University of Alabama history Professor Emeritus Marteen Ultee and Dr. Marc Jason Gilbert, professor of history at Hawaii Pacific University generously offered their encouragement along with helpful critiques.

I also gained perspectives from others who were part of the 1960s at Alabama. Nancy Taylor Krenkel, a high school classmate and lifelong friend, provided insights into sorority life. Dag Rowe, another childhood friend, offered his perspective on fraternity life during the 1960s. I wish I could thank Tom Hall. He grew with the times and our relationship matured over the years from when we met at freshman orientation, through graduate school, and into the 1970s when we renewed our friendship while working in Omaha. Tom's early demise in 2001 prevents me from thanking him personally. It is to Tom that I dedicate this book and the four years of work that went into researching and writing it.

I cannot possibly thank all the faculty members, administrators, and former students with whom I shared the turmoil, hopes, and fears of the 1960s. Hopefully, some of them will see their role in *Turning the Tide*. If they do, I hope I prompted a few memories. For those who are gone, and the number inevitably grows, we have the closing line of our alma mater, "Until in heaven we meet."

TURNING
THE TIDE

Introduction
To Preserve the Unhindered Pursuit of Knowledge

The Capstone

Shortly after becoming president in 1912, George Hutcheson "Mike" Denny referred to the university as "the Capstone" of public education in the state of Alabama. The appellation remains popular to this day.

By 1962, Alabama alumni and students possessed a passion for football verging on the religious. Even prior to the 1960s, the annual gridiron showdown between Alabama's Crimson Tide and their cross-state rival, the Auburn University Tigers, united and divided the state's citizens. Some more moderate (or weak-kneed) fans, then as now, might claim to cheer for both teams until the annual late-November showdown forced their true allegiances. Real Bama fans claimed to "bleed" crimson and white and flatly declared, "I'm for two teams: Alabama and whoever plays Auburn."

For a very long time this football clash was in hiatus. After a forty-one-year gap, caused by a dispute over money, the series resumed in 1948. Subsequently, Alabama won five of its first six meetings, but in 1954 the Tide's faltering football fortunes resulted in five straight losses to its bitter rival. When Auburn claimed its first national championship in 1957, many Tiger fans believed they had arrived in an orange-and-blue promised land. Even then they could not have known the sun was about to set on Auburn's glory days and would not rise again for nearly three decades.

In the autumn of 1962, the University of Alabama's administration and faculty braced for desegregation, an event constituting what historians call a "watershed," a point demarcating dramatic shifts in the social and cultural landscape. Leadership would be critical in meeting this challenge. Accordingly, in June 1957, the Alabama Board of Trustees anticipated this challenge by calling Frank Anthony Rose, president of Transylvania College in Lexington, Kentucky, to step into what most board members believed was the failed presidency of Oliver Cromwell Carmichael, whose leadership proved inept during the turmoil that accompanied the first attempt at racial desegregation in February 1956.

Understanding the inseparable bond between gridiron fortunes and the university, even before Rose moved into the President's Mansion, he hired Coach Paul W. "Bear" Bryant away from Texas A&M University. Bryant, who played on the 1934 Alabama Rose Bowl national championship team, had a solid reputation for turning around football programs. He did it first at the University of Maryland, then at Kentucky, and, since 1954, at Texas A&M where, in just three seasons, Bryant transformed the Aggies from Southwest Conference cellar dwellers into league champions.

The inauguration of Frank Rose in May 1958, followed by the turnaround 5–4–1 autumn football season, marked the start of a decade of progress both for the University of Alabama and its Crimson Tide. During the first four years of the Rose administration, the university built twenty-five new buildings, including new men and women's dormitories. These were constructed to accommodate an increase in the student body from around 6,500 in 1958 to over 9,700 when the first wave of the baby-boom generation, youngsters born between the closing months of World War II and 1964, arrived for the 1964–65 academic year.[1]

When the class of 1963 entered the university in September 1959, Dwight David Eisenhower resided in the White House. For them, life at the Capstone in the late 1950s and early 1960s was not much changed from what students experienced a generation earlier. There were football weekends, fraternity parties, and candlelight initiations in the houses along sorority row. While rock 'n' roll had replaced the big-band sound of their parents' generation, the "gentleman's C" approach to higher education was only just feeling the effects of the new urgency in American higher education spurred by the Soviet leap into space in October 1957 with the launch of Sputnik, the first man-made satellite to orbit the earth. All in all, as the old decade melded into the new, life was good at the University of Alabama.

The majority of students came from comfortable middle-class homes. Some hailed from Alabama's larger cities like Birmingham, Montgomery, and Mobile. Others made their way to Tuscaloosa from smaller towns like Tuscumbia, Town Creek, Foley, Centreville, or Enterprise. On campus, major fraternities allied with students at the University of Alabama School of Law to constitute the "Machine" that ran campus politics through the Student Government Association (SGA). Even George Wallace, the state's most successful politician, succumbed to the power of the Machine. After winning the presidency of his freshman class in 1937 by pure force of his political will (a harbinger of things to come), Wallace, who couldn't afford to join a fraternity and thus secure the backing of the Machine, never won another campus election.[2] Nevertheless, in January 1963, as students who arrived in the summer of 1959 entered their last semester, the same George Wallace became governor of Alabama.

A Meeting in Morgan Auditorium

On the chilly afternoon of November 14, 1962, more than six hundred faculty members and administrators gathered in the auditorium at Morgan Hall, a yellow brick building nestled at the northwest corner of the Quadrangle near the Gorgas House, one of four buildings to survive the razing of the university during a raid by Union troops in April 1865. Built in 1911, Morgan Hall housed the English Department and also included an auditorium large enough to accommodate the faculty. President Rose presided over the meeting called by the local chapter of the American Association of University Professors (AAUP) to consider a resolution supporting "the maintenance of peace and order" on campus when the Capstone desegregated.

Ten days earlier, the student legislature adopted a resolution stating, "Law and order should be maintained at all times on the campus in order to uphold the high standards of academic excellence this university has enjoyed since its founding in 1831."[3] The violence six weeks earlier in nearby Oxford that marked the enrollment of James A. Meredith, the first black student at the University of Mississippi, weighed heavily on the minds of administrators and faculty in Tuscaloosa.

Prior to the 1954 Supreme Court decision in *Brown v. Board of Education*, most whites across the Deep South nestled comfortably in the established traditions and customs attendant to their racially segregated society. The following winter, Alabama's white population became increasingly apprehensive when Martin Luther King Jr., the charismatic pastor at the Dexter Avenue Baptist Church in Montgomery, led that community's black population in a boycott of city buses to eliminate longstanding Jim Crow restrictions that separated passengers by race.

Additionally, many among the faculty and administration recalled the mob violence that wracked the campus after the first attempt at desegregation six years earlier in February 1956. Vice President J. Jefferson Bennett and Dean of

Women Sarah Healy remembered vividly the mob that almost overwhelmed them as they escorted Autherine Lucy to class. The riots at Ole Miss reminded many of what took place at the Capstone earlier and they feared it might happen again.

The horrific violence at Ole Miss shocked the nation. On Sunday, September 30, the night before Meredith's scheduled enrollment, a mob consisting of students and townspeople overwhelmed some 500 federal agents including prison guards, border patrolmen, Federal Bureau of Investigation (FBI) agents, and US marshals escorting and protecting Meredith. Klansmen from both the Mississippi White Knights of the Ku Klux Klan and the Tuscaloosa-based United Klans of America reinforced the mob. By dawn a jukebox salesman and a British journalist were dead. Of the 500 agents sent to protect Meredith, 160 were injured, including 28 wounded by gunfire.[4] The following night, as a fiery cross cast ominous shadows across a field outside Tuscaloosa, Imperial Wizard Robert M. Shelton of the United Klans of America offered to send reinforcements to Oxford.[5] Shelton, who lived in nearby Northport, connected the violence in Oxford to the Tuscaloosa campus.

In the wake of the tragedy at Ole Miss, Frank Rose was determined to maintain order at the Capstone when its time came. He faced formidable challenges, foremost among them the potential for Klan involvement. There was also Governor-elect George Wallace, an avowed segregationist who promised to physically block federal court-ordered desegregation. Rose knew that after breaking the racial barrier at Ole Miss, civil rights leaders had turned their sights clearly on the University of Alabama. President Rose needed support from local business and civic leaders. Members of the university community also had to be brought on board, including the alumni, students, and faculty. On that chilly November afternoon Frank Rose focused on solidifying faculty support.

After calling the meeting to order at four o'clock in the afternoon, President Rose introduced John Henderson, president of the local chapter of the AAUP. Professor Henderson then put the following resolution before the assembled faculty:

We the faculty of the University of Alabama hereby affirm these truths:

That it is the duty and purpose of this faculty to teach all the students enrolled at this institution.

That learning can flourish only in a peaceful environment free from the threat of violence.

As teachers and scholars persuaded by these truths, we commend President Rose, the Board of Trustees, and the alumni to maintain peace and order on this campus and to preserve the unhindered pursuit of knowledge at this university.

Following a brief discussion, the faculty endorsed the resolution.[6] Twenty minutes after they assembled, the scholars and administrators walked out of Morgan Hall and onto the campus just beginning to feel the chill of the approaching November evening.

Deep in the Heart of Dixie

Alabama lies deep in the heart of Dixie. In 1962, like today, most state license tags included a brief motto at the bottom. In Tennessee, which for many years issued license plates shaped like the state, the inscription read, "The Volunteer State." Alabama's tags carried the motto, "The Heart of Dixie."

Alabama used only rear license tags, freeing the front bumper for personal expressions. Around the Capstone, the preponderance of front tags consisted of the single word, "ALABAMA" or "BAMA" in white letters across a crimson field or vice versa. Elsewhere throughout the state, many cars, pickup trucks, and sedans driven by Alabama State Troopers made their way along two-lane highways and dusty red clay backroads behind front license plates depicting the Confederate battle flag.

Southerners constituted the majority of the university's faculty and administration in 1962. President Frank Rose hailed from Meridian, Mississippi. Standing at his right hand as vice president was J. Jefferson Bennett, a native Kentuckian who grew up in Bay Minette and Fairhope, Alabama. Shortly before World War II, Bennett graduated from the university with a degree in commerce. After service in the Marine Corps, including fighting on Guadalcanal, Bennett returned to the Capstone to earn a law degree in 1948. Before Frank Rose arrived at the university, Bennett served as assistant dean of the law school and as executive assistant to President Carmichael. A devout Episcopalian, Jeff Bennett sat on the advisory committee for Canterbury Chapel, which hosted a group called the "Forum" consisting of a handful of politically involved and more liberal faculty and students.[7] Rose and Bennett felt uneasy with the racial status quo that linked the state's history to its present.

The South's peculiar history fosters a deeper reverence for the past than found in many other parts of the republic. Southerners endured something their fellow American citizens have never known: total military defeat and the humiliation of occupation during a period of reconstruction. Southern historian C. Vann Woodward wrote in *The Burden of Southern History*, "Nothing in its history was conducive to the theory that the South was the darling of divine providence."[8]

Even in the 1960s, for many Southerners the words "the war" referred to the American Civil War and not the recently won victories over the Axis powers. In 1962, to one degree or another, almost all Southerners—whites very differently from blacks—carried a spiritual legacy from "the war." Many white Southerners harbored lingering perceptions of injustices inflicted on their forbearers by carpetbaggers and scalawags during reconstruction. Legitimate or not, these perceptions were deeply rooted in the hearts of white Alabamians.

By the 1960s, however, the South was re-emerging as a viable economic and political entity. Although another generation passed before prosperity made its way into its smaller towns, the state's vast resources and industry-friendly labor and tax policies assured a future brighter than the past. By the end of the 1960s, the number of jobs in Alabama would grow two times faster than in New England and four times faster than in Pennsylvania.

Frank Rose, his administrative team, and the faculty members who gathered in Morgan Hall that November afternoon believed education provided the key to socioeconomic progress. But they had other factors to consider. Students, the vast majority of whom came from Alabama and whose parents had just elected George Wallace governor, constituted one unknown. The people of Tuscaloosa and nearby Northport made for another. Above all, racism presented the most volatile and unpredictable factor. Blind, unreasoning racial prejudice ignited the conflagration at Ole Miss. Many feared it might do so in Tuscaloosa.

Although well educated and committed to teaching, many among the faculty, administrators, and the board of trustees in 1962, if not segregationists, were inclined to remain cautiously silent on racial matters. There were, of course, exceptions like Dean John Blackburn and one of the bright and shining stars of the History Department, Professor John F. Ramsey. While some who found the racial situation in Alabama intolerable departed for opportunities on more liberal campuses (which also probably paid more for their services), most of the faculty seemed content.

Although George Wallace disingenuously maintained segregation was foremost a constitutional and states' rights issue, race lay at the crux of the matter for his more adamant supporters. Wallace's racist animus fed upon and sustained something more ominous than racial prejudices. The tinder that made for a potentially explosive situation when desegregation reached the Capstone was the almost unreasoning fear among many that lowering segregation's barriers would foster what Wallace called "race mixing."

While emotions associated with race ran high in 1962, Frank Rose, along with most of the administration and faculty understood the inevitability of desegregation. Within a week of the violence at Ole Miss, a *Tuscaloosa News* editorial stated, "Next year generally is considered to be 'Alabama's year' in the school desegregation movement."[9] As of 1961, only seventeen school districts in the South had been desegregated. During the following year, the pace quickened exponentially when 166 additional districts desegregated, most of them peacefully. Nevertheless, only 1 percent of black children living in Dixie attended school with whites.[10] At the University of Alabama, that was about to change. The question confronting Frank Rose and the faculty in November 1962 was what that change might involve.

1
The University of Alabama
From Slavery to Desegregation

Rolling with the Tide

Beginning in the autumn of 1958, the rising tide of gridiron victories washed away the bad memories of football defeats during the mid-1950s. From that point into the summer of 1963, the University of Alabama rolled along on the fortunes of the Crimson Tide and the growing level of achievements across the campus.

In September 1962, as the class of '63 entered its senior year and the class of '66 strolled to their first classes, the University of Alabama continued its upward trajectory. The student body at the Capstone numbered just over eight thousand with six thousand additional students matriculating at extension centers in Birmingham, Mobile, Gadsden, and Huntsville, as well as at the medical and dental schools in Birmingham. The autumn leaves of the oaks on the campus in Tuscaloosa fell across 455 acres, its classrooms and dormitories still separated from the Warrior River by thick woods bounding the university's northern perimeter. A golf course and arboretum sat on a nearby tract and married student housing and storage facilities were on 150 acres constituting the Northington campus, also located in Tuscaloosa. The Capstone itself was comprised of 285 buildings, including 25 built during the first four years of Frank Rose's presidency.

In addition to new construction, President Rose also raised the university's academic standing by increasing the intellectual rigor of existing programs. In an effort to couple the university's teaching culture to research, Rose attempted to hire younger faculty just out of graduate school whose pursuit of tenure required publication. The administration and faculty had achieved much since Rose's inauguration in May 1958. By 1962, the University of Alabama, with its rich history, was well worth protecting and preserving.

A Matter of History

During the Civil War, so many cadets ran off to fight for the "Glorious Cause," that the university was forced to counter this drain on the student body by admitting boys as young as fifteen.[1] Even though the state legislature's decision to turn Alabama into a military school had more to do with disciplining the high-spirited sons of the planter class than it did with producing military leaders, the university's contribution to the Confederacy made it a target of a Union army raid, an extension of General William T. Sherman's "March to the Sea" during the closing months of the Civil War. On the night of April 3, 1865, Union troops occupied Tuscaloosa, and after a brief skirmish with cadets from the university, who were withdrawn by President Landon Cabell Garland in an effort to avoid unnecessary bloodshed, the next morning the raiders burned most of the university, sparing only four buildings: the President's Mansion, a private house on campus known to this day as the Gorgas House, an observatory, and a small, white roundhouse armory. In the twenty-first century, they connect the modern university to its historic past.

The university did not reopen until 1870 and rebuilding was a struggle given the poverty extant throughout the state and the South. It remained an all-male military school until ten females were admitted in 1893 due to the lobbying of Julia Tutwiler, a Tuscaloosa native who studied at Vassar College and Washington and Lee University before serving as president of Livingston State Normal School (now the University of West Alabama), from which Alabama's first ten female students had graduated.

This volume concludes at the end of the 1969–70 academic year in the aftermath of campus disorders in May 1970. There were, however, two earlier significant instances when student dissent turned violent: one in 1900 and the other fifty-six years later.

In December 1900, a cadet revolt that involved students barricading themselves in Woods Hall, the first building erected in the aftermath of the Civil War, led to the abolishment of the military system in 1904. From that point on, the University of Alabama was a coeducational, nonmilitary institution, although Army Reserve Officer Training was reestablished in 1917 and expanded to include an air force detachment in 1947.

The second University of Alabama struggled into the twentieth century with a student body hovering at barely four hundred students in 1912 when George Denny accepted the presidential medallion as the university's fourteenth president. At the end of his remarkable twenty-six-year tenure the student body numbered nearly five thousand. President Denny's vision transformed the University of Alabama from a sleepy backwater academic institution into a relatively sophisticated university, one competitive with similar institutions across the Deep South. Denny's combination of football and recruiting out-of-state students provided the money to fuel modernization and expansion. This approach proved efficacious. Frank Rose revived it in 1958 and his successors continued it into the twenty-first century.

In 1922, Alabama's football team defeated the University of Pennsylvania Quakers, a major powerhouse of the era. Three years later Coach Wallace Wade took Alabama to the Rose Bowl where the Crimson Tide edged the University of Washington 20–19 to claim the first of twelve national championships in the twentieth century. There were subsequent trips to Pasadena in 1926, 1930, and 1934.

To increase enrollment, President Denny placed ads in northern newspapers, especially in New York, New Jersey, and Pennsylvania, touting the University of Alabama as a place offering a good education at an affordable price in a friendly, pleasant, and safe environment. By the mid-1930s, out-of-state students, many of whom were Jewish, comprised nearly one third of the student body. This provided the Capstone, which would not admit the state's African Americans for three more decades, a measure of diversity and sophistication not found on most other southern campuses. Additionally, when Denny retired at the end of 1936, women constituted a third of the 4,897 students matriculating at the university.

During the Denny years the university grew from nine to twenty-three major buildings. Alabama established the School of Commerce, a School of Home Economics, and a graduate program in chemistry. The School of Commerce produced business leaders destined to lay a firm foundation for future financial support. Two of the university's more recognizable symbols, Denny Chimes and Bryant-Denny Stadium, honor his contributions.[2]

World War II and Its Immediate Aftermath

In the brief tenure of Denny's successor, Tuscaloosa businessman Richard Clarke Foster, the university built the Amelia Gayle Gorgas Library, six men's and two women's dormitories. When Foster died suddenly on November 19, 1941, the trustees turned back to Mike Denny as an interim president. Less than a month later, when the United States entered World War II, the student body stood at just over 5,000 students, including 1,500 women.

The preponderance of young men in the demographic did not augur well for the university. Volunteering and conscription reduced enrollment to 1,800 regular students by 1944. The university, under the direction of President Raymond Ross Paty, kept enrollment up with what later would be known as "nontraditional students." Army training programs, ranging from flight training and map reading to combat engineering courses, prepared military personnel for a plethora of positions needed by the Industrial Age armed forces of the era. Additionally, the traditional Army ROTC program continued to produce officers. More than 8,000 officers commissioned through Alabama's ROTC from 1917 to 1945 served in World War II, and 350 alumni made the supreme sacrifice.[3]

In December 1946, President Paty resigned to become chancellor of the University System of Georgia. Dean Ralph E. Adams, a 1926 Alabama alumnus, served as interim at a time when enrollment burgeoned to over 8,500, the increase fed by veterans taking advantage of GI educational benefits. From January 1948, just after the trustees elevated engineering professor John M. Gallalee to the presidency, until June 1950 when the Korean conflict broke out, enrollment in undergraduate, graduate, law, and medical school programs climbed past ten thousand. For the most part, these were older, more serious-minded students anxious to graduate and enter careers in business, education, legal, and medical professions.

Happy Days at the Capstone

By the early 1950s, the Capstone's inclination to the liberal arts and business made it the place to go for young men aiming to take over the family business or seeking a career in law, medicine, or dentistry. Alabama's School of Education provided young women an opportunity to obtain a teaching degree; given the attitudes of the era, stereotypically considered a backup if they failed to find a husband during their four years on campus. A degree from the Alabama School of Law was a plus for anyone considering a career in state politics.

At the start of the 1952–53 academic year, undergraduate enrollment decreased from a high of 9,000 in 1948 to 6,500, two-thirds of which were male. In part this was due to the graduation of former servicemen who had completed their education along with increased conscription to meet the needs of the Korean War. Male students of the early 1950s seemed more mature than those of the prewar era perhaps owing to the way the military draft, like the gallows, focused their minds.

Four years after the university established its first doctoral program in 1951, terminal degrees were available in biology, chemistry, English, history, political science, and, at the Medical College in Birmingham, in biochemistry and pharmacology. An EdD in education was also offered in Tuscaloosa.[4]

The Capstone in 1955 nestled in its intrinsic idyllic beauty and intellectual tranquility. Students were hardly distinguishable from their counterparts a generation earlier. Being younger and less mature, they were not as focused on their studies as the veterans who flocked to the university in the immediate aftermath of the war. But neither were they as frivolous and rebellious as the post–Great War generation epitomized by Alabama's Zelda Fitzgerald. There was something almost prosaically traditional about the white sports coat and pink carnation pre–rock and roll student body, whose silver-screen heartthrobs included the young Marlon Brando and James Dean, killed at the age of twenty-four in a car accident on September 30, 1955.

When the Mob Ruled

In 1953, Alabama's trustees named Oliver C. Carmichael president. A 1911 alumnus, Carmichael was serving as president of the Carnegie Foundation. As he settled into his new job, a lawsuit brought by attorney Arthur Shores of Birmingham on behalf of two young black women, Pollie Anne Myers and Autherine J. Lucy, made its way through the courts. In October 1955, the US Supreme Court upheld rulings in the lower courts barring the university from denying admission based on race. While the university managed to exclude Pollie Anne Myers because she had borne a child out of wedlock, Autherine Lucy was admitted, although she was denied a dorm room and cafeteria privileges.

The Supreme Court decision in *Brown v. Board of Education* in 1954 struck down the separate-but-equal provisions of *Plessy v. Ferguson* in 1896. This, coupled with the Montgomery bus boycott of 1955, sent waves of alarm throughout the state's white population. Many white Alabamians thought blacks no longer "knew their place." The university's administrators failed to heed the intensity of racial unrest extant in the state at that time.

On Friday, February 3, Autherine Lucy attended her first class in Smith Hall without incident, except when geography professor Don Hays called the roll and a male student sprang to his feet, raised a clenched fist, and marched out shouting, "For two cents I'd drop this course!"[5] That evening, after Lucy had gone home to Birmingham, a small band of drunken students burned a cross in the middle of University Boulevard.

Nothing untoward happened on Saturday when Lucy returned for a morning class. That evening, local high school students and townspeople swelled a crowd of students who gathered after a basketball game. Led by a sophomore named Leonard Wilson, the mob moved up University Boulevard to downtown Tuscaloosa where some attacked cars driven by blacks. The mob then returned to campus, gathered on the lawn in in front of the President's Mansion, and booed Carmichael as he pled with them to "think about what you are doing."

Sunday passed quietly. But on Monday morning, with Lucy back for classes, a mob of students and townspeople congregated outside Smith Hall. Jefferson Bennett, Carmichael's top assistant, and Dean of Women Sarah Healy moved a very frightened Autherine Lucy out the back door and into Healy's Oldsmobile just as assailants, having spotted them, hurled rocks as the car sped off for Bibb Graves Hall. Bennett guided the Oldsmobile into the parking lot behind Bibb Graves before the mob got across the Quad. Healy escorted Lucy into the safety of the classroom. When the mob surged into the parking lot they attempted to overturn the car driven by Bennett, but he managed to drive away as a brick smashed the back window.[6]

If it had not been for the brave actions of Reverend Emmet Gribbin, Episcopal rector at the Canterbury Chapel, who, while distracting the mob's attention, also incurred a beating by a Klansman named Robert "Dynamite Bob" Chambliss, Autherine Lucy might well have been lynched. Instead, Dean Healy shoved the young woman onto the back floor of a police car that then drove her to safety.

That evening the trustees suspended Autherine Lucy "for her own safety and the safety of the student body."[7] Meanwhile, back on campus, the Confederate flag-waving mob set off firecrackers and torched some supposedly "Communist literature" published by the National Association for the Advancement of Colored People (NAACP). They then moved to the President's Mansion, demanding to speak to President Carmichael. When campus police chief Allan O. Rayfield and Mrs. Carmichael came onto the balcony to explain that the president was not in, a fusillade of rocks and eggs forced them back inside.

Forrest David Mathews, a sophomore majoring in history with a minor in Greek, whose future would be inexorably entwined with the University of Alabama, experienced an epiphany as he watched these horrific events. Over half a century later he recalled, "People you thought were normal began acting like idiots. The power of the mob on human beings was remarkable. I saw hate written all over the faces of people I had thought were normal human beings. The experience was transforming."[8] What David Mathews learned he applied years later when in May 1970, as president of the University of Alabama, he confronted campus unrest and disorder.

The university expelled the rabble-rousing Leonard Wilson. He later achieved a modicum of notoriety as a leading figure with the Alabama Citizen's Council, a group formed in Mississippi in 1954 that used social, political, and economic pressure to maintain segregation. Several other students received suspensions ranging from a semester to two years. After the trustees suspended Autherine Lucy, her attorney filed a suit charging university officials with conspiring to create disturbances to facilitate her removal. The trustees responded by expelling Autherine Lucy for making untruthful charges against university officials.[9]

On Tuesday, February 7, the morning after the mob nearly lynched Autherine Lucy, Buford Boone, the publisher of the *Tuscaloosa News*, wrote a front-page editorial titled, "What a Price for Peace." It concluded, "What happened here is far more important than whether a Negro girl is admitted to the University. We have a breakdown of law and order, an abject surrender to what is expedient rather than a courageous stand for what is right. Yes, there is peace on the University campus, but what a price has been paid for it."[10] The editorial won him the 1957 Pulitzer Prize for Editorial Writing. When the university faced its next crisis of conscience, Buford Boone would again speak out forcefully for law, order, and doing the right thing.

Oliver Carmichael's mortally wounded presidency limped along until the start of the fall semester when he announced his resignation effective January 1, 1957. James H. Newman, the dean of administration, served as interim president. When faced with a major crisis, it is best to prepare for the worst that might happen. Not doing that, perhaps, was Carmichael's gravest mistake. For the next president and his staff, failure to learn from those mistakes would have held the potential for even worse consequences.

Interlude

In the spring of 1956, a discussion group called the "Open Forum" organized around Canterbury Chapel. In February 1957, the Student Government Association (SGA) approved its charter thus giving the forum access to university facilities for meetings and programs to carry out its stated purpose of discussing issues of interest to students and faculty. At the end of the first week in May, the Open Forum, still meeting off campus at the Canterbury Chapel, held a panel discussion on "academic freedom." An estimated 120 students and faculty attended. Seventy members of the Ku Klux Klan also showed up.

Judy Means, out-going editor of the *Crimson-White*, was at the meeting. According to a front-page editorial, the Tuscaloosa police, although informed of the event and the possibility of harassment by the Klan, arrived after the robed demonstrators had departed. An accompanying photo showed one Klansman came armed with a pistol.[11]

The next Tuesday, the student legislature of the SGA voted 24–2 to revoke the Open Forum's charter, stating that the group had not lived up to its stated purpose of holding "free and open discussion of current topics to cover all fields." Supposedly, in its first five meetings, the forum focused only on issues attendant to racial desegregation at the expense of a broader range of topics like the Eisenhower defense budget. "Life is a practical matter," stated one of the legislators, "when we get out of school we're going to have to find jobs. . . . We're representing the majority of students. If the organization is not in the best interest of the majority, it is our right and duty to withdraw its charter."[12] The administration did not intervene to save the Open Forum. Consequently, over the next four years the discussion of matters related to desegregation receded at the University of Alabama.

Two Key Hires

Even without the botched attempt at desegregation and the accompanying anarchy that made the university a spectacle of bigotry and intolerance, President Carmichael might have faced another issue fatal to his tenure: a football program in disarray. In 1955, Carmichael, overlooking Coach Jennings B. "Ears" Whitworth's losing record at Oklahoma A&M, hired Whitworth as head football coach. Whitworth, who played at Alabama in the 1930s, posted a miserable four wins, two ties, and twenty-four losses in three years as head coach at the Capstone. The university needed new leadership in offices of both the president and head football coach.

In the summer of 1957, Ernest Williams, a trustee and member of the presidential search committee, traveled to Jacksonville, Florida, to attend the annual meeting of the Kappa Alpha (KA) social fraternity. There he heard an address by KA brother Frank A. Rose, president of Transylvania College in Lexington, Kentucky. In his sixth year at Transylvania, the thrity-seven-year-old, tall, dark-haired, and well-spoken Rose impressed Williams as a possible replacement for Carmichael.

Frank Rose, a native of Meridian, Mississippi, spoke eloquently because he was a preacher. After graduating from Transylvania with a degree in philosophy, Rose earned a divinity degree and then served several years as a pastor in Danville, Kentucky, before Transylvania named him president at the age of thirty-one. In addition to youthful good looks, eloquence, and experience, Rose had one other thing to recommend him: service on a commission studying how to desegregate Kentucky public schools.

Culpepper Clark, in his study of desegregation at the Capstone, *The School-house Door*, claimed, "A lore had developed that the trustees brought Rose in to take care of desegregation and manage the transition." Clark doubted this was so because Rose did nothing obvious to foster or support desegregation between 1958 and 1962.[13]

While Frank Rose did not overtly attempt to end segregation until compelled to do so by its inevitability, in a 1990 interview with John Blackburn, Rose maintained that he was hired to facilitate it. According to Rose, it was the trustees' argument that "only a Southerner could do the job," that convinced him to accept the presidency.[14] In the same interview, Rose said that when he met with Governor James E. Folsom shortly after accepting the presidency, the out-going governor told him he wanted the university desegregated. Furthermore, Rose disclosed that his friend Nelson A. Rockefeller urged him to meet with George Wallace, who served with Rockefeller on the board of trustees at historically black Tuskegee Institute. According to Rose, at their 1958 meeting Wallace told him the time had come to desegregate the university of Alabama. This is not as far-fetched as it may seem since Governor Folsom appointed Wallace to the Tuskegee board. At that time Wallace, along with Folsom, were thought to be "moderate" on racial issues.

In early September 1957, after the trustees offered Frank Rose the presidency, he went to work even before leaving Lexington. During this period, he spent his weekends and sometimes Mondays in Tuscaloosa and then returned to his job at Transylvania for the rest of the normal workweek. It was in the autumn of 1957 that he and Ernest Williams persuaded Coach Paul W. "Bear" Bryant to leave Texas A&M and come home to Alabama.[15]

President Rose assumed office on January 1, 1958. Five months later, at the May commencement, the university conferred upon him the honorary degree of Doctor of Letters or LittD, to make him "Dr. Rose." Meanwhile, Coach

Bryant had sized up the team during spring drills and dubbed them "a fat, rag-gedy bunch."[16]

A Time of Rebuilding and Preparing

The first four years of the Rose presidency was a time of rebuilding the foot-ball program, rehabilitating to the extent possible the university's tarnished reputation, and new construction in anticipation of future growth. Although Frank Rose's presidency proved pivotal and set the tone for successive admin-istrations, changes during his tenure were not so much a result of reform as an evolutionary process attendant to growth.

Coach Bryant's "fat, raggedy bunch" improved enough to post five victories against four losses and a tie in his first year. In the 1959 season, seven wins, one loss, and two ties got the Tide into the inaugural Liberty Bowl, played in Philadelphia, where they faced the Penn State Nittany Lions. Since a handful of those lions were black, Bryant asked Governor John Patterson, a determined segregationist, if he should accept the invitation. Patterson not only approved, he attended the game. This did not prevent the White Citizens Council of Tus-caloosa from sending Coach Bryant a threatening telegram.[17]

The following year, the Tide rolled through an 8–1–1 season capped with a Bluebonnet Bowl invitation. Then, in 1961, the undefeated Southeastern Con-ference (SEC) champions bested Arkansas 10–0 in the Sugar Bowl to win Bry-ant's first national championship as head coach at the Capstone.

Sports history is a form of cultural history. In the case of Alabama, Crim-son Tide gridiron victories not only kept the university in the good graces of many, if not most, of the state's white citizens and state legislators, it also served to divert their attention from a process of liberalization on campus. While Paul Bryant turned the Crimson Tide's gridiron fortunes, Frank Rose turned a greater tide by placing the University of Alabama on a new institu-tional course, doing so against a rising current of racism. It wasn't that football was used as a politically neutralizing factor. Such a strategy probably never oc-curred to Frank Rose or Coach Bryant. The reality was that winning football made a lot of people happy, not only alumni but also the vast majority of white Alabama fans who were not yet ready to place laurel wreaths on black heads.

In the 1958 gubernatorial race, John Patterson blatantly played to the fes-tering racial prejudices among the electorate to garner enough Klan support to defeat George Wallace in a runoff election. In the aftermath of the Mont-gomery bus boycott of 1955 and the failed attempt at desegregating the university the following year, racial animosity rose among Alabama's white voters. Patterson, however, a Phi Beta Kappa graduate of the Capstone, supported the university's budget requests in the state legislature.[18] Throughout his first four years as president, Frank Rose avoided contentious issues attendant to desegregation and focused on new construction and enhancing the faculty.

Twelve days before President Rose's November 14, 1962, meeting with the faculty, he delivered his annual "State of the University" report to the trustees gathered for their yearly meeting on the Friday prior to homecoming. Rose acknowledged the tranquility that marked the first four years of his presidency was about to end. "I am fully aware," he told the trustees, "that I do not know when we will be faced with the problem of enrolling a Negro student. . . . I have been assured by our authorities that the state will use every force at its command to see that we do not have violence." Rose noted that heightened admission standards adopted in 1958 compelled the university to turn down more than three thousand applications and that "we have not had one (black person) to complete his registration since 1956."[19]

Indeed, the Rose administration chalked up some notable successes during this relatively tranquil period. In 1960, the College of Arts and Sciences introduced an honors curriculum and initiated an American Studies Program. The same fall semester, the College of Engineering installed a common curriculum for freshmen. Additionally, during the first five years of the Rose presidency, the university increased its doctoral level offerings from twelve major fields to twenty-three areas of specialization by 1962.[20] Frank Rose, along with many other well-meaning and dedicated people at the Capstone and throughout the state, resolved to continue the university's pursuit of excellence.

The Ole Miss Specter

For the first two years of the 1960s, while the university enjoyed its tranquility in seeming isolation from the verities of Cold War events, the still relatively new Democratic administration in Washington experienced a series of setbacks in Laos, Cuba, and increasingly in South Vietnam, where in late 1961, the Kennedy administration decided to make a stand. In the coming years the ramifications of that would affect events at the Capstone as much as the immediate concern over desegregation.

Students returned to campus in September 1962 to the usual round of fraternity rush parties made all the better after the Crimson Tide traveled to Athens to open the football season by ripping the Georgia Bulldogs 35–0. Meanwhile, the violence that accompanied the desegregation of the University of Mississippi shook the nation and grabbed the attention of Frank Rose, members of his administration, as well as business and civic leaders in Tuscaloosa.

Melvin Meyer, the son of a Jewish newspaper editor from Starkville, Mississippi, served as the editor of the *Crimson-White*. In mid-September, before the riots associated with the admission of air force veteran James Meredith, when officials at Ole Miss restated their determination to resist desegregation, the *Crimson-White* published an editorial titled, "A Bell Rang."

The editorial took on the South. "Bias is a force that strikes at one and all. We have come much too far, and fought much too long, to abandon our democratic system to appease the great god, Expediency." It concluded, "We lost something American in Oxford this week, and every American is the less for it."[21]

Three nights later, Klan imperial wizard Robert Shelton addressed his robed congregants in a field outside Tuscaloosa illuminated by a fiery cross. He referred to the *Crimson-White* editorial, declaring, "I have taken steps in the form of contacting influential people in Alabama to see that such a situation does not develop where an outsider can come into the state and try to use his influence to change our way of life."[22] Ironically, the "outsider" in question (Meyer) came from neighboring Mississippi to which Shelton that same night urged his "Kohorts" to throng in support of Governor Ross Barnett, "outsiders" though these Klansmen would be.

Telephoned threats to Meyer compelled Frank Rose to hire private detectives to protect the editor. Melvin Meyer did not write the editorial. As is the case with most newspapers and journals, editorials are unsigned, and while ultimately bearing responsibility for whatever is published, the editor may or may not have written a particular piece. Robert E. Roberts, a senior majoring in history and political science and soon to be commissioned a US Air Force second lieutenant, wrote "A Bell Rang," the title taken from a popular folksong, "If I Had a Hammer."[23]

Frank Rose knew he needed the support of Tuscaloosa's business and civic leaders to prevent the local Klan from wreaking the kind of havoc that rocked Oxford. George LeMaistre, a law professor turned bank president and an elder at the First Presbyterian Church, feared Governor-elect Wallace's resistance to federal court orders concerning desegregation might imperil future economic progress. In November, LeMaistre spoke to the Tuscaloosa Civitan Club. "No state official," he declared, "has the right to put himself above the law, and that includes the governor." After a moment of embarrassed silence, one person clapped. Another joined in. Others added applause and as it swelled many rose in support.[24] This was no endorsement of integration. Rather, it was a vote for economic progress unimpeded by the prejudices that ignite the flames of violence.

Toward the end of November, things did not seem as bleak for Frank Rose. He had signed resolutions of support from student leaders and faculty. Local business leaders, including *Tuscaloosa News* publisher Buford Boone, had stated their determination to stand against violence. On Thanksgiving Day, the Crimson Tide thrashed Auburn 38–0.

An Orchid in Cottondale

A member of the class of 1962, quoted in *Mahout*, the university's humor magazine, noted that taking a class from history professor John F. Ramsey was like "finding an orchid in Cottondale."[25] A specialist in modern European history, Ramsey joined the faculty in 1935 after earning his doctorate at the University of California at Berkeley. Wise university presidents listen to professors like John Ramsey. His long tenure, impeccable service to the university, along with his popularity among students and alumni enabled him to stride boldly where most of his colleagues feared to tread even gingerly. Frank Rose appreciated his worth.

One of the means the university used to thwart applications by African Americans was to close registration when faced with a qualified black applicant. In December 1962, when the administration suddenly closed enrollment for the following semester, figurative red flags went up among those faculty members anticipating possible desegregation in the upcoming spring semester. Professor Ramsey expressed their concerns in a letter to President Rose. "Their [the faculty's] concern stems from three sources: 1. the possibility that the University will be in a weaker position by next fall; 2. the comfort and encouragement that the recent decision on the Negro applications will give to the worst elements in the state; 3. the inability of the faculty to make these sentiments known to you *before* [underlined in the letter] this recent action was taken."[26]

President Rose replied immediately, informing Ramsey that delays in construction of a new women's dormitory prompted the early closure. He added that only one black applicant was a "serious contender for admission, and that she is being advised by militant Negro groups to continue agitation but not seek to enroll before September, 1963." Rose further explained he closed enrollment early for another reason he could not share but added, "It would mean the difference between a serious crisis in February and preparations for order at a later date."[27]

Between Athena and Dionysus

While Alabama was a long way from Berkeley both geographically and academically, by 1962 the intellectual atmosphere at the Capstone was improving. When Frank Rose spoke of the "pursuit of excellence" it was more than a rhetorical flourish. Nevertheless, at the University of Alabama there was a tension between acquiring wisdom and having fun, a conflict as eternal as the Greek myths. In this case, the contest was between the ancient Greek deities Athena, the goddess of wisdom, and Dionysus, the spirit of revelry and ribald debauchery.

As regards wisdom, in February 1962, the Graduate Council, responsible for matters attendant to intellectual vitality and academic achievement, unanimously recommended students admitted conditionally to any master's program sustain a "B" average during their first twelve hours or be dropped. All graduate students had to have a "B" average at the completion of their master's coursework to be admitted to candidacy regardless of discipline.[28] Meanwhile, undergraduates needed an overall "C" average to stay in school with at least a "C+" in their major to graduate. Although grade inflation would set in by the end of the decade, in 1962 and 1963, the average was acceptable to many Alabama students.

The Greek system was entrenched at the Capstone. It fed the Machine in a symbiotic relationship between the more prestigious fraternities and the Alabama School of Law. Male students in the College of Commerce and Business Administration used fraternity ties to gain influence in Alabama's business community, extending the reach of the Machine while also building a powerful cohort of support for the university. The non-Greek majority lived in a parallel universe.

Male students with political ambitions understood that joining the right fraternity opened the door to participation in the Student Government Association. Being part of SGA enabled the astute campus mover and shaker to build alliances helpful to future political ambitions. While most Alabama politicians, at least at the county and state levels, were not Alabama alumni, eight of Alabama's twenty-three governors in the twentieth century were. The Machine produced seven of the eight, the exception being George Wallace. By contrast, only two Auburn graduates were elected governor. Additionally, as Wayne Flynt, one of the state's most distinguished historians, has noted, many of its congressmen and US senators were products of the Machine. More specifically, in the mid-1960s both US senators and seven of the eight congressional representatives hailed from the Capstone. In addition Governor Wallace, Lieutenant Governor Albert Brewer, and Alabama Attorney General Richmond Flowers were Alabama Law School alumni.[29]

It was important that the university attain as much support as possible with lawmakers. One way to do this was to win football games. Another way was to avoid antagonizing their constituencies with controversial issues related to race. Consequently, university officials did little to push desegregation, especially in the first four years of the Rose presidency, during the governorship of arch-segregationist John Patterson.

If Athena had a heart for politics, Dionysus had prerogatives as well. In August 1962, the campus police, noticing a car blocking the driveway behind the Phi Delta Theta house, knocked on the door during a rush party. When the door opened, a well-inebriated brother greeted the officers by mooning them. The next day, Dean Blackburn suspended the offending brother along with the fraternity's charter. The Phi Delta Thetas previously established their "zoo fraternity" bona fides in the autumn of 1961, by routinely serving alcoholic beverages to underage pledges and their dates. A year earlier, the brothers got in trouble when they blindfolded drunken pledges and their inebriated dates and then forced them to crawl around on all fours while pledges attempted to identify their dates by biting them on their "rear extremities."[30]

Blackburn used the "August moon" incident to order the Inter-Fraternity Council (IFC) to propose reforms in pledge policy as a first step in overhauling the Greek system. Throughout the remainder of the decade, while the university moved in a more progressive direction, Bama's Greeks upheld the Capstone's reputation as one of the South's leading party schools.

As final exams neared in December 1962, few seemed aware of the building sense of drama attendant to desegregation. The Crimson Tide, with only one blemish on its 1962 record, played in the Cotton Bowl on New Year's Day 1963. Led by sophomore quarterback Joe Namath, the Tide handed the Oklahoma Sooners a 17–0 defeat with President Kennedy on hand to witness it. A few weeks later George Wallace took the oath of office as governor of Alabama. From that moment, Alabama's governor and the federal government headed toward a confrontation.

Springtime in Alabama: 1963

In the spring of 1963, fraternities and sororities held ceremonies turning pledges into actives. There were formal dances at which couples often became engaged. The Army and Air Force ROTC units held their annual military balls complete with cadets outfitted in dress uniforms and their dates resplendent in cocktail dresses. As the afternoons warmed, Capstone students often congregated on the banks of nearby Hurricane Creek for a ritual known as "creek banking." This involved a couple, their blanket, a portable radio or phonograph, and either a six-pack of beer—Pabst Blue Ribbon being a perennial campus favorite—or some other concoction usually mixing Coca-Cola or Pepsi with Rebel Yell bourbon.

Governor George C. Wallace's first Governor's Day, an annual spring event at Alabama, was held on April 30, 1963. Army and air force detachments assembled on the Quadrangle alongside the Million Dollar Band. Following a nineteen-gun salute, cadets paraded past Governor Wallace, First Lady Lurleen B. Wallace, President Rose, and other dignitaries. After the parade, the governor addressed cadets (a mandatory formation for which they were excused from classes) and interested students in Foster Auditorium. Cadet Colonel Robert Roberts, author of "A Bell Rang," served as the governor's escort.

In his speech that morning, after boasting that 127 new industries had been attracted to the state during his first four months in office, Wallace then attributed the state's historic lack of economic progress to injustices suffered during Reconstruction and oppression by northern industries. "It was the people of the South who were the architects of freedom," Wallace proclaimed. He then warned of "forces lined up against us . . . centralizers, spenders and wasters who regard your tax money as something to siphon off and give away to the do-gooders who think our unique gifts belong fully to the whole world."[31]

Perhaps as a portent of events beginning to simmer around the university, SGA president Donald Stewart sharply criticized Wallace in a speech delivered to members of the Men's Residence Hall Council, taking the governor to task for "railing out against so-called inequities that have long been imposed on us" and by "harkening to that glorious past which some say still sustains us." Stewart urged residence hall leaders to be ready to bear their responsibilities when faced with the challenges of desegregation.[32]

For many students in the spring of 1963, the biggest issue on campus involved the accusation that Coach Bryant and Georgia's athletic director, Coach

Wally Butts, conspired to fix the previous September's Alabama-Georgia game that the Tide won 35–0. Bryant denied the charges and lodged a ten-million-dollar lawsuit against the *Saturday Evening Post* for publishing "The Story of a College Football Fix," in its March 23, 1963, issue. He also sued the *Atlanta Constitution* and sportswriter Furman Bisher for hitchhiking on the story with an article on Bryant's purported brutal coaching style. Eventually, both Butts and Bryant were exonerated, and Bryant settled with the *Saturday Evening Post* for three hundred thousand dollars.[33]

No university president welcomes controversy in the athletic department, especially with a football program as extraordinary as Alabama's. This one occurred at a most critical time because, by late April, Frank Rose and the administration knew the Capstone faced desegregation in early June at the beginning of the summer session.

Not "If" but "How"

Tension heightened throughout the state and at the university during the spring of 1963 as the question became not if desegregation was coming but how it would be accomplished. Sixty miles east of Tuscaloosa in Birmingham, the most segregated major city in the South, its black community challenged the business-oriented pragmatism of the city's relatively moderate mayor, Albert Boutwell. He was not, however, the most powerful man in Birmingham's white power structure. That distinction belonged to Commissioner of Public Safety Eugene "Bull" Conner, whose duties included administrative oversight of the city's police and fire departments.

Bull Conner had an ally in Colonel Al Lingo, the state's director of public safety, whose twofold qualifications for the job included a short stint as a highway patrolman in the 1930s and his friendship with George Wallace. When Birmingham's black community took to the streets to protest discrimination in hiring by local businesses, along with the city's rigid system of segregation in public facilities, Colonel Lingo gladly sent state troopers to support Bull Conner's police force with its propensity for using water hoses and police dogs to subdue demonstrators.

The Reverend Martin Luther King Jr., having moved from Montgomery to Atlanta, came to Birmingham to support the black community. After demonstrators took to the streets, many hoped that the images of African American youngsters being savaged by dogs and rolled down city streets by powerful fire hoses might rivet the attention of the nation on the injustices endured by Alabama's blacks and, additionally, compel the Kennedy administration to greater efforts in civil rights.

The violence in Birmingham heightened racial tensions across the state even as George Wallace remained determined to make good on a campaign promise to block desegregation even if it meant physically standing in the schoolhouse door.[34] In April, Attorney General Robert Kennedy flew to Montgomery to make a brief "courtesy call" on Governor Wallace aimed at determining the extent to which the governor might go with his promised "stand." The meeting did little to allay Kennedy's apprehensions, and Kennedy came away from the encounter believing Wallace relished the confrontation as a political plus.

And there were reasons to be uneasy. The upper crust of the Tuscaloosa community benefited from the university's sophistication, something that covered the town with a veneer of civility. Rose later admitted he misjudged the depth of passion many Alabamians felt on the racial issue.[35] For instance, the inside decor at a barbeque restaurant just off campus included cartoon-like portraits of "Martin Luther Koon." In addition to succulent chicken and sauce-dripping pork ribs, the restaurant also sold novelties including black dolls attached to nooses and "nigger hunting licenses."

Frank Rose and George Wallace represented two distinctly different types of southerners. Rose epitomized the concept of "southern gentleman." As articulate as he was handsome, Rose's charm obscured his substantial toughness. Wallace, on the other hand, cultivated his populist image to court a political constituency comprised of folks who, like him, thought hamburger smothered in catsup epitomized fine dining. During the weeks before desegregation, a struggle developed between these two very different men, one that continued throughout the remainder of the decade. While George Wallace was playing to a larger audience on the national political stage, Frank Rose was cultivating far more extensive connections with the media and in Washington.

From the autumn of 1962 to June 1963, Frank Rose moved with steady determination not to "keep Bama white," but to keep Bama safe. President Rose and Dean Blackburn called in student leaders to demand (not ask, but demand) their help in maintaining campus calm. When an undergraduate from Fort Lauderdale was caught distributing a racist pamphlet titled, "The Rebel Underground," he was expelled for untruthfully representing university policy; the same charge used to expel Autherine Lucy nine years earlier.[36] The pace of events quickened on May 16, when US district judge H. Hobart Grooms informed the university that the original injunction ordering Autherine Lucy admitted was still in effect and that any administration official violating that order would be jailed.[37]

On Sunday, May 19, Wallace called Rose and the trustees to Montgomery. By then, it was certain that three black students would be enrolled, two in Tuscaloosa and one at the Huntsville extension. Wallace made clear that while no one would attempt to thwart desegregation, he intended to fulfill his promise to stand in the schoolhouse door.[38]

The following weekend, Frank Rose and Jeff Bennett flew to Washington, DC, to attend a meeting of the National Capital Chapter of the Alabama Alumni Association. The meeting was important for three reasons. First, the chapter was awarding its first ever "Distinguished Alumni Award" to author Harper Lee. Her novel, *To Kill a Mockingbird*, had just hit the silver screen with Gregory Peck in the starring role of Atticus Finch, a small-town lawyer defending a black man unjustly accused of raping a white woman. Second, that Alabama alumni were honoring this noted writer offered an opportunity for positive press coverage for the university, something that might distance it from George Wallace. Third, the trip provided Rose and Bennett a chance to touch base with Robert Kennedy one last time before June 11, 1963, the date Vivian J. Malone and James A. Hood would register for summer classes.

On Saturday morning, May 26, Rose and Bennett visited Hickory Hill, the McLean, Virginia, home of Robert and Ethel Kennedy. Rose's relationship with Robert Kennedy went back nearly a decade when they were both named by the Jaycees as among the "Ten Outstanding Young Men in America." Over breakfast, Bennett suggested that the attorney general not bring in federal troops from Fort Benning in the upcoming confrontation with Wallace. Instead, he suggested federalizing the Alabama National Guard whose local boys (all of whom were white) would be less likely to inflame the population. After breakfast the threesome took the suggestion across the Potomac to the White House.

Attorney General Kennedy escorted Rose and Bennett to the Oval Office. After a while, a clearly agitated President Kennedy emerged from an adjacent room. In a meeting just completed with the Soviet ambassador, Kennedy had protested the unacceptably slow pace of missile withdrawal from Cuba. Fearing a possible renewal of the previous October's Cuban missile crisis, President Kennedy suggested desegregation of the university be postponed because he feared riots in Alabama would divide the nation at a critical time. Rose protested, stating such a delay would encourage Wallace and his supporters, perhaps intensifying their opposition, and assured the president that desegregation would proceed peacefully. President Kennedy turned to his brother, "Bobby, what do you think?" The attorney general replied, "If Frank says there will be no trouble, you can bank on it."[39] That out of the way, President Kennedy endorsed the idea of federalizing the Alabama National Guard and Bobby Kennedy offered to send extra FBI agents to Tuscaloosa to intimidate local Klansmen by interviewing them.

The Birth of the Third University of Alabama

While the second University of Alabama rose from the ashes of the Civil War, the third University of Alabama was born when the legacy of that war, racial segregation, ended on June 11, 1963. For all of the hype, largely a result of George Wallace's determination to use the events surrounding desegregation to feed his own political ambitions, the registration of Vivian Malone and James Hood occurred peacefully.

Wallace's stand in the schoolhouse door served three purposes. First, he substituted himself for the mobs that thwarted desegregation eight years before, enabling Alabama to escape the violence that occurred at Ole Miss the previous October. Second, Wallace made sure there was enough force on hand, including state law enforcement officers as well as five hundred members of the Alabama National Guard involved in Task Force Tusk to deter any mischief from students or outsiders. Third, George Wallace's stand in the schoolhouse door catapulted him into the national political limelight.

While Wallace focused figuratively on the schoolhouse door, in the Tuscaloosa community as well as inside the very real doors of the university, many good people stepped forward to keep Bama safe. From October 1962, Frank Rose gathered support among critical constituents including faculty, alumni, and, closer to time, student leaders. Tuscaloosa community leaders like Buford Boone, bank president George LeMaistre, and realtor Henry Pritchett convinced local businessmen that resisting desegregation could be economically consequential. Furthermore, the impact of Frank Rose's personal friendship with Robert Kennedy, and to a lesser extent his association with President Kennedy, proved helpful. Rose also adroitly worked between opposing interests posed by Montgomery and Washington.

Alabama's student body played their part as well. In early 1956, before the first attempt at desegregation, President Carmichael obtained support from SGA president Walter Flowers and the leader of the Associated Women's Student (AWS) organization but did not go beyond them to include other campus leaders.[40] In the spring of 1963, President Rose and Dean Blackburn reached much deeper into the student power structure to gain the support of a wide range of student leaders.

David Mathews, who witnessed the anarchy of February 1956, after a brief stint in the army returned to campus in February 1960 to work in the Dean of Men's office. Mathews focused on integrating male students living off campus into the greater college environment. In 1962, he left for Columbia University to pursue a doctorate in the history of higher education. At the behest of Blackburn, Mathews returned to Tuscaloosa to help mobilize male students in preparation for the arrival of James Hood. He moved young men he trusted to act civilly into dormitory rooms around and above the one slated for Hood. By noon on June 11, James Hood was eating lunch in Paty Hall and nobody threw food.[41]

Two days later and 150 miles to the north, Dave McGlathery enrolled at the university's extension in Huntsville. Other than an anonymous caller phoning to tell him how "ugly" he was, McGlathery experienced no problems registering or starting classes. While FBI agents shadowed him, there was not the show of force or security that accompanied Malone's and Hood's registrations at the Capstone. There was no need. Registering Vivian Malone and James Hood desegregated the University of Alabama; McGlathery's entry into the Huntsville student body marked the start of a long, slow process of integration.

Desegregation at the Huntsville campus went more easily for several reasons. First, Wallace's presence in Tuscaloosa drew the media there, focusing attention on Foster Auditorium. Second, the space program mushroomed Huntsville's population with an infusion of newcomers, including people from northern states. The Klan, while powerful in neighboring towns like Cullman and Decatur, was not as prominent in Huntsville. Third, University of Alabama in Huntsville (UAH) did not possess the Capstone's long history as the state's "flagship university." There was no large alumni base or an emerging group of "subway" alumni drawn to it, nor was there a sports tradition around which to coalesce. Finally, UAH was a "commuter campus" catering to part-time students, some like McGlathery, taking courses to further their careers with the National Aeronautics and Space Administration.

On a turning tide, the University of Alabama launched a new era of progressive growth under the aegis of the pursuit of academic excellence envisioned by Frank Rose. At the Capstone, because good people worked hard to achieve a noble goal, civilized behavior triumphed where otherwise mayhem might have reigned.

2
Ebb Tide
June 1963 to September 1964

The Third University of Alabama

More than eleven years passed from the time Autherine Lucy's application for admission reached the University of Alabama's registrar's office in 1952 and the day the university desegregated successfully on June 11, 1963. Integration, being different from desegregation, took a lot longer. Desegregation fulfilled legal and moral imperatives through policy changes allowing blacks to attend the university. Integration proved far more difficult since it involved changing cultural norms and breaking down barriers erected by generations of prejudice.[1] As late as 2001, only one previously all-white fraternity at the Capstone had pledged an African American.[2]

Nevertheless, the tide ebbed on the hot afternoon of June 11, 1963, after Governor Wallace pulled out of town leaving Frank Rose and his team back in control. Three companies of Alabama National Guard and around eight hundred state agents, the most proficient being the contingent of state troopers, supported the university's small campus police cadre. During registration, when only students were allowed to enter dormitories, the fathers, mothers, and brothers looked on helplessly as their daughters and sisters struggled in the exhausting heat while lugging armfuls of clothing, heavy luggage, portable radios or record players, and hair dryers into their dorms. A few beefy law enforcement officers stepped forward, adding their sweat and sacrificing a bit of their dignity to help out. "Nobody told us to do it," one sweaty trooper grinned, "but how y'all gonna let a little girl carry all that stuff with no help?"[3]

Female students, used to dealing with university regulations constricting their social life, coped with the temporary curfew that applied to males and females alike and was in place from ten o'clock to six o'clock in the morning better than males who lived relatively free from rules. One young lady commented, "Sure it upset me, but my mother has been waiting for a curfew like this for years." A male student, using a metaphor perhaps lost on post–Cold War generations, felt differently. "You feel like you've got to rush it because the Brandenburg Gate slams shut at ten."[4]

Students who rushed to beat the curfew may have taken in Joanne Woodward strutting to the heavy beat of the Dave Rose Orchestra's rendition of "The Stripper" in a motion picture of the same title playing at the Bama Theater on Greensboro Avenue. Or a couple of blocks away at the Capri Theater, students might watch Sean Connery establishing himself as the quintessential James Bond in "Dr. No."

While the Capstone appeared safe during the first week of summer school, appearances may have betrayed reality. On June 12, one official found only two of the twenty-six checkpoints set up to verify the credentials of students or faculty entering campus occupied. In fact, Governor Wallace was in the process of withdrawing state troopers and had already wired President Kennedy to inform him that the federal government bore full responsibility for keeping the peace on campus. He also stated that 288 state security personnel would be off campus by two o'clock in the afternoon of June 12, with the remainder gone four days later, Sunday, June 16. That left campus security to the university police and five hundred guardsmen of Operation Tusk.[5]

Fortunately, the extensive measures in place on June 11 dissuaded any local extremists who might have taken advantage of lapses occurring in the immediate aftermath. The university dodged a bullet . . . perhaps many bullets. Nevertheless, the campus was safe and calm. At the end of the month, Frank Rose wrote a friend declaring, "Things are relatively quiet on campus and we have returned to normalcy."[6]

As summer moved into its dog days, something between chaos and serendipity happened. Initially, James Hood settled well into university life. So well, he penned a guest editorial for the *Crimson-White* titled, "Needed: More Students, Less Pickets." Its publication initiated a series of events culminating in Hood's abrupt departure. Ironically, the editorial read more like something written by a segregationist than a young man who had just broken the color barrier at the Capstone.

Hood wrote that although black leaders were accomplished men, "the bulk of these people involved in the organizations are students and uneducated people." He added, "Civil rights groups thrive on conflict and will continue to exist so long as they are able to instigate conflict." Hood concluded, "There must be more time spent in the classroom and less time wasted on picket lines."[7] The following day the *Birmingham News* reprinted Hood's editorial.

Were Hood's words a matter of conviction? Or was this an attempt to curry favor among fellow students, his newfound white friends? Hood claimed that the editorial was given to the *Birmingham News* without his knowledge, implying he naively expected its circulation would be limited to the university community.[8]

Having dug himself into a hole, Hood shoveled deeper. On July 16, speaking at a civil rights rally in his hometown of Gadsden, Hood tried to justify his editorial. He accused university officials of attempting to trick him into expulsion and charged the administration with pressuring a professor to lower his grade. Hood also claimed Al Lingo cursed him. Finally, he denied ever writing the editorial. Unbeknownst to Hood, state investigators in the audience recorded his remarks, which they then released to the *Montgomery Advertiser.*[9]

Alabama's trustees turned the matter over to Dean John Blackburn who sent a letter to James Hood instructing him to report to his office at two o'clock on August 12 to discuss the situation.[10] Iredell Jenkins, in his capacity as an acting assistant dean, wrote a memorandum to Blackburn urging leniency. "I am very confident that the expulsion or even suspension of Jimmy Hood would have a serious deleterious effect on our faculty morale; and furthermore, that it would make it difficult to secure new faculty. It is even likely to lead to a further wave of faculty resignations."[11]

James Hood saved himself from added embarrassment and the university from a potentially difficult situation. The day before the scheduled meeting, Hood's attorney announced his client's withdrawal "to avoid a complete mental and physical breakdown." According to an article in the *Birmingham News*, an unnamed trustee confided that Hood's allegations constituted grounds for suspension if not expulsion.[12]

When the fall semester began on September 20, the start of the Capstone's first academic year as a desegregated institution, Vivian Malone was its only black student. A few welcomed her, most kept their distance. She lived in a private room in Mary Burke Hall and, throughout the first semester, US marshals escorted her to class. When she socialized, it was with students at nearby Stillman College.

Attitudes among white students varied. Many shared the prejudices extant throughout the state. Most had no interaction with Vivian Malone. But to some degree all were affected by the presence of National Guard troops and some resented the intrusion. Racist venom continued to spew from the *Rebel*

Underground. A late summer issue celebrated the withdrawal of James Hood with a "One Down, One to Go" headline.[13]

George Wallace's vitriol fed the base instincts of a people facing social changes with, at least from their perspective, enormously ominous implications. On the last Sunday before the beginning of the new academic year, September 15, 1963, an explosion ripped apart the basement of the Sixteenth Street Baptist Church in Birmingham. Four young black girls died. Ku Klux Klansman Robert "Dynamite Bob" Chambliss was later convicted of planting the bomb.[14]

Summer into Autumn: Thank God for Frank Rose and BOMB

At the start of the fall semester, renewed violence in Birmingham compelled the university to shore up its preparations in anticipation of trouble. At registration, students were encouraged to sign a pledge foreswearing disorderly conduct. Dean Blackburn issued a memorandum prohibiting students from drinking beverages from paper cups publicly while on campus. The switch from soft drink vending machines dispensing bottled soda to machines providing soft drinks in paper cups, a precaution taken prior to June 11 to eliminate a source of bottles that might be used as missiles, also made it difficult to determine what was being quaffed; a simple soft drink or one laced with bourbon or rum.[15]

More was at stake than compliance with local drinking ordinances. Officials in the dean of men's office knew fraternity parties loomed. As the revelry wore on and the effects of imbibing took hold, groups of students often wandered between fraternity houses. This, the administration feared, might lead to the formation of mobs. Violators risked penalties ranging from probation to suspension. After the first weekend, thirty young men faced disciplinary action. University officials also hoped the crackdown on drinking might reduce the university's party school reputation.[16]

Carol Ann Self was among the entering freshmen in the class of '67. A majorette at Central High School in Phenix City, Alabama, "going Greek" seemed the thing to do. Meeting the sisters at the various houses came easily to the petite brunette with a pixie-like face and dark brown eyes. At the end of rush week she received a bid from Kappa Kappa Gamma and then settled into the school year, residing in Martha Parham Hall. Over the next four years as Carol Self gained iconic status as an "Alabama coed," she was also changing as the turmoil of the 1960s illuminated and altered her worldview.[17]

Across campus, Jack Drake, a freshman from Birmingham's working-class neighborhood of Gardendale, checked into Somerville Hall, a men's dorm across from Paty Hall. A political science major, Jack enrolled in a six-year program that bypassed the bachelor's degree while resulting in a law degree. Given his family's relatively modest financial situation, going Greek was not an option. Additionally, his independent temperament and argumentative nature did not jibe with the conformist attitude embraced by fraternities. Instead, Jack joined the Capstone's cinema society and got involved in campus politics. Over the next six years the futures of Jack Drake and Carol Self converged amid the changing times that lay ahead.[18]

As September waned, if students did not embrace the changing order, at least they tolerated it. Although most behaved well, opposition to integration continued. On October 14, the SGA House of Representatives unanimously approved a resolution commending President Rose for his handling of desegregation. Two nights later, the SGA Senate rejected the resolution by a vote of 10–6 with one abstention. Jim Henderson, graduate representative to the senate, led the effort to kill the resolution. He stated as his reason, "It would be interpreted as an expression of student opinion and, at this early date, I don't believe we know what students think."[19]

The following week, president pro-tem of the Senate, Harry McCrary, reiterated Henderson's point concerning the divided nature of student opinion. McCrary expressed his own personal opposition to integration and also criticized the "coercive elements involved in convincing the University to make this move."[20] McCrary added, "For the record, thank God for Frank Rose."

On the first weekend in November, the university celebrated its annual homecoming, the highlight of which was the Saturday afternoon football game with Mississippi State University. The student homecoming committee selected "BOMB," an acronym for "Bama Orbits, Maroons Blasted," as the 1963 homecoming theme. A *Crimson-White* editorial chided the committee stating, "To the people of the rest of the United States it probably seems appropriate that the theme for the University of Alabama's homecoming is 'BOMB.' After all, most of the publicity about Alabama has the same theme."[21] While the choice of themes might have seemed inappropriate given the September 15, 1963, Klan bombing of the Sixteenth Street Baptist Church in Birmingham, previous years' themes included BEAR, HOBO, BAM, and STORM.

On Friday night, Governor Wallace, President Rose, and Coach Bryant spoke at a pep rally in Foster Auditorium. Incapable of separating politics from sports, Wallace noted, "I stand with Mississippi in everything except when it comes to football."[22] Wallace then joined the crowd on the Quadrangle for the annual bonfire rally where Pat Trammell, quarterback of the 1961

National Championship team and at the time a student at the medical school in Birmingham, spoke. The following day the Crimson Tide eked out a 20–19 victory.[23]

Scrapping Sisters, Real Bombs, and a Friday to Remember

The National Guard presence notwithstanding, life on campus was not much different from previous autumns. More than five hundred male freshmen "went Greek," a slight increase over the previous year. The Sigma Chi Derby, an annual event at the Capstone, took place the week following homecoming.

The 1963 derby involved sorority sisters snatching derbies from the heads of Sigma Chi brothers as they walked across campus. The sorority collecting the most derbies won. Supposedly, this contest provided a little harmless fun, but in the autumn of 1963, something went wrong.

Early in the contest, fights broke out among competing sisters. The deteriorating situation prompted Dean Healy to phone the fraternity's social chairman to demand he call off the festivities, but he was unavailable to take her call. Meanwhile, the pilfering sisters pilfered on.

In a particularly nasty incident reminiscent of something out of a female version of William Golding's *Lord of the Flies*, sisters from one sorority held down a member of a rival sorority as they shouted, "Kick her! Kick her! Kick her!," while a booted sister punted away at the hapless victim. In another, a Kappa Kappa Gamma (Kappa) bit Zeta Tau Alpha (Zeta) Sally Wahlsen. The Kappas called a truce and, according to a sorority spokesperson, Kappa representatives resolved the unpleasantness with the Zetas. Soon thereafter, the injured Zeta raised a bandaged hand to swear she "couldn't remember such a thing ever happening." Meanwhile, Kappa sister Betty Vines reported, "I was trying to get a derby off one of the Sigma Chis when I slipped and fell." Probably due to the release of adrenalin, sister Betty didn't notice her injury until that weekend after she returned home to Birmingham. By then the Kappas had snatched their way to victory.

A Sigma Chi offered this succinct analysis. "I guess sorority girls at Alabama are just vicious." An Alpha Delta Gamma sister, whose sorority avoided participation in such revelries, provided an epitaph to the whole affair, "It was an ugly, ugly thing, and it is best forgotten."[24]

Such behavior was uncharacteristic of Alabama coeds known for their modesty, decorum, and gentility. Indeed, university in loco parentis regulations applicable to female students sought to perpetuate those qualities. Until the end of the decade, female students were required to wear dresses or skirts and blouses to class. Blue jeans, allowed for male students, were forbidden to females except in art class. Even so, women in jeans or shorts bound for art or physical education classes were required to don a raincoat or overcoat for the walk.

Even for young women of legal age, university rules forbade the consumption of alcoholic beverages along with visiting male students in their off-campus apartments. These rules, although unevenly enforced and largely ignored, nonetheless remained on the books. In many ways the Capstone was a bastion of propriety, if not always sobriety.

During the fall semester, the Cotillion Club booked a number of acts into Foster Auditorium. The Smothers Brothers appeared in late October and, the second week in November, sexy singer-actress Julie London cooed her way through "Cry Me a River." Meanwhile, Joan Baez canceled her scheduled appearance because she feared the audience at the University of Alabama would be segregated.[25]

The BOMB theme at homecoming and "rampaging" sisters on sorority row presaged a return to normalcy, almost. In early November, the Department of the Army announced two of the three companies comprising Task Force Tusk would be deactivated at the end of the month, leaving 125 guardsmen on duty at the university. The deactivation, however, affected more than 220 men from the Tuscaloosa area.[26] In the predawn hours of Saturday, November 16, a stick of dynamite tossed from a speeding car awakened many of the young women sleeping in Mary Burke and Martha Parham. The blast left a small hole in the pavement on a street just east of Mary Burke Hall where Vivian Malone slept. The following night, someone threw a stick of dynamite from a car into the parking lot of an African American nightclub on the outskirts of Tuscaloosa.[27] Early on Tuesday morning, November 19, a third explosion, this one on Tenth Street just four blocks from Mary Burke Hall, shattered windows in that black neighborhood. In the aftermath, Dean Blackburn urged male students not to rush to the scene of future bombings, both for their own safety and because congregating around the scene of an explosion might hamper firefighters and other emergency responders.[28]

Local authorities impaneled a grand jury to investigate the bombings. In December, four guardsmen were arrested and then charged with setting off the three explosions. One of them claimed he did it to support Governor Wallace because "it took a lot of courage for him to make his stand." Another suspect expressed a more pragmatic motivation. He wanted to remain on active duty because the activation of the guard in June cost him his sawmill job.[29]

The deactivation of the guard continued despite the bombings. In appreciation for their contribution to keeping Bama safe, President Rose hosted a dinner at the Indian Hills Country Club for the officers commanding Task Force Tusk and their wives.

By noon on most Fridays, students shifted their attention from studies toward the weekend's partying, dating, watching television, and catching up on sleep. On Friday November 22, Capstone students also anticipated an easy week ahead because classes dismissed at their conclusion on the Wednesday before Thanksgiving. They also looked forward to the annual gridiron contest with archrival Auburn played, until 1965, on Thanksgiving afternoon at Legion Field in Birmingham. Students eating lunch in the Supe Store cafeteria inside the Alabama Student Union building (now Reese Phifer Hall), in dormitory dining facilities at Mary Burke and Paty Halls, and in various fraternity and sorority houses, perhaps heard snatches of news bulletins coming out of Dallas. It was around one o'clock in Tuscaloosa when reports confirmed the assassination of President Kennedy. While a few students cheered, many more wept.

The following week the *Crimson-White* ran a two-page spread featuring photos of President Kennedy accompanied by notable quotes. An analysis suggested that while Kennedy was an eloquent speaker, Lyndon Johnson might more effectively move civil rights legislation into law.[30] It was a prescient piece.

Along the Difficult Road to Academic Excellence

At the start of the fall semester, a *Crimson-White* editorial called on the university to extend the library's night hours from ten o'clock to eleven o'clock. The rationale for closing the library so early was that female students faced an eleven o'clock curfew on weeknights. Since it took less than ten minutes to walk from the library to any dormitory or sorority house, the editorial argued it made sense to lengthen the hours, noting the extra time "might mean the difference between passing and failing an examination or completing a term paper."[31] In February, in addition to purchasing the library's first Xerox electronic copying machine, the university extended library hours to eleven o'clock Sunday through Friday nights.[32]

Meanwhile, George Wallace parlayed his stand in the door at Foster Auditorium into enough political capital to burst onto the national conservative scene as either a kingmaker or potential spoiler in what shaped up as a contest between the Democratic incumbent—at the time, President Kennedy—and Arizona's Republican senator Barry Goldwater. Indeed, a political shift away from the Democratic Party's hold on the South appeared possible, maybe even likely. Accordingly, in early November the Alpha Lambda Delta female freshman honorary society hosted a panel titled, "Liberalism versus Conservatism." Historian John Ramsey presented the case for liberalism while political science professor Walter Bennett explained the conservative perspective. The History Department's Thomas B. Alexander moderated the panel. What ensued was more discussion than debate since Ramsey and Bennett held moderate rather than extreme political views. Bennett, although presenting the conservative viewpoint, also conceded, "Some people in the United States are living in the nineteenth rather than the twentieth century." Ramsey offered, "Extremes of either position are bad." Alexander opined that southerners tended to be liberal on almost all issues except race. Ramsey agreed, adding that the South also remained a bastion of conservative Christianity.[33]

Professors of the quality of Ramsey, Bennett, and Alexander inspired and mentored students smart enough to recognize the value of their wisdom. Nevertheless, many undergraduates simply wanted to get through the curriculum with as little effort as possible. Graduate School of Arts and Sciences dean, Frederick W. Conner, in a letter to President Rose, urged the administration to stand firm in upholding academic standards or risk impeding "the progress along the difficult road to excellence which we are all anxious to make."[34]

The road to excellence included taking steps to encourage increased faculty research and publication. A new sabbatical policy adopted in May 1964 represented a step in that direction. Under this initiative, faculty with six years at the university could apply for one semester away from teaching at full pay or two semesters at half pay. Normally, professors might use sabbaticals to research and write a book or series of scholarly articles or, perhaps, prepare a new course. The policy also allowed faculty and administrators to work on or complete their terminal degrees.[35]

The state's reputation on racial matters made it difficult to attract and, in some cases, retain highly qualified faculty. With the peaceful transition to integration under way, attention turned to bolstering the quality of faculty. This is not to say the university was bereft of fine scholars before or during the Rose era. Ann Gary Pannell, who received her D.Phil. from Oxford in 1936, taught history at Alabama from 1939 to 1949 and then left for the presidency of Sweet Briar College. Ralph L. Chermock, internationally noted for his study of butterflies, was a member of the biology faculty from 1947 to 1966.

Increased compensation offered one way to attract new faculty and helped to keep good scholars already on board. Accordingly, in 1963 faculty salaries ranged from $5,100 for instructors to $11,500 for full professors. Raises for top performers ran between $500 and $1,000. Nevertheless, at the end of the 1963–64 academic year, President Rose lamented that faculty salaries still lagged behind other southern public universities.[36]

In the annual "State of the University Report," delivered to the trustees at their meeting over homecoming weekend in November 1963, Frank Rose noted eighty-five new hires for the year, which offset seventy-nine losses due to retirement, resignation, and death, a net gain of six. While only twenty-nine possessed terminal degrees, that still represented a positive increase in the percentage of faculty holding doctorates. New faculty directly from graduate studies who had not done so would be expected to complete their dissertations in the foreseeable future.[37]

By the mid-1960s, higher education in the United States had become more affordable. The constant median dollar income of the American family increased more than 100 percent between 1928 and 1964, while the constant dollar cost of college tuition, room, and board rose only 25 percent.[38] Because the University of Alabama provided a good education at a reasonable price, President Rose considered it a state treasure. To sustain progress, the trustees raised tuition from $125 to $150 per semester for Alabama residents. Out-of-state students paid twice that figure. A double-occupancy dormitory room ran $200 per semester and a men's food contract in Paty Hall cost $420. Women students paid $20 less for a semester's food contract. A telephone cost $28.50 per semester. Even with the increases, a Capstone education totaled less than $2,000 a year in tuition, room, board, and extraneous fees.[39]

By the autumn of 1963, Coach Bryant had brought Alabama back to national football prominence. In that critical year, with racial tensions percolating in Birmingham and threatening to spill over into Tuscaloosa and onto the Capstone, the Tide won eight games while losing only two. In October, the Florida Gators visited Denny Stadium where quarterback Steve Spurrier, destined to become one of the finest collegiate football coaches of his time, guided the Gators to a 10–6 victory. Stunned fans could not know that eighteen seasons would pass before the Tide suffered another defeat in Denny Stadium when, late in the 1982 season, in the last game Bryant coached at home, Southern Mississippi prevailed 38–29. In the 1963 Thanksgiving weekend game at Legion Field, Auburn delivered a 10–8 defeat. Alabama went on to face Ole Miss in the Sugar Bowl, where sophomore quarterback Steve Sloan, substituting for a suspended Joe Namath, guided the Tide to a 12–7 victory over the Rebels.[40]

Distant Thunder and Continuing Traditions

During the university's first year of desegregation, events in faraway Vietnam seemed remote. Amid the excitement of June 11, 1963, when Malone and Hood registered for classes, few associated with the university noted the monk in Saigon who burned himself to death that same day, doing so to protest the policies of the South Vietnamese government of Ngo Dinh Diem, a regime supported by the United States. On November 2, 1963, in a coup d état approved by the United States, the South Vietnamese army removed Diem from power.

In 1963, campus unrest over the war in Vietnam lay in the future but would not reach Tuscaloosa for nearly five years. The southern military tradition was strong at Alabama where all able-bodied freshmen and sophomore males who had not completed military service were required to take four one-hour credit courses in basic military science or aerospace studies, offered respectively under the auspices of Army and Air Force ROTC. While some freshmen and sophomore men groused about "Rotcy," especially the wearing of old, sometimes poorly fitting wool uniforms on Tuesday and Thursday "drill days" and suffering through orders barked by cadet officers a year or two older than themselves, most figured out that little more than polished shoes on drill days and steady class attendance produced an easy "A" with three accompanying quality points. Generally, students handled ROTC with grudging grace. A few used the opportunity to gain entrée into meaningful military careers.

Grumbling among freshmen and sophomores over "Rotcy" notwithstanding, until the end of the decade most students and faculty respected military service. In the early 1960s there were many veterans of the Second World War among the faculty and administration. Some like university registrar Hubert E. Mate, a captain in the Naval Reserve, held reserve commissions. Additionally, Maxwell Air Force Base, located one hundred miles south of Tuscaloosa in Montgomery, was the center for all Air Force professional military education, including ROTC. Frank Rose also served on the Air University Board of Visitors, a group roughly equivalent to a university board of trustees, chairing it in 1963. The following year, the Secretary of the Army invited Rose to join the Advisory Panel for Army ROTC, an invitation he readily accepted.[41]

The Capstone's brigade benefited from the presence of a veteran of the war in Southeast Asia when Capt. William J. Yantis reported for instructor duty following a tour as an advisor to the Royal Laotian Army. Accordingly, the commander of the Army ROTC detachment presented Captain Yantis with his Combat Infantryman's Badge for service rendered in his previous assignment. The award, one coveted among career officers, required participation in at least five combat engagements.

Captain Yantis put his unconventional warfare expertise to use by establishing an Army ROTC counterguerrilla unit. In addition to studying guerrilla tactics and ways to counter them, this elite unit wore snappy black berets and "bloused" their trousers over highly polished combat boots. At Bama Day in early May 1964, the "Black Berets" demonstrated small unit tactics and hand-to-hand combat outside Tuomey Hall, the Army ROTC headquarters located on the Quadrangle next to the Amelia Gayle Gorgas Library.[42]

As the decade unfolded and the war in Vietnam intensified, relations between many universities and government agencies associated with national security, including the intelligence services, deteriorated. Not so at the Capstone. Recruiters from the National Security Agency (NSA), the ultrasecret agency charged with gathering electronically transmitted information and developing it into intelligence, administered their professional qualifications test to interested applicants on December 7, 1963.[43]

On Sunday, February 9, 1964, just as second semester got underway, the British rock group the Beatles made their American debut on the *Ed Sullivan Show*. During the days and weeks that followed, many American teenage boys fluffed their hair as best they could and stood before the bathroom mirror mouthing, "I want to hold your hand! I want to hold your hand!" Across America, teen girls swooned while their mothers seemed resigned to the relative innocence of the lads from Liverpool. Compared to the gyrations of Elvis Presley and the raunchiness of some of Jerry Lee Lewis's songs, Beatles love songs seemed almost—if not completely—cherubic by comparison. In the spring of 1964, as the Capstone entered its first full calendar year as a university for all Alabamians, a similar innocence prevailed.

On Tuesday, February 11, Katherine Ann Porter, author of *Ship of Fools*, the best-selling novel of 1962 and soon-to-be major motion picture, spoke to an overflow crowd in Morgan Hall Auditorium. "If we didn't know evil we wouldn't need good," Porter informed the audience. That same week the University Players performed, "Waiting for Godot," an avant-garde drama by Samuel Beckett.[44] Freshman Jack Drake attended both these events.

In March, the Detroit Symphony held a concert in Foster. On April 2, 1964,

Johnny Cash and June Carter performed in Foster, followed a few days later by the piano team of Ferrante and Teicher.[45] On April 9, folk singer Joan Baez, who earlier canceled her performance at the university, played nearby Stillman College. She told her audience, "I prefer it here at Stillman because it is integrated. The University wouldn't really be integrated." Indeed, a number of Alabama students sat in the audience.[46]

In addition to opportunities for cultural enrichment, the university offered traditional kinds of fun associated with fraternity parties and dating. Beginning in March 1964, the administration extended weekend curfews at women's dormitories and sorority houses from eleven thirty to midnight.[47]

Selection of next year's "Miss Alabama" took place just before the end of the spring semester. In the absence of majorettes, a "band sponsor," dressed in a two-piece crimson-and-white suit and cradling a bouquet of white chrysanthemums, led the Million Dollar Band. In May 1964, the band elected Carol Self from a field of candidates nominated by sororities and other groups to march at the head of the Million Dollar Band for the forthcoming school year. The *Crimson-White* reported, "While the band played 'Yea Alabama,' Miss Self managed a nervous smile and fidgeted with a bouquet of red roses, often biting her lip to fight back possible tears of happiness."[48]

The US Surgeon General's report definitively connecting cigarette smoking to lung cancer did not come out until summer, and even after it did, smoking among students and faculty was common. In those days, little tin ashtrays sat on most desks in almost every classroom. Often professors—especially the younger, "cooler ones"—lit up while they lectured.

Other than cigarettes and the excessive consumption of alcohol among some portions of the student population, the only other drug of concern was Dexedrine. Amphetamines, readily available as diet pills, enabled students to cram through the night for exams or finish a term paper too long delayed. With final exams approaching, Assistant Dean of Men Ray Swords conducted a panel in Paty Hall to discuss "Dex" as students called it. The panel, consisting of a local physician and a PhD candidate in psychology, concluded that coffee and over-the-counter caffeine pills provided safer and more predictable stimulants.[49]

Looking Ahead by Looking Back

Completed in 1963, Marten ten Hoor Hall, the new College of Arts and Sciences building named in honor of Dean Emeritus Marten ten Hoor, was ready for dedication. A three-day symposium titled, "Conference on the Social Sciences and the Development of the New South" marked the occasion set for late April 1964. Former president Oliver Carmichael returned to deliver the keynote address. The conference symbolically recognized the birth of the third University of Alabama, although no reference was made to it as such. This birth, a spiritual rather than a physical one, reflected the changes initiated by the end of segregation and anticipated many more to come.

President Rose invited Governor Wallace to participate in the dedication of Marten ten Hoor Hall. Courtesy and propriety demanded he do so since Wallace served as ex officio chairman of the University of Alabama Board of Trustees. Wallace declined stating, "As you know, I have entered several Presidential primaries and am now engaged in a campaign in Indiana."[50]

In the keynote address, Carmichael noted, "It is not inconceivable that if attention were focused upon excavation of ideas buried in history, literature, philosophy and art, a new source of interest and motivation might be discovered."[51] John Bloomer, managing editor of the *Birmingham News*, joined Philip Hoffman, president of the University of Houston on a panel addressing the place of social sciences in academia. Professor Hudson Strode, recently retired from the Alabama English faculty, and Walter Sullivan of Vanderbilt University both questioned whether southern literature was becoming less southern. On Friday evening, April 25, Secretary of Commerce Luther H. Hodges wrapped up the conference with an address in Morgan Hall where, seventeen months earlier, the faculty voted to support Frank Rose in his determination to affect a peaceful desegregation.[52]

The first full year of desegregation went relatively smoothly. Seniors who graduated in May probably did not find their last year at the Capstone much different from when they entered in September 1960. Reports and rumors indicating five to eight additional black students were slated for enrollment in September caused nary a ripple among the student body.[53]

White Sheets at Home and Dark Clouds across the Pacific

Two events during the summer of 1964 held both immediate and long-range implications for the university. Ku Klux Klan–inspired mob action in downtown Tuscaloosa in July and picketing of various businesses, including Morrison's Cafeteria at the edge of campus, constituted the first event. The second, with longer-term implications, took place the following month in the Gulf of Tonkin off the coast of Vietnam.

In early June, when "whites only" signs went up on bathrooms and water fountains at the new Tuscaloosa County Courthouse, irate black citizens formed the Tuscaloosa Citizens for Action Committee, headed by Reverend T. Y. Rogers, pastor of the First African Baptist Church, to challenge such racially discriminatory practices. After a series of demonstrations, culminating in a confrontation between blacks and the Tuscaloosa police on June 9, 1964, in which ninety-one protestors were arrested, a federal court ordered the offensive courthouse signs removed. The next challenge would be to force local compliance with the Civil Rights Act, still being filibustered by southern senators.[54] Figurative battle lines were drawn between the Klan and the Tuscaloosa Citizens for Action Committee.

On July 2, 1964, President Lyndon Johnson signed the Civil Rights Act of 1964, a bill outlawing racial discrimination in public schools, libraries, playgrounds, and in places of public accommodations including restaurants, theaters, hotels and motels, along with waiting rooms in bus terminals, airports, and railroad stations. The new law also forbade racial discrimination in hiring.

Two days later, on the afternoon of Independence Day, a handful of black Tuscaloosans entered previously "whites only" restaurants and theaters for the first time. The Reverend T. Y. Rogers and the Reverend Charles L. Hutcheson broke the color barrier at Morrison's Cafeteria. They ate lunch and then left without incident. A few hours later a handful of black patrons who showed up for dinner found the cafeteria closed. That same afternoon, between two thirty and four thirty, the Capri Theater admitted about twenty-five African Americans. White moviegoers simply moved, leaving black patrons by themselves. After the movie, the theater quietly emptied. It was a peaceful start to a tumultuous week in T-Town. It was the fourth of July but the day wasn't over.

Around nine o'clock at night, a crowd gathered in the vicinity of the Capri after it was rumored black patrons had entered the theater. The crowd, many of them people leaving the theater at the end of the early evening show, dispersed after an hour. The rumors proved false.

Meanwhile, Fred Barton, manager of the Bama Theater, told the *Tuscaloosa News* that the chain owning the Bama and Capri would comply with the new civil rights law. Earlier that day, Morrison's Cafeteria head office in Mobile announced its chain of restaurants would serve all customers regardless of race.[55]

Some restaurants took down their "whites only" and "we reserve the right to refuse service to anyone" signs. The relatively peaceful nature of Saturday may have been due to its being Independence Day, a time when most people were celebrating with their families at home or at newly desegregated, but still not integrated, local parks. It may also have been that initial efforts at desegregation so soon after the passage of the Civil Rights Act caught local white supremacists—including the Klan—by surprise.

The following day, the situation deteriorated. Nine students joined with Professor James R. Jaquith and his wife to brave a Ku Klux Klan picket line to attend a Sunday matinee at the Capri. Among the picketers were two Klansmen carrying signs that read, "Why spend a dollar to sit next to a nigger?" and "This establishment serves niggers, please stay away."[56]

Picketers hurled insults at the students, the professor, and his wife as they entered the Capri. Several Klansmen used syringes to spray oil of mustard on them. The crowd outside the theater grew larger during the movie. Following the film, seven university students stayed in the relative safety of the Capri while two students joined the Jaquiths as they pushed through taunting Klansmen outside. Once free of the crowd, they then dashed for the professor's nearby Volkswagen, pursued by several Klansmen. Upon reaching the vehicle, they discovered all four tires slashed. One Klansman remarked, "That was a real expensive movie."[57] The Tuscaloosa police were conspicuous by their absence.

The incident involving the university professor, his wife, and students who accompanied them was no happenstance. On that same Sunday morning, the letters to the editor section of the *Tuscaloosa News* published a submission by Mrs. Jaquith in which she wrote, "Americans in Tuscaloosa will be ceded their first class citizenship, but how? Will it be accompanied progressively and honorably or with the strident and unyielding savagery of those committed to a moribund dreamlike past?"[58]

On Monday, Klansmen in full regalia showed up to picket Morrison's, a favorite of students and faculty because it served good food at reasonable prices. In the days to come, Klan picketers outside the cafeteria, while avoiding violence, nevertheless attempted to intimidate would-be patrons. As an out-of-town couple and their son visiting Tuscaloosa to check out the campus before the young man enrolled in September neared the picket line, they warily eyed a Klansman carrying a sign that warned, "You might be eating off the same plates niggers did." Undaunted, the trio walked into the picket line. A hulking Klansman snickered, "Y'all must be some kind of nigger lovers." The father, a Presbyterian minister from Leighton, Alabama, and a former collegiate football lineman, stopped. He turned and faced the Klansman, fixed him with a cold, unblinking stare, and then answered in a measured and unwavering voice, "You bet." The Klansman stepped back. As my family entered Morrison's, I was proud to be the son of that Presbyterian minister.

Although my father didn't know Buford Boone, the intrepid publisher of the

Tuscaloosa News, they were kindred spirits.[59] In a front-page editorial published on July 7, Boone warned of the potential threat of mob violence. He pointed to "elements of the white mob . . . busy-bodying around a cafeteria which was complying with a new law because it had to do so" and decried the fact that "a group invaded a private business and forcibly ejected colored patrons who had been seated and who were about to be served." Then Boone thrust home. "Supreme commander of these reckless irrepressible white elements is a sickly-looking pitiable little man named Robert Shelton . . . living as a human jackal on a racket known as the Ku Klux Klan."[60]

The description of Shelton as "sickly-looking" and a "human jackal" resulted in a million-dollar lawsuit for libel. In 1965, a Tuscaloosa court awarded Shelton a pitiable five-hundred-dollar award as compensation. Buford Boone paid the court-ordered compensation the same day.[61]

Meanwhile, Klansmen policing the streets of Tuscaloosa drove around town in sedans with long "whip" antennas. This effort at intimidating blacks along with any white supporters drew scorn from Boone. In a front-page editorial titled, "Lullaby and Good Night," he wrote, "Sleep well tonight, the Grand Wizard and his plug uglies will be patrolling the streets of our city." He continued, "The Grand Wizard glides up to a trouble spot, radio antenna whipping the clean breeze above his command vehicle. . . . He steps out . . . looking like an owl in his dark glasses."[62]

On Thursday night, July 9, only the intervention of the Tuscaloosa police prevented what might have been the lynching of actor Jack Palance, his wife, and three children. The Palances were visiting relatives in nearby Northport when, on their last night in town, the family went to see "The World of Henry Orient" playing at the Druid Theater. They walked through a Klan picket line for the nine o'clock showing.

Soon after the Palance family settled into their seats, a rumor spread that the actor was encouraging compliance with the Civil Rights Act. A mob gathered outside the Druid. Projectiles and curses flew through the air. A brick shattered the theater marquis. The manager took the family into his locked office for their protection while police used tear gas to clear the streets. After the mob scattered, the police escorted the actor and his family to safety. Palance later told the *Tuscaloosa News* he was unaware of protests and demonstrations surrounding the civil rights law.[63]

Referring to this incident in his fourth and final front-page editorial of the week, Buford Boone lamented, "We nearly mobbed Jack Palance. . . . We have let mobsters project the image of our community. This must end now." Boone called on both the Klan to stop picketing and black leaders to cease their demonstrations and boycotting of local businesses.[64] Meanwhile, the city commissioners established a curfew from eight o'clock at night to six in the morning for anyone less than twenty-one years of age. The curfew did not apply to the university campus.

The University of Alabama remained at the periphery of downtown violence, although Morrison's was located at the edge of campus. Nevertheless, Capstone officials acted cautiously. On the Monday morning following the Sunday afternoon incident at the Capri, Jeff Bennett summoned student leaders to the vice president's office. Although Bennett assured them the administration would not forbid students to patronize local businesses, he also advised them not to provoke situations that might reflect badly on the university. Bennett suggested students avoid going to theaters and restaurants in groups larger than two or three so as not to appear provocative.[65]

Things quieted down the following week. On Monday, July 13, the Tuscaloosa Citizens for Action Committee called off their boycott of white businesses. "All we are asking is that merchants and their clerks be courteous to our people."[66] Additionally, black citizens made fewer attempts to test their newly acquired civil rights. Accordingly, Klan picketing dropped off.

As the summer of 1964 moved into its dog days, members of the incoming class of 1968 attended one of three freshmen orientation sessions. During the three-day sessions, students underwent a battery of aptitude tests. Frank Rose's efforts to expand the university's facilities anticipated a sharp increase in enrollment coming with the first wave of the baby-boomer generation. Large auditoriums in ten Hoor Hall handled hundreds of freshmen crammed into required courses like Western Civilization taught by brilliant young professors like David McElroy and Hugh Ragsdale. What could not be anticipated were the changes in student culture that would transpire before the freshmen of '64 walked into Denny Stadium for commencement three years and eight months later. In August, as the last freshmen cycled through orientation and others, in cities and towns across the state, busied themselves saying goodbye to former high school classmates, events taking place on the other side of the globe would shape and alter them over the next four years while also transforming student culture at the Capstone.

On August 4, 1964, several North Vietnamese torpedo boats attacked two US Navy destroyers operating off the southern coast of North Vietnam. President Johnson, soon to be locked into presidential campaign electioneering against his Republican challenger, Senator Barry Goldwater, having posited himself as the "peace candidate" who "sought no wider war," chose not to retaliate. However, after confused reports concerning a possible second wave of attacks the following night, Johnson ordered retaliatory air strikes. Accordingly, sixty-four US Navy strike aircraft flew from two aircraft carriers stationed in the Gulf of Tonkin to bomb radar installations, petroleum storage facilities, and the naval base at Vinh. North Vietnamese gunners downed two planes. Congress responded with the *Gulf of Tonkin Resolution*, providing President Johnson authority to conduct military operations in Vietnam without a formal declaration of war. US policy in Indochina went in a new direction. Students, faculty, and the administration would feel its effects in coming years. And the Tide rolled on.

3
An Oasis of Modern Thought in
a Sea of Reactionism

The Baby Boomers Arrive

In July and August the heat and humidity in Tuscaloosa reach their heights. Even at eight o'clock in the morning, prospective male students sweated profusely as they trekked from Paty Hall across campus to the Alabama Union for summer orientation. Young women walking from nearby Mary Burke and Martha Parham Halls suffered nearly as much.

Freshman orientation occurred simultaneously with summer school, which proceeded more or less normally, despite civil rights demonstrations downtown and Klansmen picketing Morrison's Cafeteria. It was the absence of national guardsmen and US marshals that distinguished the enrollment of three African American students in June 1964 from the previous summer when Vivian Malone and James Hood registered. At the start of the summer session, a *Crimson-White* editorial noted, the mixed metaphor notwithstanding, "Perhaps the University has reached a point in its thinking whereby it can become an oasis of modern thought in a sea of reactionism."[1]

September's entering freshman class was part of a record 9,724 undergraduates and graduate students matriculating at the Capstone, an 18.3 percent increase over the previous year, reflecting the arrival of Alabama's baby-boom generation. When added to the enrollment at the extension centers in Huntsville and Birmingham and at the medical school in Birmingham, the total reached 15,867. Furthermore, graduate and law school rolls, congruent with a national trend, were up 21 percent at the Capstone.[2] Since Frank Rose's arrival in 1958, the faculty had increased from 536 to just over 700 with 68 percent possessing terminal degrees, a higher figure than the national average for state universities.[3]

In May 1964, the trustees approved building a new sports complex consisting of a massive field house with a basketball arena seating fifteen thousand, a large weight-lifting room, a smaller gym with an additional basketball court, four indoor tennis courts, film-processing and viewing rooms, and provisions for television and radio coverage. A year later, the university signed a $3,294,000 contract with a Birmingham company to build what eventually was named "Coleman Coliseum."[4]

The baby boomers were the children of parents for whom the Great Depression and the Second World War were formative experiences. After defeating Nazi Germany and Imperial Japan, surviving servicemen returned to a revitalized economy able to employ them to produce consumer goods ranging from appliances and furniture to automobiles and baby buggies. Nineteen years after the end of the war, the young men and women entering the nation's colleges and universities in 1964 had grown up during the unparalleled prosperity generated by a post-war economic boom.

Although not a threat to social stability at Alabama, a cold wind blew from the north. In early June 1962, a small group of college and university students, members of the Students for a Democratic Society (SDS), met in Port Huron, Michigan. Their "Port Huron Statement," completed on June 15, began, "We are people of this generation, bred in at least modest comfort, housed now in universities, looking uncomfortably to the world we inherit."[5] The forty-page statement revealed their disenchantment with American liberalism, especially the Kennedy administration's opposition to Fidel Castro's regime in Cuba and the focus on fighting insurgencies in Southeast Asia. They also were concerned with class-related issues noting that "a gulf" had developed between the ideal that all people are created equal and the realities of racial bigotry in the South. It took more than five years for a hint of what SDS stood for to reach the Capstone, where it manifested itself among a relatively small number of students.

Capstone Greeks under Fire

One of the main points of the "Port Huron Statement" was that the cultural and educational focus of American academe perpetuated the status quo by encouraging conformity to established values and political institutions attendant to middle-class notions of citizenship. The entire SDS ethos diametrically opposed everything the Greek system at Alabama embraced and revered.

In 1962, John Blackburn tasked the interfraternity council with devising a "Four-Year Fraternity Self-Study Evaluation Program." An interim two-year report, completed in July 1964, concluded that fraternities at the University of

Alabama were anti-intellectual, encouraged mass stratification, and were "inclined to live in the past."[6] It further admonished Alabama's Greek system for fostering a "group-think" mentality by encouraging members to avoid taking positions on controversial issues that might jeopardize their career aspirations.[7]

Dean Blackburn instructed the IFC to recommend remedies. This resulted in suggestions like shortening the pledge period from the entire freshman year to one semester and forbidding harassment. The IFC failed to address matters attendant to intellectual growth, diversity of opinion, and the widespread abuse of alcohol.[8] The changes that occurred over the next two years mostly focused on rush-related issues like limiting each fraternity to one rush party in the spring semester.[9]

Alabama's well-entrenched Greek system remained impervious to immediate change. Significantly, Frank Rose was a dedicated member of the Kappa Alpha Order, a fraternity founded in December 1865 at Virginia's Washington College, now Washington and Lee University, and also located exclusively at schools below the Mason-Dixon Line. When visiting another campus, Rose often dropped in on the local KA chapter. At Alabama, and other campuses, the fraternity was known for celebrating "Old South Week" during which pledges were inducted amid ceremonies marked by brothers accoutered in Confederate army uniforms with their dates attired in antebellum dresses. The practice, increasingly seen as insensitive if not inappropriate, continued into the twenty-first century.

In addition to the bad press generated by the state's racial strife, many academics considered the University of Alabama little more than a football-party school located in a politically antediluvian state governed by racist rednecks. That reputation made it difficult both to recruit the best students in Alabama and attract the high-caliber faculty Rose sought. Bombings in Birmingham, Klansmen picketing in Tuscaloosa, and mobs threatening theater patrons compounded the difficulty.

In mid-July 1964, Thomas B. Alexander, president of the local AAUP chapter, wrote Tuscaloosa mayor George Van Tassel emphasizing the importance of maintaining law and order. Alexander warned that failure to do so would prove detrimental to recruiting and keeping first-rate scholars. "University faculties must be recruited and retained against attractions from all sections of the country." Alexander wrote, "We cannot impress upon you too forcefully the baneful, long-range consequences of even a brief period of unfavorable notoriety for Tuscaloosa."[10]

Fall 1964

Other than that the class of 1968 was the largest in the university's 133-year history, the freshmen were merely younger versions of the sophomores, juniors, and seniors who awaited them. In many respects, getting a college education at the University of Alabama involved an intensification of the high school experience. This was more the case for students from urban areas, whether large or small, than for youngsters raised in rural settings. For the most part, once on campus, new students discovered a familiar value system, one that encouraged gravitating toward cliques defined by their interests and socioeconomic status. With some exceptions, youngsters from affluent backgrounds were more likely to "go Greek," while others—indeed most—remained independent.

Young men, with neatly cut hair, some still sporting crew cuts, wearing madras jackets or dark blazers, button-down collar Gant shirts, and neatly pressed trousers riding just above cordovan loafers, made their way through closed and open rush, hoping for a bid to a top fraternity. Over on sorority row, freshmen women wearing skirts and neat Villager blouses, or dressed in primly tailored shifts, strolled from house to house where sisters performed skits depicting each sorority's history and character. At the end of rush, some shrieked with joy while others, inevitably, shed tears of disappointment.

Freshmen men and women checked into dorms and then wandered around campus locating academic buildings, various libraries, and Foster Auditorium where registration yielded a packet of computer punch cards along with information specifying class meeting places and times. They then endured long lines at bookstores to complete their first steps in matriculating at the Capstone. Given the late summer heat and high humidity, this proved a hot, sticky ordeal that was at once confusing, scary, and exciting.

Wise freshmen walked through their schedules timing how long it took to get from one classroom building to the next. The night before classes began, while some freshmen partied, others trekked downtown since cars were forbidden until their sophomore year. At the Bama Theater, in air-conditioned comfort, they watched George Peppard and Elizabeth Ashley in *The Carpetbaggers*. Returning to campus in the evening, they found darkness brought some relief from the oppressive heat of late summer. The baby boomers of the class of 1968 had arrived.

Vice president for Student Affairs, C. T. Sharpton, opened the required freshman convocation. "Look to your right. Look to your left. Four years from now, two of the three of you won't be here." Common wisdom, partially derived from rumor among freshmen, was that the university lacked enough facilities, classrooms, and other resources to accommodate the surge of baby boomers. Therefore, the faculty winnowed the chaff by making freshman courses purposefully difficult.

David McElroy's class in Western Civilization met in the first floor auditorium at ten Hoor Hall. McElroy, a young assistant professor specializing in modern European history, walked into the auditorium followed by his graduate assistant, a PhD student in his mid- to late twenties who seemed bent on imitating his mentor in speech and attitude.

"I'm Dr. McElroy," he announced, pausing a few seconds while he eyed the class with an air of disdain. "Welcome to History 101, Western Civilization. This isn't high school. I will lecture twice a week. The other day you will meet in smaller laboratory sections with my assistant, Mr. Britton. You will be on time and in your seats before I begin my lectures. Immediate, unendurable physical distress is the only acceptable reason for leaving class during a lecture. My hours are posted on my office door. If you have a problem, see Mr. Britton first. If phoning me at home will save your life, then by all means call. Otherwise, don't." After a pause, he turned to his notes, stating, "We begin our discussion after the fall of the Roman Empire."[11] Students reached for notebooks and pens.

Freshman core courses in zoology and botany met in Nott Hall. English courses, in Morgan and B. B. Comer Halls, focused on grammar and composition. Geography and geology classes convened in Smith Hall. By the end of September, the class of '68 was off and running. Midterm exams in October gave credence to any who doubted the admonition that two-thirds of the entering freshman class would not be around to graduate in May 1968.

Student Life in the Autumn of '64

Opportunities for distraction abounded. On Tuesday, October 6, the Al Hirt Jazz Show performed in Foster. Two days later, Miss Nell Rankin, a native Alabamian and soprano with the New York Metropolitan Opera, sang in the Capstone's Concert and Lecture Series season opener. At the end of October, the Japan Philharmonic Symphony Orchestra performed.

Opera and violin concertos probably were a bit "haute" for many, if not most, Alabama students. That being the case, Grand Ole Opry performers Lester Flatt and Earl Scruggs entertained in early November. According to the *Crimson-White*, although a good crowd turned out, editor Bill Plott apologized for the rudeness demonstrated by some students. Plott noted that as the two performers concluded their last number and started off stage, before applause subsided, many students had left their seats and headed for the exits. This proved embarrassing because when Flatt and Scruggs returned for an encore, there were students standing in the aisles and lollygagging at the exits. Plott lamented, "The really sad fact is that this incident is not unusual. . . . It is a frequent occurrence at many concerts and lectures here. They don't even do that at Auburn, an institution we like to call a cow college."[12]

In the autumn of 1964, with student discontent stirring on campuses elsewhere, the Tuscaloosa campus seemed stuck in a less contentious time. Those who knew about SDS and the "Port Huron Statement" could have convened in a small seminar room in ten Hoor Hall with seats to spare. For the most part, Alabama undergraduates were far more concerned about the next football game.

After Lyndon Johnson won the November election, the American presence in South Vietnam transitioned from what historians call the "advisory phase" to a higher level of commitment, one that involved the "escalation and Americanization" of the war. These would be well underway by March 1965. But for the time being, the war seemed remote from fraternity parties, dances, dating, and football.

Riding with the Tide and Going with the Flow

Football, not opera singers—whether from New York or Nashville—stirred the souls and moved the hearts of most Alabama students. The Crimson Tide, led by senior quarterback Joe Namath, opened the season by trouncing the Georgia Bulldogs 31–3. At the fourth game of the season, when North Carolina State's Wolf Pack visited Denny Stadium, the undefeated Tide had racked up ninety-one points to their opponents' nine. North Carolina State went down 21–0. Unfortunately, so did Joe Namath. The knee injury he suffered would plague him through the remainder of his football career.

After defeating Tennessee 19–0 on the third Saturday in October, the Tide entertained the Florida Gators who had administered a 10–6 defeat in their previous encounter with the Crimson Tide. The theme chosen for the 1964 homecoming was CAGE: Crimson Avenged, Gators Exterminated.[13]

Festivities started on Friday evening, October 23, with the annual pep rally and bonfire on the Quadrangle. At ten o'clock the following morning, the Million Dollar Band, with Carol Ann Self strutting in front, led the homecoming parade. As the parade proceeded from Denny Chimes along University Boulevard toward downtown Tuscaloosa, it first passed the fraternity houses. After leaving campus, it continued past Morrison's on the left and the many eateries and shops that later came to be known as "the Strip." The parade made its way up the hill and then wound along past the antebellum University Club that once served as the residence of Alabama's governors before the state capital moved to Montgomery. Then it flowed into downtown Tuscaloosa. Convertibles carried members of the homecoming court and various fraternity sweethearts who waved to the crowds. There were fraternity and sorority floats as well as a trailer-truck bed hauling drunken law school students in tuxedos and top hats along with their inebriated dates, an Alabama tradition.

When the Tide played at home, whether at Denny Stadium or at Legion Field in nearby Birmingham, it made for a festive weekend atmosphere on campus. Everyone, be they students, returning alumni, or fans, attended games dressed in their Sunday clothes. Young men accoutered in sports jackets pinned corsages on the cocktail dresses or suit jackets of their dates. No one stripped to the waist and painted himself crimson and white. The only unusual headgear was perennial gubernatorial candidate Shorty Price's top hat, not a roll of toilet paper next to a box of Tide detergent signifying, "Roll Tide." Shorty, however, got drunk. Many would say that until Shorty in his top hat and tux was cuffed and carried away by police, "it wasn't really a football game." But Shorty wasn't the only one getting "blitzed." Many students from the 1960s would not see an Alabama football game sober until later in life, for some, much later.

At homecoming in 1964 the Tide avenged its previous year's loss to the Gators with the outcome decided only after Florida missed a last minute field goal that would have tied the game. Alabama won 17–14 and then rolled through the rest of the schedule undefeated and favored in its annual Thanksgiving Day grudge match against Auburn played at Birmingham's Legion Field.

The Bama Mascot Swings His Chicken on National TV

In mid-November, when the American Broadcasting Company (ABC) scheduled the Alabama-Auburn game for a national television audience, Frank Rose welcomed the opportunity to use the ninety-second promotional allowed each school to present the university to America in a positive light.

From the debut at the 1979 Sugar Bowl, Big Al, the Alabama mascot, became a much-loved, colorful character portrayed as a pot-bellied, mischievous, gray pachyderm sporting a crimson jersey. In 1964, long before Big Al began to evolve, the Alabama mascot was a student dressed in a red elephant suit. A large, red-painted papier-mâché head gave the mascot a vaguely ominous appearance. Before this Thanksgiving afternoon was over, Frank Rose might well have deemed the red figure "demonic."

During the halftime, when the Auburn band marched onto the field, the red elephant pranced ahead of its band major and majorettes. Around and around, above the elephant's head, the mascot swung a live chicken by its legs, wings flapping. This was, as everyone in the stadium understood, an act mocking Auburn's "War Eagle" fight song and trademark cheer. People watching on national television across the rest of the nation may have wondered what form of southern Celtic barbarism they were witnessing. High up in the president's box, an astonished President Rose dispatched an assistant to stop the rampaging, chicken-swinging mascot.

To clarify, the origins of "War Eagle," like "Roll Tide," are varied. Auburn's mascot is a tiger, while Alabama's is an elephant. Alabama calls itself the "Crimson Tide," and Bama fans yell "Roll Tide." Auburn fans bellow "War Eagle" and use the phrase "War damn Eagle" to add emphasis. Alabama fans greet each other, toast one another, or say farewell with "Roll Tide." For emphasis, Bama fans expand it to "A big Roll Tide, y'all." To outsiders this can be as baffling as watching someone in a red elephant suit swinging a live chicken over its head. To Alabamians, however, it's a "southern thing" and therefore entirely understandable.

By Monday, letters of outrage filled President Rose's inbox. One stated, "The young man who treated the live foul so brutally should be talked to." Rose replied, "We have had a session with the young man involved and I don't think it will happen again."[14]

The much admonished student apologized to the president of Auburn's SGA, "Caught up in the feeling of the day, I didn't realize how antagonistic my actions were."[15] In the end, while the chicken-swinging mascot ate crow, it went down easier with the Tide's 21–14 victory over the Auburn Tigers.

On the Monday following the game, the Associated Press and football coaches' polls declared the Crimson Tide the 1964 National Champions. A disappointing 21–17 loss to the University of Texas Longhorns on New Year's Day made for a letdown. Nevertheless, the national championship, Alabama's second of the decade, belonged to the Crimson Tide.

The Louis Armstrong Controversy

Seniors might well have thought the autumn of 1964 resembled that of their freshman year in 1961. Back then there was no imminent anticipation of desegregation, as there was at the beginning of their sophomore year in 1962 when the turmoil at Ole Miss warned of what could happen at Alabama. The presence of guardsmen and US marshals escorting classmate Vivian Malone to and from her classes, bomb blasts at the edge of campus in November, and the assassination of President Kennedy marred the autumn of their junior year. The Tide also lost to Florida—and worse—to Auburn. By comparison, during the autumn of 1964, as time with its campus rituals rolled along, it was great to be an Alabama senior or, for that matter, a junior, sophomore, or even a lowly freshman.

The Cotillion Club, the student organization charged with spending the activities fee portion of student tuition costs, began securing performers during the fall semester in preparation for their opening session on February 17, 1965. After efforts to bring in Henry Mancini and his orchestra foundered over money, they turned to Ray Charles, a popular black entertainer, but negotiations stopped in early November after his arrest on drug charges. The search then shifted to booking Louis Armstrong and the All Stars for the seasonal debut. On the last Wednesday in November, as students departed for Thanksgiving, the president's office instructed the Cotillion Club to stop negotiating with Armstrong's agent. No reason was given.

The first assumption might be that this was another example of racism at the University of Alabama. That explanation, however, seemed incongruous since African American bands often played fraternity parties. Additionally, the accountant in the university's comptroller's office in charge of the Cotillion Club's account, C. J. Compton, recalled the cheers that greeted "Satchmo" Armstrong when, as legend had it, he strolled into Foster in 1955, his trumpet blasting out, "When the Saints Go Marching In."[16]

Word of the cancellation spread rapidly among students returning to campus at the end of Thanksgiving break. In the Tuesday edition of the *Crimson-White*, Dean Blackburn explained, "This is not a decision against Negro entertainment, but taking into consideration all the problems relative to his performance, we thought it unwise to bring Mr. Armstrong to campus at this time," adding, "We need a plan to bring in less controversial colored entertainment."[17]

Since Armstrong was not associated with any civil rights groups, students thought it odd he would be considered so controversial. One rumor suggested the administration feared negative media attention if demonstrators from nearby Stillman College, carrying signs accusing Armstrong of being an "Uncle Tom," picketed outside Foster Auditorium. That, however, seemed far-fetched. University regulations forbade demonstrations by anyone unaffiliated with the institution. Although written in the aftermath of the riots of 1956 to prevent Klansmen from picketing on campus, university and Tuscaloosa police would have enforced those regulations against Stillman students, and probably done so vigorously.

It may have been that administration officials recalled the reception accorded Montgomery native Nat King Cole when he attempted to perform at Birmingham's Boutwell Auditorium in April 1956, shortly after the failed attempt at desegregating the Capstone. Cole, like Armstrong, was a nonpolitical, mainstream entertainer. His easygoing style made him one of the first "cross-over" black entertainers transitioning into a white market. Cole's apparent cultural assimilation, which exceeded that of Armstrong, didn't stop three Klansmen from jumping the stage to attack him. In this case, assumed threats of demonstrations by Stillman students or potential Klan violence and the media attention these might have drawn, put an end to Louis Armstrong's booking.

Events from 1956 may not have been as fresh in the minds of students Mike Thompson, Joe Putnam, and Bill Youngblood when they started a petition drive. On Friday, at a table outside the Supe Store, they gathered over six hundred student and faculty signatures. With uncharacteristic dissention increasing among the student body, President Rose summoned Thompson, Putnam, and Youngblood along with SGA president Don Siegal to his office where he told them that Louis Armstrong's race played no part in his decision. Instead, he acted on the possibility that outside forces might cause trouble. Thus reassured, the students suspended their petition drive.[18]

Nevertheless, the controversy simmered on. Art students hung a banner across the third-story balcony at Garland Hall proclaiming, "Louis Armstrong YES! Censorship NO!" The banner came down shortly after Theodore E. Klitzke, chairman of the Art Department, received a call from the assistant dean of Arts and Sciences reminding him of university regulations forbidding the posting of political statements on campus. The *Crimson-White*, weighing in with the first of several critical commentaries, noted, "For the first time the majority of students seem to be in accord on an issue concerning racial problems."[19]

On Saturday, December 12, at the request of the SGA, Frank Rose met with members of the student legislature. Ground rules included no note taking or recording of what was said during the meeting. It was to be strictly off the record. After hearing Rose's explanation, and following whatever discussion ensued, the legislature unanimously passed a resolution supporting the administration.[20]

Meanwhile, Vice President Bennett, looking for help in finding "suitable" black entertainers, turned to ABC Television, where the university had a connection through its president, Thomas W. Moore, a childhood friend of Frank Rose. ABC responded with a list that included Johnny Mathis, Nat King Cole, Ella Fitzgerald, Lena Horne, Harry Belafonte, and Count Basie and his orchestra.[21]

The *Crimson-White* was not through. The paper questioned the "closed-door" aspects of the meeting between Rose and the student legislature. It characterized the protest generated by the Armstrong controversy as "a sign students here are not apathetic" and also noted that while Alabama students used petitions to request explanations from the administration, they avoided disruptive demonstrations like picketing, sit-ins, and riots.[22]

Indeed, student reactions during the Louis Armstrong controversy never approached the intensity of unrest emerging on many other campuses. Nevertheless, the administration kept a tight rein on events. Although university officials engaged in a dialogue with student leaders, they never backed down or modified their original decision. Rose explained his reasons and, remarkably, the students agreed not to reveal them.

Rose's correspondence provides hints as to why he cancelled Armstrong's performance. Trustee Gessner T. McCorvey grew up on the university campus, where his father taught mathematics during the post-Reconstruction era. During his student days, McCorvey played on the 1903 football team. A long-time trustee, McCorvey let Rose know what he thought on almost any and every issue. "I applaud your action in barring that repulsive looking baboon, Louis Armstrong, from performing at the University," McCorvey wrote, adding, "I sincerely hope something can be done to see that the editors of the *Crimson-White* have proper respect for those in authority at the University."[23]

In a letter, marked "confidential," Rose replied, "I must confess, we may have made a mistake." He admitted the primary reason for forbidding Armstrong's performance was that he feared it might result in picketing and bad publicity. "It turned out we got the bad publicity anyway, and it certainly hurt the University."[24]

Rose was right. The media responded sharply, evidenced by a blast against the university issued by a radio station in Lexington, Kentucky, reported to Rose by a friend who heard it. Rose defended his actions to his friend, pointing out that forty-one African American students were studying at the university or its extensions around the state. Rose added that he thought it vital that no one whose presence might stir up trouble be allowed on campus before the beginning of the next academic year. "We feel our best interests will be served by sticking with our present program and plan." He concluded, "There are always a few students who want to run the institution and this is not going to happen at the University of Alabama."[25]

Indeed, it did not happen. The Louis Armstrong controversy simmered down over Christmas break and was forgotten by the time classes resumed in early January. The 1965 edition of the *Corolla*, the university's yearbook, didn't mention it, not even a photograph of the banner slung so briefly across the balcony at Garland Hall. The annual did, however, feature photos of Johnny Mathis performing in a March 1965 event at Foster Auditorium.

Winter into Spring

Hardly noted in the uproar over Louis Armstrong was an article on page three of the *Crimson-White* revealing something many students knew or suspected: Alabama fraternities and sororities existed in three distinct classes. According to the article, a freshman coed's likelihood of being pledged to a top-tier sorority depended largely on her family's social standing and economic circumstances. Additionally, "big sisters" in the best sororities not only warned their pledges about dating independents, they discouraged them from dating men in lower-tier fraternities.

The article also revealed some class two and three sororities challenged their pledges to date among top fraternities as a means of increasing their particular sorority's standing. For instance, a tier three sorority pledge might earn five points for going out with someone from a top fraternity but garner only two or three points for dating a brother from a lower-ranked house. Since a pledge needed around two hundred points to be initiated, the incentive was useful. Pledges might also acquire extra points for attending parties at the better fraternity houses, a football game, or some other event with a fellow from the right Greek-lettered organization. While this news confirmed the suspicions of some, it shocked no one.[26]

The shock of losing to Texas in the Orange Bowl affected the student body more than the loss of Louis Armstrong in the upcoming Cotillion event. When students returned to campus in early January, final exams loomed a fortnight away, adjusting priorities and focusing minds. After the finals, the survivors—and most survived—were ready to move from winter into spring. Life at the Capstone resumed its rhythms of fraternity parties, basketball games, and spring dances.

Selma and the Capstone

A hundred miles south, in Dallas County, life seemed hardly so idyllic. Selma, the county seat, and neighboring Lowndes County, where not a single black was registered to vote, epitomized the segregated South. In the winter and early spring of 1965, attempts at voter registration and accompanying demonstrations fostered racial violence that once again brought the state to the forefront of the kind of national attention that did the university no good.

As classes resumed after Christmas break civil rights leaders in Selma planned a series of demonstrations, one of which, held in Marion, Alabama, on Saturday night, February 18, turned violent when Alabama State Troopers and members of the Dallas County Posse used clubs and electric cattle prods to attack demonstrators. After twenty-six-year-old Jimmy Lee Jackson intervened to prevent the beating of his elderly grandfather, a trooper shot him in the abdomen. Jackson died several days later.

The following day, Martin Luther King Jr. dispatched his deputy, C. T. Vivian, from Atlanta to Selma. Veterans of the previous summer's Mississippi voter registration drives, along with blacks and whites from as far away as Berkeley and Boston, Detroit and Washington, converged on Selma. So did a small number of University of Alabama students and three professors: Ted Klitzke, the increasingly outspoken progressive head of the Art Department, Frederick Kraus, and Ed Carlson.

On Saturday, February 25, they joined a march through downtown Selma. By five thirty that afternoon, even before Klitzke, his colleagues, and the students had returned to Tuscaloosa, university officials learned of their participation when a *Tuscaloosa News* reporter phoned Jeff Bennett with an inquiry concerning the administration's policy on professors participating in civil rights demonstrations. Bennett worked out a position congruent with the AAUP's 1940 statement on academic freedom holding that professors should be free to participate in "lawful activities subject to recognizing their responsibilities for restraint and accuracy by reason of their special place in society." He included it in a memorandum submitted to President Rose on Monday morning. In it he stated, "This is the principle of student and faculty rights to which we are committed."[27]

The demonstrations and the brutality continued into March. On Sunday, March 7, the Edmund Pettus Bridge spanning the Alabama River and linking Selma to the rest of Dallas County became a symbol in the struggle for human rights in America. On that day, Alabama State Troopers and members of the Dallas County Posse, some on horseback and others on foot, used clubs and cattle prods as they surged into demonstrators while they knelt in prayer on the bridge. Martin Luther King Jr. flew to Alabama the next day. Events culminated with the Selma-to-Montgomery march that occurred between March 21 and 24. Before it was over, two more people were killed. Reverend James Reeb, a Unitarian minister from Boston, was beaten to death after he and two other ministers, returning to their hotel after dinner at a soul food restaurant, walked past the Silver Moon Cafe, a Klan hangout. On the final night of the march, a carload of Klansmen shot and killed Viola Liuzzo, a white Detroit housewife, as she drove demonstrators back to Selma from Montgomery.

Back in Tuscaloosa, President Rose received numerous letters and telegrams, the majority hostile to the Alabama professors who participated in the Selma demonstrations, some urging they be fired. Most writers indicated they resented taxpayers supporting the "subversive" behavior of university employees. In most cases, Rose used a standard reply, changing the name, address, and date as appropriate. He thanked the writers for taking time to contact him, and assured them the university was giving "the problem" its attention.[28]

President Rose's response to letters of outrage directed at the violence more accurately reflected his true feelings. Margaret Chamber Rainey, a Montgomery native and university alumna, sent Rose a telegram stating, "I'm ashamed of brutal police action in Selma and am sure responsible citizens join me." Rose replied, "I want you to know it was just as disturbing and disheartening to us as it was to you. We have been assured that this kind of activity will never happen again."[29]

A Turning Point

The events in Selma initiated a historical turning point for the university. It started with a small act of compassion. Reverend Robert Keever, pastor at the Westminster Fellowship, the Presbyterian ministry to students located on Eighth Street a couple of blocks west of Denny Stadium, studied at Princeton Theological Seminary with James Reeb. The day his classmate died, Keever started a fund drive to support the fallen minister's wife and children.[30]

In February 1962, after the First Presbyterian Church in Tuscaloosa threatened to charge Stillman students with trespassing following attempts to desegregate Sunday services, the Westminster Fellowship welcomed them.[31] This prompted a confrontation between Keever's predecessor, the Reverend Ed Payne Miller, and the denomination's Synod Committee on Campus Life. Complaints to the synod from influential members of First Presbyterian, people who disapproved of the fellowship's interracial initiatives, fostered this confrontation.[32] In June 1962, as a result of the turmoil, Reverend Miller resigned.[33]

Bob Keever's first day on the job was Tuesday, June 11, 1963, the day George Wallace stood in the door at Foster Auditorium. Keever watched the whole thing from Emmet Gribbin's office window in Canterbury Chapel across Hackberry Lane from Foster. For the present, in an attempt to improve relations with First Presbyterian Church, Keever discouraged Stillman students from attending services at Westminster Fellowship. Nevertheless, Keever and a handful of students continued to meet secretly with Stillman students. "They really let us have it!," Keever recalled nearly a half century later, "They told us how painful, humiliating, and demeaning it was to be a black person in Alabama. We were shocked. I was deeply, profoundly affected by their outrage and pain."[34]

Keever also expressed regrets for not joining the small number of university students and faculty members who participated in a protest and sympathy march in downtown Tuscaloosa.[35] On Friday, the day after James Reeb died, a crowd estimated at more than 1,200 walked four abreast and hand in hand from the First African Baptist Church to the intersection of Greensboro Avenue and University Boulevard, where they knelt in prayer before returning to the church.[36] Three participating university students reported that while there was no violence during the demonstration, hecklers hurled verbal abuses like, "Where are you nigger-lovers from, New York or Illinois?" According to one student, "That was for openers. It got coarser."[37]

After the demonstration, the students, walking from the church to their parked cars, noticed three white men following them. As the men drew closer, they broke into a run, followed closely by their white pursuers, barely reaching the car and locking the doors before the thugs caught up. One pressed his face to the driver's side window as he muttered something unintelligible into the glass. As the car pulled away, he flicked a lighted cigarette onto the windshield. It could have been a lot worse, and while this incident disturbed the students, what they found more galling was that many of their classmates subsequently "ranked us beneath snakes and lizards."[38]

On Monday evening, March 22, 1965, just as the Selma-to-Montgomery march got started, approximately 150 students and faculty gathered in the art gallery at Clark Hall to hear the Reverend T. Y. Rogers speak about current racial tensions in Alabama. Prior to accepting the call to the First African Baptist Church in Tuscaloosa, Rogers served as the associate pastor at the Dexter Avenue Baptist Church in Montgomery during the 1955 Montgomery bus boycott led by Martin Luther King Jr. He told the group, "We must be agitators. There's a lot of dirt in this city. It takes agitators to clean the dirty clothes."[39]

Two days later, on Wednesday, the Discussion and Leadership for Human Rights Group submitted a petition requesting a charter from Alabama's SGA. Professor Clarence Mondale, director of the American Studies program, presented the charter request. After explaining the organization's goals, Mondale concluded with, "All we ask is the right to hold discussions." Student legislators then engaged in a heated debate focused on whether the group's constitution adequately described its mission and goals, along with whether activities like tutoring local African American children served the interests of the university. After the debate, the SGA denied the charter by one vote.[40]

Undaunted, the following Monday an estimated 125 students and faculty convened to reorganize the group into the Human Rights Forum. This new iteration differed from the earlier one by abjuring group participation in any off-campus civil rights activities and confining its role to providing a forum for discussion. It also established a steering committee consisting of professors John Ramsey and Harold Nelson, along with students Mike Thompson, Kay Harris, and Ralph Knowles.[41]

The Human Rights Forum resubmitted a revised and more detailed charter to student legislators at their May meeting, the last one of the 1964–65 academic year, where it was referred to committee. There the bill remained throughout the summer. The issue did not die in the interim. At the first SGA meeting of the fall semester, the bill, with some amendments, passed the house and the senate, albeit by small margins. With that, the University of Alabama officially sanctioned the first campus group dedicated to exploring civil rights matters.[42]

Vietnam Intrudes

On March 2, 1965, as events intensified in Selma, half a world away the United States escalated its participation in the Indochina conflict with Operation Rolling Thunder, a bombing campaign aimed at North Vietnam that lasted three years and nine months. The start of Rolling Thunder also marked the beginning of the antiwar movement on American campuses. On March 24, 1965, the University of Michigan held the first "teach-in," an event that spread to other colleges and universities, although not as far south as Tuscaloosa.[43]

Several years passed before teach-ins reached the Capstone. Nevertheless, over time, Alabama students became aware of—and concerned about—the war in Southeast Asia. On the night of March 25, the Student Government Association's Debate and Symposium Series hosted a panel discussion featuring Alabama's Senator John Sparkman, Senator Ernest Gruening of Alaska (who was one of two senators to vote against the Gulf of Tonkin Resolution), and Senator Frank Church of Idaho. After dinner with students and faculty at the Indian Hills Country Club, the panel convened in the auditorium at Morgan Hall to address the topic, "What's Next in Vietnam?"

While the panelists agreed the United States should seek a negotiated end to the war, they disagreed on how that might be done. Senator Sparkman believed the way to compel Hanoi to negotiate was through increased military pressure. He also saw the future of South Vietnam as key to the security of all of Southeast Asia, including Indonesia and the Philippines.

Senators Church and Gruening both thought the United States made a mistake by assuming the French struggle after 1954. Frank Church differed from Ernest Gruening by maintaining that once American forces were committed, with national credibility and prestige at stake, pulling out was unacceptable. Senator Gruening disagreed sharply, "We have been aggressors just as surely as the North Vietnamese. . . . I also think it is a war we cannot win."[44]

Less than a week later, on April 1, Howard University professor Bernard Fall, probably the leading US expert on Vietnam, spoke on campus. The author of three classics on the French Indochina war and its aftermath, *Hell in a Very Small Place: The Siege at Dien Bien Phu*, *Street Without Joy: The French Debacle in Indochina*, and *The Two Vietnams: A Political and Military Analysis*, told the audience that a million soldiers and twenty-three billion dollars would be needed to win the conflict in Indochina. He added that even that level of commitment was unlikely to suffice because, "While we may get the Viet Cong to bow to us for a while . . . within two years of our departure, they will reappear."[45] In the spring of 1965, the majority of Alabama students supported US policy in Southeast Asia. Doubts were few and expressions of disagreement muted.

Familiar Rituals of Spring

With teach-ins growing elsewhere in the spring of 1965, the Capstone remained highly patriotic. Air Force ROTC Cadet Major Ronald E. Clary, commander of the local chapter of the Arnold Air Society, an AFROTC honorary, wrote President Rose asking him to invite Bob Hope to campus for an event cosponsored by the Cotillion Club and the Arnold Air Society. Rose responded immediately with a letter of invitation to the legendary entertainer. "The University has some 10,000 students on the main campus and we would consider it a great honor to have you with us."[46]

While Bob Hope could not work Tuscaloosa into a schedule that increasingly included performances at places named Da Nang, Pleiku, and Bien Hoa, the Billy Graham Crusade visited the Capstone on Monday night, April 26, 1965. Students and townspeople packed Denny Stadium to hear bass baritone George Beverly Shea sing his signature hymn, "How Great Thou Art." When he got to, "I see the stars, I hear the rolling thunder," although there were no stars to be seen, plenty of thunder rolled as lightning streaked the skies. Seconds after Frank Rose introduced Billy Graham the heavenly floodgates released torrents of rain. Graham cut his message to a few short sentences. "God loves you. His son died for your sins. God bless you and good night." Frank Rose wrote Billy Graham, "I regret the rain did not allow you to finish your message. We are looking forward to your return to Montgomery in June."[47] When the Billy Graham Crusade visited Montgomery a few weeks later, during the nationally televised service Carol Self and Crimson Tide quarterback Steve Sloan gave their personal testimonies before a racially integrated audience.[48]

Although the Human Rights Forum represented a new departure presaging a shift in student culture, only a tiny portion of the university community comprised its membership. Meanwhile, life at the Capstone rolled along through the spring semester much as it had in years past. On Friday night, April 2, Foster Auditorium was the scene of the annual Sigma Chi Derby. Bama Day took place the following weekend. President Rose dismissed classes at noon and the parade started at one thirty in the afternoon with the Million Dollar Band marching along University Avenue, followed by the drill teams from the Army and Air Force ROTC. Convertibles carried "Miss Bama Day" contestants, who waved to onlookers gathered along the sidewalks. After the parade, Joe Namath, Paul Crane, and Ray Ogden, cocaptains of the 1964 national championship team, put their cleat- and handprints into the cement around Denny Chimes. Attention then turned to the parking lot behind Martha Parham Hall, where carnival rides and games offered diversions for students soon to be faced with final exams.[49]

The following Tuesday, April 13, Air Force and Army ROTC cadets formed on the Quad for Governor's Day ceremonies. After Governor Wallace pinned medals on forty cadets, the Million Dollar Band led the parade past the reviewing stand. The governor and the official party then left the Quadrangle for Foster Auditorium where more than 2,800 ROTC cadets, for whom this was a "mandatory formation," heard George Wallace deliver the annual address.

Two years had passed since Wallace's first Governor's Day address. In April 1963, with desegregation looming, he fumed defiance. Perhaps reacting to the bad press generated by the violence in Selma, Wallace spoke more moderately, focusing on his administration's support for education. He pointed to the fourteen new junior colleges and fifteen trade schools established across the state during his administration, which he predicted would make Alabama the "Athens of the South." Wallace announced a one-hundred-million-dollar construction program for higher education and credited the 29 percent raise in teachers' salaries during the past three years with "helping our state take its place in the sun."[50]

In reality, Wallace used the system to pay off political cronies with lucrative state posts. Among the junior college and trade school system, only three presidents possessed earned doctorates; most had no educational experience beyond secondary school administration. Faculty and administrators at Alabama and Auburn privately groused about the waste of money and duplication of effort.[51]

A Turning Tide

Racial strife that inevitably tarnished the state's reputation also affected the university and its football team. *Los Angeles Times* sportswriter Jim Murray minced no words when explaining why he didn't cast his vote for Alabama as the 1964 national champions, "I didn't care for the school colors: solid white." According to Murray, while publishing his feelings elicited an onslaught of hate mail from Alabama fans, he also received a letter signed by Alabama quarterbacks Joe Namath and Steve Sloan politely asking him to watch the game. Murray did.

"Alabama was the better team," Murray admitted in his January 5, 1965, column. He also predicted, "Within a few years, the backfields of Southern state universities will be as integrated as their buses. . . . when that day comes, stars will really fall on Alabama."[52]

Melvin Durslag, one of Murray's colleagues on the sports beat at the *Los Angeles Times*, remained unconvinced that any good could come out of Tuscaloosa. In April 1965, when Coach Bryant made a recruiting foray to Los Angeles in search of a junior college prospect, Durslag blasted Alabama for its racism, associating the Crimson Tide with all that he held abhorrent in the state. After interviewing Bryant, Durslag wrote, "Not surprisingly, Bear doesn't wish to come out of Dixie and enter into a discussion of local conditions there." When Durslag tried to elicit Bryant's views on racial matters, the coach responded, "We are as out of contact with the trouble in our state as you are in Los Angeles. I learn about it mostly by watching television out of New York."[53]

The race issue dogged Alabama while it fielded all-white football teams for the next six seasons. In the last two years of the decade, the Crimson Tide's gridiron fortunes waned with sliding numbers in the win-loss column. Klan bombings and murders, along with outrages like the incident at the Edmund Pettus Bridge, coupled with George Wallace's insatiable need to keep his ultra–states' rights message before the American people, provided the university with significant public relations challenges. Frank Rose supported his vision for the University of Alabama with a hard-nosed, carefully crafted, yet dynamic strategy to achieve his goals. The environment in which the university existed, a veritable slough of prejudice, fed the efforts of people committed to making the Capstone an island of liberal inquiry in a sea of conservatism. Nevertheless, Frank Rose stepped cautiously and, above all, intelligently.

Rose was politically adroit. After the death of President Kennedy, he needed to build a relationship with President Lyndon Johnson, with whom he had no close ties. President Johnson, however, was determined to implement the Great Society as a culmination of Franklin D. Roosevelt's New Deal. Frank Rose, a classic progressive, intended to capitalize on the significant educational component inherent in Johnson's vision for America. Accordingly, he cultivated his personal relationship with Johnson to the ultimate benefit of the university. By February 1965, this strategy was paying dividends. "I have just returned from Washington," Rose wrote to his friend David Nevin, a reporter at *Life* magazine, "and found that the University of Alabama is held in high regard by all the government agencies and in the White House." He added, "I found . . . they were willing to put millions of dollars into the expansion of our programs."[54]

Robert Kennedy could not have helped Rose much given the antipathy that existed between Kennedy and Johnson. Rose turned to Douglass Cater, a special assistant to the president responsible for educational policy. Born in Montgomery and educated at Harvard, Cater was also married to the former Libby Anderson, a 1946 graduate of the university and the first woman to serve as SGA president.

Frank Rose put Alabama on board with the Great Society by making the university's research and teaching resources available to President Johnson's antipoverty program. Reducing poverty was something all Alabamians, black and white, could support since doing so benefited everyone. Accordingly, in late 1964, Rose quickly formed a committee comprised of all the academic deans, principal administrative personnel, and student representatives and commissioned them to devise a plan to implement programs under the auspices of the Economic Opportunity Act of 1964.[55] During the spring and summer of 1965, through Head Start, one of the initiatives authorized by the Economic Opportunity Act, the university trained over 1,700 teachers from across the South.[56] Rose's efforts paid off. His access to the president enabled him to tap the cornucopia of federal dollars flowing out of the coffers of the Great Society. In 1965, the Johnson administration committed forty-three million dollars in federal funds to support construction and research at the University of Alabama.[57]

In addition to providing funds, Rose's close relationship with the Johnson administration also distanced the university from the antifederal antipathy spewing from the governor's office in Montgomery. Frank Rose believed it imperative that the university set itself apart from the racial bigotry endemic to Alabama's political and cultural scene. Accordingly, he planted himself—and by extension the University of Alabama—-firmly on the side of the Johnson administration by making the Capstone's resources available to Johnson's Great Society.

Another way to distinguish the university from the state was to garner favorable media coverage. The May commencement provided an excellent opportunity because Vivian Malone would be among the 1,725 students receiving degrees. Indeed, *Newsweek* published a long article detailing her saga at the university. A very positive piece, the article began with Malone's "role as a supporting actress in a theater of the absurd" with George Wallace "posturing in the schoolhouse door," and concluded with the university offering her a job upon graduation.[58] *Newsweek* also noted that fifty-seven African Americans had followed Vivian Malone to the Capstone and its six extension programs across the state.

Additionally, *New York Times* feature writer Gay Talese, a 1953 Alabama alumnus, wrote an article praising his alma mater's progress in race relations. He noted that while the university remained basically conservative, some Alabama students risked ostracism by socializing with Stillman students. He also praised Ted Klitzke for participating in the Selma demonstrations, which Talese covered as a reporter. While concluding that even though apathy still existed, change was evidenced by the fact that student leaders, including the president of SGA and the editor of the *Crimson-White*, were unaffiliated with fraternities.[59]

Frank Rose asked his childhood friend, Thomas Moore, the president of

ABC Television, to deliver the commencement address. Moore, who subscribed to progressive racial views congruent with Rose's, sent a draft of his commencement remarks asking that he eliminate anything that might be overly sensitive. Rose excised one sentence that stated the trustees enthusiastically supported desegregation in 1963.[60] Although every board member except the ex officio chairman, Governor Wallace, signed a memorandum agreeing not to oppose desegregation, their acquiescence was a matter of necessity rather than enthusiasm. Otherwise, Rose left untouched a draft focused sharply on race and civil rights.

With over 1,700 graduates and thousands of parents and relatives on hand, along with the board members, distinguished alumni, local dignitaries, and the press, Moore spoke both bluntly and eloquently. "You, the class of 1965, are the inheritors of a sad tradition and a heavy burden. It is no secret that the present image of your state, and for that matter the entire South, is in deep disrepute." Moore was only warming up. "Who should speak for the South? Not merely the loudest among us, the most belligerent, or the most extreme. But all the people who are between now and never, the great majority of the South." He continued, "If the Negro is not prepared for equality, we must raise him up emotionally and economically until he is ready. But let us start now."[61]

It was no coincidence that ABC reporters and television crews roamed the campus for several days prior to commencement. Ten days after Moore's address, a documentary titled, *Southern Campus: A Quiet Revolution*, aired on the ABC news program, "Scope." The opening scene showed George Wallace defiantly blocking the entrance to Foster Auditorium two years earlier. The next scene switched to Vivian Malone in her baccalaureate robe as she walked gracefully into Denny Stadium. Interviews with Rose, top administrators, faculty, and students told a story of tolerance and progress at the Capstone, with comparisons drawn to the intolerance and intransigence extant throughout the state.

According to Rose, with a few exceptions, reactions across Alabama and from around the nation were overwhelmingly positive. Reverend Lawrence E. McGinty, a Unitarian minister from Birmingham wrote, "As a white Southerner, I received special delight in hearing progressive views voiced in the thickest Southern drawls." Rose replied, "We have received a splendid response from the people of Alabama. I believe the tide is finally beginning to turn."[62]

Frank Rose and Governor John Patterson chair a board of trustees meeting early in Rose's tenure. Patterson was determined to keep Bama white during his tenure. (Hoole Special Collections Library, University of Alabama)

Alabama alumnus and Marine Corps veteran J. Jefferson Bennett served the university in various administrative capacities from 1947 until 1969. (Hoole Special Collections, University of Alabama)

Dean of Men John
L. Blackburn allowed
dissident student leaders
to use the system to affect
change without resorting
to violence. (Hoole Special
Collections Library,
University of Alabama)

Dean of Women Sarah
Healy served Presidents
Carmichael, Rose, and
Mathews before retiring
in 1969. She and Jeff
Bennett teamed up to
save Autherine Lucy's
life in February 1956.
Healy later worked
to integrate black
women into the student
body. (Hoole Special
Collections Library,
University of Alabama)

The friendship between Frank Rose and Robert Kennedy proved especially critical to breaching the racial barrier in June 1963. Kennedy delivered the keynote Emphasis addresses in 1966 and 1968. (Hoole Special Collections Library, University of Alabama)

Sorority sisters welcome new pledges at the conclusion of rush week in 1964. (Hoole Special Collections Library, University of Alabama)

Miss Alabama Carol Ann Self leads the Million Dollar Band down University Boulevard, homecoming 1964. The lone band sponsor, nominated by sororities and elected by the band members, were unique to Alabama until replaced by majorettes in 1970. (Hoole Special Collections Library, University of Alabama)

Representing Kappa Kappa Gamma, Carol Self was band sponsor for the 1964–65 school year. (Photograph courtesy of Carol Ann Self)

"Dress that line, mister!" On a cold November afternoon in 1965, an Air Force ROTC cadet officer barks orders during "Leadership Laboratory," more popularly known as "drill." (Hoole Special Collections, University of Alabama)

Carol Ann Self and Bubba Brewton team up as cheerleaders in the fall of 1966. (Photograph courtesy of Carol Ann Self)

Frank and Tommye Rose welcome the first lady of the United States, Lady Bird Johnson, to campus for the Alabama Women's Leadership Conference in February 1966, an event that coincided with the start of Lurleen Wallace's bid to succeed her husband as governor. (Hoole Special Collections Library, University of Alabama)

Cordial smiles hide an increasingly antagonistic relationship between President Rose and Governor Wallace as the board of trustees welcome governor-elect Lurleen Wallace to the annual homecoming meeting in November 1966. (Hoole Special Collections Library, University of Alabama)

Changing Leadership. Vice president David Mathews and president Frank Rose host governor Albert Brewer after he succeeded Lurleen Wallace who died of cancer in May 1968. A period of improved relations between the university and Montgomery followed. (Hoole Special Collections Library, University of Alabama)

Jack Drake at the Alabama Student Union's Supe Store. By 1968, Drake had become a leader among Alabama's small number of determined student dissidents. (Photo courtesy of Jack Drake)

4
Toward a New University of Alabama
Building a Team for Excellence and Competence

Dean John L. Blackburn turned forty-one years of age in December 1964. After serving in the China-India-Burma Theater during the Second World War, he earned a bachelor's degree in science at Missouri Valley College and then completed a master's in education at the University of Colorado. Blackburn accepted his first job in higher education as assistant dean of men at Florida State University (FSU), until 1948 the Florida College for Women. Blackburn's task was to integrate men, outnumbered four-to-one, into the fabric of student life. By 1955, with that done, Blackburn decided to study for his PhD at Columbia University. Then in March 1956, he received a call from the dean of men at the University of Alabama.

The riots a month earlier immediately came to mind as soon as Dean Louis Corson identified himself. According to Blackburn, when Corson asked if he might be interested in the assistant dean of men's job at the Capstone, "I laughed. Alabama was on television every day with scenes from all these riotous conditions. I asked, 'Why in the world would I want to work at a place like Alabama?'" Louis Corson responded, "I thought you were concerned about the race issue in America. If so, where else would you want to work?" Blackburn abandoned his Columbia plans and headed for Tuscaloosa. "When I arrived, there were Klansmen marching at the edge of campus. I wondered, 'What have I gotten myself into?'"[1]

By 1965, with higher education becoming more specialized and President Rose committed to increasing the academic qualifications of faculty and staff, John Blackburn needed to complete the doctorate he had been working on part time at FSU. Accordingly, in January, he asked for a one-year leave of absence to return to Tallahassee. The value of Blackburn's research, focused as it was on student-administration relationships at the University of California at Berkeley, appealed to Frank Rose. Blackburn suggested David Mathews, then finishing his PhD in the history of American higher education at Columbia University, be named acting dean of men in his absence.[2]

It didn't take Frank Rose long to appreciate John Blackburn. As soon as Corson retired in 1959, Rose elevated Blackburn to the dean's post. Shortly thereafter, in February 1960, David Mathews, who earned his master's degree in education the year before, found himself in the job market after completing a short tour with the army. "There was nothing available in my hometown of Grove Hill, Alabama, and I was thankful when John Blackburn gave me my first job at Alabama."[3] His responsibilities included handling issues attendant to male students living off campus.

In 1962, Mathews took a leave of absence from the university to work on his doctorate. In May 1963, Blackburn called him back to campus to help prepare student leaders for the arrival of Vivian Malone and James Hood. That done, Mathews returned to New York to complete his dissertation, "The Politics of Education in the Deep South." In March 1965, Frank Rose offered him the position of interim dean for the coming academic year, with a follow-on job as his executive assistant in charge of legislative matters.[4] It was a propitious hiring. Four summers later, in June 1969, the Alabama Board of Trustees named David Mathews to succeed Frank Rose as president of the university.

From 1965 to the end of the decade, while Frank Rose was still at the helm, a consensus emerged throughout higher education as to what constituted a "model university." First, the better universities expanded their faculties to accommodate the growing number of undergraduate and graduate students with increasingly diverse academic interests. Second, they engaged in research programs attracting conspicuous federal funding. Third, model universities committed to ambitious building programs for housing, classrooms, and research facilities.

By 1965, to varying degrees the University of Alabama qualified in all three categories. Despite President Rose's increasingly contentious relationship with George Wallace, a supportive legislature committed twenty-one million dollars to support new construction. There also was an 8.5 percent increase in the 1965–66 budget for normal appropriations allowing an across-the-board hike in faculty salaries. Additionally, Rose secured copious federal funding, enabling the university to embark on a ten-year, seventy-five-million-dollar building program. Rose admitted to a friend, "We are having a wonderful time spending all this money," while also noting, "We are going to use most of it to build as much excellence and competence as possible."[5]

Plans for expansion included an addition to the administration building, a new Alabama student union, new fraternity and sorority houses, more residence halls, a large field house and coliseum complex, vast increases in facilities at the medical center in Birmingham, and expanding the seating capacity of Denny stadium from forty thousand to sixty thousand. Rose anticipated that within a decade, by 1975, enrollments would top fifteen thousand at the Capstone with a total enrollment of forty-one thousand, with the extension centers included.[6]

To improve efficiency, Rose streamlined the administration. He reduced the number of people reporting directly to him by rerouting the chain of command to Alex Pow, who assumed the new position of vice president for academic affairs. Additionally, C. T. Sharpton became vice president for institutional research and physical planning with responsibility for controlling and allocating the vast sums projected for research and construction. Raymond F. McLain, formally joined the faculty as dean for international programs on February 1, 1966. This resulted from a courtship between Rose and McLain going back to 1963 when the latter left the presidency of the American University in Cairo to assume chancellor's duties in Washington, DC, where he remained until moving to the University of Alabama in 1966.[7]

While the university's future looked bright in the summer of 1965, there were potential mine fields through which Rose stepped cautiously. Rose was wary of how George Wallace might respond to the remarks made by commencement speaker Thomas Moore and, also, to the airing of *Southern Campus: The Quiet Revolution*. As a hedge against possible repercussions and with characteristic diplomatic aplomb, Rose invited President Ralph W. Adams, president of Troy State College, to deliver the August commencement address. Rose knew Adams's friendship with Wallace went back to their student days at the Capstone and that the honorary doctorate he received at the ceremony would emboss his credentials as a college president.[8] There is no record of Wallace reacting to Moore's commencement remarks or to the documentary.

No Berkeley on the Warrior

George Wallace's passion for politics could have made him a tyrannical demagogue. Tyranny, however, was not the stuff of which Wallace was made, if only because tyrants revel in the details of governing. Wallace's passion was running for office and getting elected. As governor, Wallace devised policies and programs that catered to voters, thus enhancing his future political prospects. In his second run for governor in 1962, when it served his political interest to take an uncompromisingly racist stand, he did so, even though his fiery rhetoric in defense of segregation inspired violence from the worst elements in Alabama. The civil rights movement had come a long way since the Montgomery bus boycott of 1955, fostering fear and apprehension among many white voters. Wallace fed their fears, turning them to his political advantage, first in Alabama and then nationally.

While George Wallace extended his political ambitions beyond Alabama, the antiwar movement gained momentum. On Saturday April 17, 1965, six weeks after the start of Operation Rolling Thunder, an estimated twenty thousand demonstrators gathered on the Washington Mall to hear speeches denouncing the war. Joan Baez and Judy Collins sang the standard protest songs of the time, "If I Had a Hammer," "Blowing in the Wind," and "Where Have All the Flowers Gone?" They then helped lead a procession to the US Capitol to present congress with a petition calling for an end to the war.[9] Television transmitted the images to the nation. Scenes from antiwar demonstrations played no better in living rooms of white Alabamians than did images from the Edmund Pettus Bridge in northern parlors.

George Wallace attempted to capitalize on rising apprehensions by supporting a legislative measure to ban Communists from speaking on the campuses of state-supported colleges and universities. It seemingly did not matter that after the North Carolina legislature passed a similar measure, the Southern Association of Colleges and Universities threatened to rescind accreditation from the University of North Carolina and other state schools. While Rose thought that was unlikely, he understood such a bill would provide the state's executive and legislative branches enormous power over the university. Accordingly, Rose marshaled every available resource to oppose what became known as the "speaker ban" or "Communist ban" bill.

From the university's perspective, a state law regulating who could or could not speak on campus threatened the exercise of intellectual freedom essential to its academic credibility. Although many legislators were Alabama alumni, given the mood of the electorate, their support was uncertain. Nevertheless, a determined Rose garnered enough support in the state legislature to defeat the measure.[10]

The university's procedure for vetting speakers included a committee comprised of students and faculty who compiled a list of possible speakers and then sent it to Vice President Bennett for review.[11] If Bennett harbored doubts about a particular speaker, he consulted with President Rose who then made the final decision. Rose willingly exercised his authority in cases potentially embarrassing to the university. As demonstrated by the controversy over Louis Armstrong, Rose did not shrink from using his discretionary powers in such matters.

Additionally, Wallace didn't totally dominate the state legislature. Shortly after the speaker ban bill failed, in September 1965, he ordered the legislature to amend the state constitution to allow a sitting governor to run for a second term. Representative Ryan DeGraffenried led the effort to scotch the attempt. It was then that Wallace prevailed on his wife Lurleen to run in his place. Rose's concerns, however, focused on the potential threat to academic freedom inherent in the speaker ban bill.

Although Frank Rose believed stopping the bill was essential, he picked other battles carefully. The *Birmingham News* published an article about an antiwar demonstration held in Washington, DC, between August 6 and 9, one cosponsored by the Committee for Non-Violent Action and the Student Peace Union to commemorate the twentieth anniversary of the atomic bombs dropped on Hiroshima and Nagasaki. The article mentioned Joan Baez sang for the demonstrators.[12] Alabama Educational Television, a university initiative, had scheduled a two-hour special titled *A Room Full of Music* beginning at eight thirty on the evening of August 11 and featuring, among others, Joan Baez.

Raymond D. Hurlbert, general manager of Alabama Educational Television, was writing a memorandum to President Rose informing him of Baez's participation in the demonstration and asking if he thought it wise to air *A Roomful of Music*, when he received a call from Mr. Ed Ewing, a member of Governor Wallace's staff. Ewing spoke bluntly: Wallace wanted the program cancelled. He added, "He sincerely hopes this request will be honored." With no apparent hesitation, Rose ordered the program withdrawn.[13] Otherwise, summer school proceeded uneventfully.

A Pivotal Meeting at Ann-Jordan Farm

Over the Labor Day weekend, top university officials, including Frank Rose, Alex Pow, Jeff Bennett, and David Mathews, along with twenty-seven student leaders, traveled to the university's Ann-Jordan Farm outside Alexander City for the annual Student Leaders' Retreat. In the opening address, President Rose outlined new programs associated with the expansion of the university. Student leaders in the audience taking in Rose's remarks included SGA president Zach Higgs, vice president Allen Lee, along with Sandi Mestler, president of the Associated Women Students, and the group's vice president, Charlotte Gallogly. Bill Shamblin, editor of the *Crimson-White*, brought his associate editor, Billie Blair, and reporter Kay Gauntt. Mac Cowden, the editor of the *Corolla*, also attended along with nineteen other student leaders.[14]

Most of the students at the retreat were active in several organizations.

Some were men selected for Omicron Delta Kappa (ODK) and the Jasons, the prominent men's service and honor societies, while the women's equivalent honorary society, Mortar Board, had tapped a number of the young women present. The Jasons, for instance, a men's honorary founded at the university in 1914, annually admitted to membership only fifteen of the most outstanding male student leaders. This group of button-downed, neat, and proper students comprised the campus best and brightest. Given their tenor, it was both perceptive and prescient that David Mathews, the interim dean of men, selected as the topic for the keynote address, "Collegiate Reformers: 1965."

Mathews, whose youthful appearance made him look more like a graduate student (and a young one at that) than a dean, noted that while the vast majority of students remained quiet and uncommitted, they also were concerned about the world in which they lived. Reformers, Mathews contended, had recently taken the offensive on college and university campuses, and the majority of students, he predicted, would be "willing to follow; if not now, soon." Mathews then addressed changes in student culture. Speaking in his quiet, yet commanding, manner, his soft voice anchored in a genteel southern accent, he said, "This means traditional activities like rock and roll dances, spring festivals, and beauty contests will continue; but they will be joined by art exhibits, debates with congressmen and, occasionally, petitions and demonstrations."[15]

The young dean then addressed the student unrest at Berkeley. "They lost faith in the official governing body," Mathews posited and advised the leaders before him not to lose touch with their fellow students, even the dissidents. He further advised, "You need to see beyond your traditional roles . . . even adopt a different language in dealing with the reformers." Mathews warned against authoritarian approaches, "They may become quite upset, perhaps unmanageable if you tell them to shut up." Conversely, Mathews advised, "Dissidents might be cooperative if they felt their views were considered. And they might be reasoned with if they found principles—more than necessity—lay behind your arguments."[16] While few, if any, of the students present at the Ann-Jordan Farm that day realized it, David Mathews had nudged them into a turning tide.

Same Form, Different Temper

During the spring of 1965, the student legislature initiated a program titled, "Emphasis." Conceived as an annual event, its purpose was to bring highly qualified, even controversial, speakers to campus to discuss pertinent issues from differing perspectives. For its first year's theme, the Emphasis committee selected "The Student's Role in a Democratic Society." Ralph Knowles, who cochaired the Emphasis '66 committee with Tom Henderson, along with program director Charlotte Gallogly, were committed to providing students the opportunity to hear "those people we have seen and heard on television discuss the major issues of the time."[17] At the beginning of the fall semester, the committee set Emphasis '66 for Friday and Saturday, March 18–19, 1966.

Through President Rose, the Emphasis '66 committee secured New York senator Robert F. Kennedy to speak on the opening night. Kennedy's presence on the program enabled the committee to attract Nathan Glazer, a liberal sociology professor from Berkeley. The committee worked with Frank Rose, who had the authority to veto any speaker they might recommend. To balance the agenda between conservative and liberal voices, the committee invited Senate minority leader, Republican senator Thurston Morton of Kentucky; James J. Kirkpatrick, the editor of the *Richmond News Leader* and author of a weekly conservative, syndicated column; and the director of Internal Security at the Federal Bureau of Investigation (FBI), Fern C. Studenboecker, rounded out the list of speakers.

That autumn, as the University of Alabama inched toward liberalism, the architects of change moved cautiously. Frank Rose, fearing George Wallace might revive the speaker ban issue, determined not to provide him any excuse for doing so, whether from carelessness or imprudence. Accordingly, as a precautionary measure, in November 1965 the Student Government Association decided to modify the structure and mission of the Board of Publications, broadening its membership and providing it with more authority and faculty oversight as a "Publications Review Board (PRB)."

Some students and faculty suspected these modifications might threaten academic freedom. Hank Black, a former *Crimson-White* editor, arguing against the bill, stated, "I fear under the proposed board that the integrity of our student publications would fall, not this year or next, but they would fall." Also not unexpectedly, Art Department chairman Ted Klitzke opposed the measure, warning, "No doubt this new board will be staffed with nice people, and you will have nice publications."[18] Reflecting at least some discomfort with what they were doing, the student senate amended the bill to forbid censorship.

The reasons for restructuring the Board of Publications into the PRB mystified many since mechanisms for vetting speakers already existed. The reconstituted Publications Review Board was, essentially, a codified and expanded form of the earlier reviewing mechanism. The new iteration included among its members the presidents of the men's and women's residence halls councils,

Inter-Fraternity Council and Pan-Hellenic, SGA, and AWS, as well as one student from the SGA House of Representatives, one from the Student Senate, and representatives from the English and Journalism Departments, a faculty member chosen at large, along with the dean of men and the dean of women. The 1966 *Corolla* pictured the members of the PRB and in the caption beneath it noted that in a campus-wide referendum, the student body rejected the changes by a slight eight-vote margin. The SGA Student Court ruled the vote invalid based on evidence some ballot boxes were stuffed.[19]

The purpose of the board, by whatever name or structure, may have seemed unclear to many students. It was not entirely censorship. *Crimson-White* editorials throughout 1966 often criticized the administration, and *Mahout*, the humor magazine, edited by Scout Powers, a member of the PRB, seemed undeterred in publishing ribald material, which eventually prompted its demise. Perhaps this initiative, contentious as it seemed at the time, was meant to maintain decorum while also covering the administration in case of future controversial publications.

Life among the Quiet and Uncommitted

In the 1960s, as today, leaving home for college offered young people the opportunity to emancipate themselves from their parents and hometowns. One of the functions of higher education is to encourage students to think about issues from new perspectives. The freedom of thought essential to a liberal education, however, contains a Pandora's box of inherent dangers. Additionally, perhaps paradoxically, the excitement generated by intellectually engaged students may unsettle administrators obligated to satisfying alumni, their board of trustees, and state legislators, all of whom provide financial resources. Furthermore, into the 1960s, the University of Alabama struggled to balance its role as intellectual provocateur with standing in loco parentis, especially with its female students.

According to *The Alabama COED*, a guide given to every female student, "The biggest change from high school to college is the experience of living on your own. . . . The University of Alabama is founded on the principle that students can successfully assume the responsibilities inherent in independent living."[20] Many female students, however, thought the rules, regulations, and punishments applied to them failed to accord with the stated assumption that students can assume adult responsibilities. One female undergraduate offered, "It seems the custom in Southern universities is for the administration to try to take the place of parents. . . . I am twenty-one and I resent the University telling me I can't do things the laws of Alabama say I can do."[21]

Alabama students routinely disregarded rules forbidding the consumption of alcoholic beverages on campus along with proscriptions forbidding female students from visiting men's apartments. Nevertheless, while the university found these rules difficult to enforce, they remained on the books. Rose and the administration were steadfast in the fall of 1965 when Sandi Mestler and Charlotte Gallogly, the AWS president and vice president, presented proposed modifications.

President Rose, sensitive to the way many Alabamians felt about alcohol consumption, stood firm on rules forbidding coed drinking, but offered to study an AWS proposal allowing women to visit men's apartments. As administrators are inclined to do with such contentious issues, Rose established a committee to study the matter.[22] Both male and female students continued to drink, especially at fraternity parties. Coeds visited men's apartments, where they drank with the male occupants.

Alabama's fraternities and sororities had just entered their annual rush season when the *Crimson-White* raised the possibility that they might soon disappear from American campuses because Title IV of the Civil Rights Act of 1964 stated that institutions receiving federal funding could not practice racial discrimination.[23] Rose queried the IFC and Pan-Hellenic Association, asking if any fraternities or sororities discriminated against prospective members based on race. The response was that not a single one had written or unwritten statements or policies specifically excluding members based on their race, creed, color, or national origin.[24]

What was the purpose of this query? Surely Frank Rose, with his ties to Kappa Alpha, knew the answer before he asked the question. He must also have known that responses assuring him there were no codified policies concerning race were disingenuous.

A *Crimson-White* editorial stated the obvious. "Not to defend or condemn the Greek system, but the truth is, that it does practice discrimination."[25] It pointed out that prospective members might be rejected based on considerations ranging from financial background to personal appearance to a single member's animus for a particular pledge. In reality, they all discriminated based on race and, to varying extents, on socioeconomic standing.

The Cotillion Club, meanwhile, selected renowned African American performer James Brown to launch the 1965 entertainment season, but not without some behind-the-scene vetting. In August, Vice President Jeff Bennett asked David Mathews to look into Brown's involvement with civil rights organizations. Accordingly, Mathews contacted the appropriate authorities in venues where Brown had recently performed and found that he was not associated with civil rights organizations and that there had been no demonstrations following his performances. On October 5, 1965, James Brown performed at Foster Auditorium.[26]

The next month, the Dave Brubeck Quartet, a progressive jazz group, played at Birthright Auditorium at nearby Stillman College. About two hundred people attended, among them several white students from the university. The four musicians' repertoire included hits like "Take Five" and the crowd applauded during a ten-minute solo by drummer Joe Morellow.[27] Attending a concert at Stillman, while not necessarily a courageous act in support of social justice, seemed at least somewhat rebellious to the Alabama students who did so, if only because Tuscaloosa served as headquarters for the nation's largest Klan group.

During the autumn of 1965, Robert Shelton, imperial wizard of the United Klans of America, based in Tuscaloosa, found himself testifying before the House Un-American Activities Committee. Shelton refused to answer the committee's questions, citing the first, fifth, and fourteenth amendments to the Constitution more than 150 times.[28] In an act of moral courage, given the Klan's local prominence, the *Crimson-White* published a highly critical editorial stating, "This is not the action that should be taken by the leader of an organization that seems to deem itself 'super American.' . . . We must abolish the Klan and the group of racially bigoted officials who tolerate it, or Alabama will be abolished by this hooded band of hate mongers."[29]

Indeed, a lot remained wrong in the state of Alabama in 1965. Within the safe haven of the university, however, it was no longer anathema for students and faculty to question the injustices occurring throughout the South and to raise controversial issues, even those that troubled fellow students and university officials, constituting a shift—perhaps subtle but also significant—in the Capstone's culture.

Homecoming and Another National Championship

The homecoming committee picked "BLAST" or "Bama Launched as Seminoles Topple" for the 1965 theme. Perhaps the committee sensed what many students already felt—they were part of something special taking place deep in the heart of Dixie. Redding Pitt, chairman of the homecoming committee, reflected that feeling in explaining the "BLAST" theme. "We wanted to stress the University's dual acceleration toward excellence on the athletic field as well as its institutional development since the arrival of Dr. Rose and Coach Bryant."[30]

On Friday night, after the traditional rally on the Quad, the speeches by the usual dignitaries, the bonfire, and the fireworks, students made their way to Foster to hear Pete Fountain perform with his clarinet.[31] The administration declared a "late night" for these festivities; meaning female students were not due back inside their dorms or sorority houses until two o'clock Saturday morning.

The evening and morning before the game, fraternity and sorority members stuffed crepe paper into floats that somehow were ready an hour or so before the ten o'clock parade on Saturday morning. Then the Million Dollar Band, with Miss Alabama, Liz Freeman, in the lead, paraded along University Boulevard. Behind the band, campus beauties in stylish suits rode in convertibles, while pledges marched behind their respective fraternity or sorority floats.

That afternoon, the Tide blasted the Florida State Seminoles by a score of 21–0. The victory secured, the warm afternoon's sunset brought with it the shadows of a cool autumn evening. Festivities turned to fraternity row where bands belted out "Shout" and "Wait 'til the Midnight Hour." On Monday, the national polls placed the Tide among the nation's top ten teams.

That late in the season, Alabama looked unlikely to repeat its national championship. There was the 18–17 loss to Georgia in the season opener, and a heartbreaking 7–7 tie in the Tennessee game when substitute quarterback sophomore Kenny Stabler, with less than a minute to go in the fourth quarter and within easy field goal range, tossed the ball out of bounds to stop the clock. Stabler thought it was the right move on third down. Unfortunately, it was fourth down and the game ended in a tie.

Things broke right and at the end of the season Alabama received an invitation to play the University of Nebraska Cornhuskers in the Orange Bowl on New Year's night. Nebraska outweighed Alabama by twenty-five pounds from end to end across the offensive line and thirty-five pounds per man on the defensive side of the ball. Nevertheless, the Tide had two advantages: speed and Coach Bryant.

Nebraska's coach Bob Devaney figured Bryant would play conservatively, relying on the running game to minimize mistakes, and take advantage of any opportunities that arose. He was wrong. Bama came out passing. Bryant called tackle-eligible plays and used on-side kicks to create opportunities. The game ended with a 39–28 Crimson Tide victory. The following Monday, Alabama was voted "Number One" . . . again.[32]

The Orange Bowl game was more than a spectacular display of passing between quarterback Steve Sloan and end Ray Perkins; it turned into a demonstration of extraordinary sportsmanship, one televised nationally. At the end of every play, the Alabama players jumped to their feet and then held out a helping hand to their downed opponents, often patting them on the back as they trotted back to the line of scrimmage. Given the disparity in size, this would have been remarkable. But it was the difference in the players' color that made the gesture special. The media's focus on racial issues set up what turned out to be a public relations coup for the university and, by extension, a state much in need of positive press coverage. An Alabama alumnus living in Pennsylvania wrote Frank Rose, "As an avid Alabama football fan, I've never seen anything surpassing it. What I saw on New Year's Day was the 'real Alabama.'"[33]

Coach Bryant often spoke of the importance of "showing class," whether in victory or defeat. During the Orange Bowl, the Alabama team demonstrated something beyond class; they showed a national television audience a level of human decency most Americans were unused to associating with the state, its governor, and its public officials. Students returning from Christmas break could take pride in another national championship, and much more.

The Twilight of Apathy

Even in the idyllic autumn of 1965, it was not all "rock and roll dances and beauty pageants." The student body was, in fact, engaged with issues beyond the comfortable confines of the Quadrangle. Toward the end of the semester, the SGA called for a show of support for the troops fighting in Vietnam. Accordingly, on December 7, students rolled up their sleeves to donate 1,183 pints of blood.[34] Army PFC Dale E. Easterling of Mobile, a former student, expressed his gratitude to Frank Rose, "I am awaiting orders for deployment to Viet Nam. Needless to say, the student support made me feel good."[35]

By December 1965, two and a half years had passed since George Wallace's futile gesture in the doorway of Foster Auditorium. In June 1963, it might have seemed far-fetched that within three years an African American associated with the civil rights movement would be speaking two blocks away in the Alabama Union building. That is where, on the last Tuesday before Christmas break, the Human Rights Forum hosted John Nixon, president of the Alabama chapter of the NAACP.[36]

During this time, the American academic community turned on the Johnson White House over the war in Southeast Asia. Frank Rose, however, remained supportive. In October 1965, an Alabama alumnus suggested the SGA sponsor a rally backing the war in Vietnam. Rose acknowledged that while the majority of students agreed with US policies in Vietnam, he also feared such a rally might backfire by "attracting a group of bearded nuts to campus." He added, "We think it best to move along steadily, and not make a great deal of noise about it." Rose also wrote that at a recent White House conference of national leaders, President Johnson asked him to speak to the more than one hundred attendees. According to Rose, after telling the assembled leaders that he stood firmly behind the administration's Vietnam policy, "I received a standing ovation, and the President, on several occasions, has expressed his personal gratitude to me."[37]

Rose's response was more than an exercise in placation since, at the time, most Alabama students backed the war. In January, Rose's signature appeared first on a petition reading, "We the undersigned students and faculty of the University of Alabama support the Vietnam policies of the U.S. Government."[38] Alpha Kappa Psi, the business and commerce honorary society, sponsored the petition drive that gathered 3,312 signatures, representing over one-fourth of the student body. The society then sent the petition to the office of Congressman Armistead Selden, asking that he forward it to President Johnson.

In February, the SGA conducted a comprehensive survey aimed at assessing student behavior and attitudes on a range of issues. If the result of the Alpha Kappa Psi petition drive indicated a compliant student body, the survey showed that matters of compliance were situational. For instance, despite rules forbidding female students from visiting men's apartments, 98 percent of those interviewed admitted they regularly did.

When it came to the Vietnam War, 87 percent of students thought the United States was justified in supporting the South Vietnamese government. While a third of respondents believed policy makers "blundered" into the war, over 80 percent thought US forces should remain in Vietnam, and 70 percent supported military escalation. Only 10 percent advocated withdrawal from South Vietnam. Furthermore, 54 percent thought antiwar demonstrators on college campuses were detrimental to the war effort, but 55.7 percent also supported the students' right to demonstrate. On the other hand, 44.3 percent thought students had no such rights. When the survey asked males if they planned to volunteer for military service after finishing their academic endeavors, 27.4 percent stated that they would, or that they might consider it.[39] Tellingly, the survey story in the *Crimson-White* ran under the provocative title, "SGA Survey Claims 'Most All Coeds Do!'"

Frank Rose wanted to distinguish the University of Alabama from the state while also moving it into the mainstream of American academia. His "move along steadily" strategy complemented the generally compliant temperament of the student body. This enabled the university to take small, if increasingly bold, steps in a new direction. The first step was to invite Lady Bird Johnson, America's First Lady, to the Alabama campus.

On the last Friday in February, the university cancelled all classes between eleven o'clock and three o'clock to enable attendance at Lady Bird Johnson's keynote address to the Alabama Women's Conference symposium titled, "Women in a Changing Community." Additionally, students were invited to honor the First Lady at a reception on the lawn of the President's Mansion. Lady Bird Johnson possessed Alabama roots. During childhood and adolescence, she spent her summers visiting relatives in Mobile, Montgomery, and Prattville. Additionally, one summer studying at the university made her an alumna.[40]

After a lavish welcome at the airport in Northport, Mrs. Johnson spoke from the stage in Foster Auditorium, addressing more than 2,500 students and symposium attendees. She began by mentioning the significant contributions made by Alabama women throughout the state's history. Her list included Julia Tutwiler, who brought coeducation to the university; and Helen Keller, a Tuscumbia native, the first deaf and blind person to earn a college degree and the subject of the 1962 motion picture, *The Miracle Worker*. The First Lady also mentioned Harper Lee, a member of the class of 1940 and author of *To Kill a Mockingbird*, and Libby Anderson Cater, the first woman president of the Alabama SGA and wife of Lyndon Johnson's executive assistant, Douglass Cater. Conspicuously absent from her list was the recently announced gubernatorial candidate, Lurleen B. Wallace, a Northport native and the First Lady of Alabama, who, likewise, was conspicuously absent from the conference.

If Alabama's present and future governors had been in the audience, they might not have appreciated the First Lady's remarks. The president's wife exhorted the audience to "extend the hand of partnership to your Negro neighbors, putting aside customs and prejudice." She admitted that doing so might not be easy, but it was also "fundamental to the American experience."[41] After the address, President and Mrs. Rose hosted a reception for the First Lady. Her visit to the Capstone constituted a prelude to what followed in mid-March.

Emphasis '66

On Friday, March 18, Emphasis '66 got under way. The first speaker, Republican senator Thurston Morton of Kentucky, told the audience that 1966 was a "year of crisis," comparable to 1936, when the nation languished in the Great

Depression. He also confidently predicted major Republican gains in the 1968 elections.[42]

The crowd came to hear the next speaker, Senator Robert Kennedy, hated by many Alabamians for his role in desegregating the university. Kennedy, accompanied by his wife Ethel, began his address with his characteristic brand of charming humor, much of it at the expense of George Wallace. He told the crowd of four thousand that he needed to clear up something. "I hear people saying I'm making these speeches around the country to further my campaign for the presidency. But I'll tell you one thing," he added, with a smile, "my wife is not running for president." Loud applause greeted this obvious reference to Mrs. Wallace's announced intention to succeed her husband in office. Kennedy then leaned over the podium, looked at his wife in the front row and asked, impishly, "Or are you?" Again, the applause thundered.[43]

Kennedy then turned serious. "We can concentrate on what unites us and secures the future of all our children, or we can concentrate on what divides us and fail in our duty through argument, resentment and waste." Senator Kennedy received several standing ovations but none matched the vigorous applause when he concluded with, "It is far easier to accept and stand on the past than it is to fight for answers for the future. . . . your generation cannot afford to waste the future on a time past."[44]

James J. Kirkpatrick, conservative editor of the *Richmond News Leader* opened the Saturday session with an address titled, "The Right to Dissent." Kirkpatrick posited that McCarthyism, far from being over, still reigned on college and university campuses, where "many people who called themselves liberal are really illiberal to the right of dissent." He pointed out that conservative writers were finding it difficult to publish anywhere except in the *National Review* and added, "The great universities of our country have become delivery rooms and playpens for liberals."[45]

Nathan Glazer, a Berkeley sociologist, initially wondered why he, a noted liberal, was invited to speak at Alabama. It was more than traditional southern hospitality that surprised the Berkeley professor who, in a thank you note to President Rose, wrote, "I can certainly say I came away with a strong impression of the intellectual variety and liveliness of the campus."[46]

While Emphasis '66 wrapped up on Saturday morning, a little over a mile west, on the courthouse steps in Tuscaloosa, a reserved, wan-looking woman in a three-piece suit thanked an enthusiastic crowd of five hundred for supporting her gubernatorial campaign. Lurleen Wallace then completed her brief remarks with, "Let me now introduce you to the man who will be my number one assistant, my husband, Governor George C. Wallace."[47] While the band struck up "Dixie" to whoops and hollers of the crowd, George Wallace pecked his wife on her cheek, then coatless, with his sleeves rolled up, ripped into the *Tuscaloosa News* for not supporting his failed efforts to change the state's succession law that prohibited Alabama governors from running for two consecutive terms.

Only a handful of university students in the crowd heard Wallace attack dissent on college campuses. "I can tell you this," Wallace snarled as he pointed in the direction of the Capstone, "Any students who demonstrate on the campuses of our state colleges and universities are going to find themselves expelled, at least for a day, until the federal courts put them back in school."[48]

As springtime reached the campus, President Rose must have been pleased with the results of Emphasis '66 as indicative of progress at the Capstone. Furthermore, Lady Bird Johnson's visit strengthened his relationship with the White House. In a letter to David H. Griffin, a Meridian, Mississippi, dentist and old friend, Rose wrote, "We had to work very hard to accomplish this, but we have an excellent chance of becoming the leading university in the South and one of the best in the nation."[49]

As the semester unfolded, another controversy arose over the possibility of censorship after the administration commissioned the Student Life Committee, consisting of five students, five professors, and two representatives of the administration, to advise the administration on speakers invited to campus. The *Crimson-White* supported the administration, stating that the committee was nothing new. The editorial also pointed out, that if the university did not set up a vetting process, "there would be lots of people in state government who would be glad to step in and resolve the issue for us."[50]

The Dawn of Dissent

In his personal correspondence Frank Rose spoke of increasing antipathy between himself and George Wallace. Nevertheless, Wallace's position as ex officio chairman of the university's board of trustees required Rose's respect. Accordingly, Rose treated Wallace deferentially when it came to functions like Governor's Day scheduled for Tuesday, April 23, 1966.

At half-past nine on the appointed morning, the governor, Mrs. Wallace, and other dignitaries gathered at the Alabama Union for coffee and pastries. Shortly before the motorcade left for the reviewing stand at the east end of the Quad, five men, clean-shaven and neatly dressed in sport jackets, and one young woman in high heels and a conservative suit, walked past Denny Chimes toward the parade ground. They carried signs that read, "This is NOT George Wallace High!" and "Stand up for Academic Freedom." The pamphlets they distributed read, "We are Alabama students concerned with the detrimental effects George Wallace's actions have had on academic quality and freedom on campuses across the state."[51] Only two of the demonstrators, William E. Palya and Penny Sheehan, were enrolled at the university.

Campus police responded immediately, intercepting the picketers and ordering them to lay their signs on the ground—face down—so they could not be read. Shortly after that, the police told the six individuals to leave the Quadrangle, which they started to do, walking back in the direction of the Alabama Union. Then Col. Beverly Leigh, chief of university security, arrived.

On Colonel Leigh's orders, the police summoned the group back and asked for their student identity cards. Penny Sheehan complied and was sent on her way. Three of the five young men, after explaining they were not university students, presented driver's licenses for identification. They, too, were excused. After William Palya, a university student, and Larry Knopp, an instructor at Stillman College, refused to show any form of identification, the police arrested them for disorderly conduct. They were booked at the Tuscaloosa jail and then released on two hundred dollars bond.[52]

That night, students and faculty, most of them affiliated with the Human Rights Forum, met at Ted Klitzke's home. Law professor Jay Murphy attended along with the current and incoming SGA presidents, Zach Higgs and Ralph Knowles. Jack Drake, Knowles's recent opponent for president, also attended. Professor Murphy addressed the legal aspects of the incident, informing the group that the police had the authority to ask for identification and to arrest anyone who refused to comply. That settled, Higgs and Knowles penned a letter to the administration urging it to clarify its policy on demonstrations and also to drop all charges against Palya and Knopp.[53]

Subsequently, the city prosecutor agreed to drop the charges. That didn't matter to Judge Joe Burns, known by some barristers as "Burn 'em Burns." First, however, he ordered the blacks and whites in the court to sit in two separate sections. He then refused to drop the charges and continued the case pending a full investigation.[54]

Two days later, the Human Rights Forum addressed the issue. Some members pronounced the demonstrations counterproductive, reasoning such acts only fed the fears of Alabamians who suspected the campus of becoming a hotbed of subversion. Others worried such behavior might bolster Lurleen Wallace's chances in the upcoming Democratic primary. After much discussion, the only thing the meeting produced was a commendation for the actions taken by Higgs and Knowles after the meeting in Klitzke's house.

Meanwhile, Sheehan and Palya told their story to the *Crimson-White*, saying they wanted to awaken fellow students from their apathy and to support academic freedom, and their actions had nothing to do with the war in Vietnam or civil rights. The *Crimson-White* story and analysis praised their sincerity but criticized their lack of judgment. "People all over this state are worried about the possibility of a 'Berkeley' here. . . . They do not understand the academic reasons for the demonstration, only that the word 'demonstration' has unpleasant connotations."[55] What happened on that Governor's Day was something different, constituting both a departure point and a harbinger of things to come.

Basking in the Sunny Spring of '66

Springtime rituals affirmed the power of tradition at the Capstone. On the last night in March, the AFROTC held its annual ball in Foster. The cadets and their dates danced to music provided by the Air University Band. At the high point of the evening, cadet officer escorts presented members of the Angel Flight. Young women attending the event, in addition to enjoying a one o'clock "late night" privilege received an engraved program as a commemorative souvenir.[56]

Originally, Bama Day consisted of a Friday afternoon set aside for SGA candidates to make political pitches to students. Over the years, entertainment edged out SGA politics, turning the event into a kind of county fair. In 1966, an election year, gubernatorial candidates received invitations to speak. Candidates that spoke that year already trailed front-runner Lurleen Wallace who, once again, was conspicuous by her absence.

Classes ended at noon, providing time to see Miss Alabama, Liz Freeman, lead the Million Dollar Band along University Boulevard. Drill teams from Army and Air Force ROTC units across the state then competed on the Quad. At the climax, a flight of four Alabama Air National Guard RF-84 Thunder Flash reconnaissance jets streaked above the campus. Then it was over to the Martha Parham Hall parking lot for carnival rides, midway games, and speeches by gubernatorial hopefuls.[57]

Like Bama Day, the Sigma Chi Derby evolved after its Capstone debut in 1940. For its twenty-sixth iteration, the derby took to the stage at Foster Au-

ditorium on the last night in April. At the height of the evening, judges selected "the girl of every Sigma Chi's dream." Prior to the crowning of the coming year's Sweetheart of Sigma Chi, there were contests devised to please an
audience largely consisting of males. First, chorus lines from seven sororities
kicked their way through various routines. Then three more sororities joined
in the competitive events. At the end of the evening, Miss Mary Jo Brazelton,
the reigning national as well as chapter sweetheart, passed her crown to Chi
Omega's Nance Fisher.[58]

The following Friday night, at the annual A-Day intersquad football game,
Kenny Stabler, a rising junior, and Wayne Trimble, a soon-to-be senior, led
opposing teams. In the end, Stabler quarterbacked the "Red" team to a 26–14
victory. The 1966 version of the Tide would still be "light" by comparison to
other big-time college teams with Nathan Rustin, a 215-pound tackle, weighing in as the heaviest man on the squad.[59]

Meanwhile, at the edge of campus in the dark woods along the Warrior
River, the Army ROTC Counter-Guerrilla Battalion held its nighttime war
games. Capt. E. R. Currier, a member of the Army Special Forces and faculty
advisor to the "Black Berets," noted that several of the seniors were enrolled
in unconventional warfare correspondence courses offered by the John F. Kennedy Center for Special Warfare. Within months, some of them would be in
Vietnam doing it for real.[60]

The conflict in Vietnam, still a long way from ROTC maneuvers at the edge
of campus, nevertheless crept closer. In early May, the *Crimson-White* ran an
article on how to "beat the draft." Taken from a conscientious objector's pamphlet made available to students at Berkeley, the article noted that one way to
secure a "4-F," or "undesirable" draft rating, was to avoid bathing starting two
weeks prior to the induction physical exam. In addition to stinking, the article
suggested it might be helpful to show up with long, dirty hair, a matted beard,
and to walk barefooted with sandals slung around your neck. If that didn't work,
one could always "play the homosexual bit. Flick your wrist, look embarrassed
in front of other guys when you undress." The article helpfully suggested, "You
might ask your girlfriend to give you lessons."[61]

Meanwhile, the Million Dollar Band elected a new Miss Alabama, Halcyann
Jones, an Alpha Chi Omega from Montgomery, to lead them through the coming school year.[62] Miss Jones's election represented the continuation of a hal-
lowed tradition. For the time being, tradition, not revolution, reigned at the
Capstone.

Commencement took place the last Sunday afternoon in May. Luther Terry, former surgeon general of the United States, delivered the address. Emmet Gribbin gave the baccalaureate sermon. It was a well-deserved honor for a man who, ten years earlier, incurred a beating to distract a lynch mob while Dean Sarah Healy stuffed Autherine Lucy into a police cruiser that carried Alabama's first African American student to safety.

Vice President J. Jefferson Bennett presided because Frank Rose was in a hospital in Bethesda, Maryland, recovering from an emergency appendectomy. The forty-six-year-old Rose fell ill shortly after arriving in Washington, DC, to attend a meeting of the local alumni association. When released after a ten-day stay, Frank Rose returned to Tuscaloosa to spend most of June recuperating and relaxing at Rose Point, his lodge on Lake Martin.[63]

In June, Coach Bryant collapsed during a speech in Los Angeles. After a few days recovering from what was described as fatigue and overwork, he returned to prepare for the season opener against Louisiana Tech. In that game Bryant forsook his lucky fedora for the black-and-white houndstooth hat that became his trademark.[64]

Anticipating the return of John Blackburn as dean of men, Frank Rose named David Mathews his executive assistant. His primary duty involved working with Jeff Bennett on legislative matters. The move made sense. The Mathews family had a long association with the Alabama legislature, where his grandfather served. David Mathews also had a knack for working with people. In that regard, Jefferson Bennett, whose portfolio included coordinating legislative matters, needed help. The lion's heart that beat within Bennett sometimes led him to speak bluntly, especially when he dealt with George Wallace. "Jeff and George were contemporaries," Mathews later recalled, "He was not afraid to tell George to 'go to hell,' and he did so on several occasions."[65]

David Mathews also brought to the administration his empathy with students, with whom he enjoyed immense popularity. "Mathews is responsible for the new atmosphere of free dissent on campus," the Crimson-White opined when he moved into President Rose's inner circle. Mathews, indeed, encouraged what he called "new attitudes among an idealistic generation . . . a very American generation that sees things in moral absolutes . . . nothing gray, but in black and white."[66]

By the summer of 1966, a new University of Alabama was emerging. Nevertheless, the Capstone remained a comparatively small, traditional, conservative, party school. Furthermore, while the Crimson Tide ranked at the top of the collegiate football world, the university also was working its way out of higher education's academic backwaters.

Dissent, though not widespread, was no longer anathema and, as the Louis Armstrong controversy showed, could reach across the student body, affecting independents and Greeks. The Human Rights Forum and small anti-Wallace demonstration in April 1966 hinted at the changing climate.

The administration, while moving cautiously, stood firm on the side of academic freedom by opposing the speaker ban bill, although the issue would re-emerge in 1967 in a more virulent way. Inviting Lady Bird Johnson to open a conference on women's issues, followed by Senator Robert Kennedy's address at Emphasis '66, further reflected the vision and moral courage of Frank Rose. In the summer of 1966, the University of Alabama looked optimistically toward a future where a multiplicity of ideas and opinions might be tolerated, even encouraged.

5
A Year of Ferment and Inquiry
In Infinite New Directions

During the annual "State of the University" address delivered to the trustees on homecoming weekend in November 1966, President Rose reported, "Excellent scholars and serious students have brought ferment and inquiry to the University of Alabama." He described an institution moving in "infinite new directions" involving academic improvements along with expanded facilities. The fall semester echoed past autumns with its traditional collage of rush parties, football games, freshmen eager to fit into college life, and upperclassmen anxious to move on.[1]

In June 1966, John Blackburn completed his doctoral studies at Florida State University and then returned to his post as dean of men. Accordingly, David Mathews packed his books and office files for the short move down the hall to the presidential suite where he assumed the duties of executive assistant to Frank Rose. There was, however, no office space for Mathews who settled into the adjacent boardroom. A corner of the conference table served as the desk from whence the president's apprentice set about learning the workings of a modern state university.[2]

David Mathews served the university well during John Blackburn's sabbatical. A talented teacher who taught an American history class during his lunch hour, Mathews quickly developed empathy with students because he understood they viewed life and its issues from a perspective of "moral absolutes."[3]

It was David Mathews who legitimized dissent a year earlier with his address at the student leaders' convocation. Although dissent barely evidenced itself during his year as interim dean, Mathews, as a historian, understood that revolutionary leaders often emerged from the privileged classes rather than from the toiling masses. The winds of change Mathews sensed sweeping across the nation's campuses blew more gently at the University of Alabama.

Advent of Student Syndicalism

Elsewhere these winds swirled into storm cells of dissent. In September 1966, Students for a Democratic Society (SDS) vice president Carl Davidson wrote a paper titled, "Toward Student Syndicalism" detailing how to take over and radicalize the nation's colleges and universities. The strategy focused on seizing control of student government and then issuing nonnegotiable demands backed by the threat of strikes.

Davidson's plan involved controlling student bodies through cells or "soviets" established in dormitories. If radicals could not take over established student governing bodies normally controlled by "bourgeois elements" like fraternities, SDS prescribed demonstrations to disrupt meetings by shouting down speakers and singing the Mickey Mouse Club theme song.[4] Upon gaining power, an SDS-controlled Freedom Democratic Party (FDP) would then submit a "students' bill of rights" to the administration. If the administration balked, the FDP could respond with a general student strike.

SDS also advocated abolishing grades. To their quasi-Marxist minds, the quest for grades resembled economic competition fostering the class system, albeit one based on merit rather than wealth. Understanding that the need to "make grades" heightened anxiety, SDS reasoned the student masses would support consigning grades to the dustbin of history. Abolition of grades provided SDS with an "umbrella issue" for solidifying their power base prior to addressing more pressing matters like the war in Vietnam. The young radicals also believed that absent a means to measure achievement, a large portion of the university hierarchy would wither, freeing students and enlightened professors to work harmoniously in a classless academic utopia. Students would marginalize recalcitrant professors by disrupting their classes and refusing to do assigned work or take examinations.[5] These antics, childish as they were, baffled university administrators and intimidated some into concessions that opened the door to anarchy. Not so at Alabama.

Revolts differ from revolutions in that revolts occur spontaneously, lack clearly defined goals, often do not gain popular support, and therefore fail. Furthermore, most students—including those in SDS—were oblivious to changes taking place in undergraduate education. By the mid-1960s, even the students at Alabama, still the quintessential Deep South party school, were more competent and sophisticated than their older siblings had been just a few years earlier. This was reflected in persistent demands for relaxation of in loco parentis rules pertaining to female curfew hours and an end to proscriptions against women visiting men's off-campus apartments.

Furthermore, the initiation of academic honors programs and the tutorials undertaken by Alabama's SGA aiding disadvantaged public school students in the African American community indicated a liberal undercurrent at the university. In 1966, the civil rights movement, particularly in Alabama and neighboring states and, albeit to a lesser extent, the war in Vietnam, pulled Alabama students in a more progressive direction. Meanwhile, on campuses in the northeast and California, the pace was faster and the goals far more radical.

In the mid-1960s, the student movement slowly shifted its primary focus from supporting civil rights to opposing the war in Vietnam. To many activists, the passage of the Civil Rights Act of 1964 and the Voting Rights Act the following year marked major victories in the struggle for racial equality. Way down south in Dixie, however, progressives knew these laws did not end the struggle. Indeed, attempts at enforcing and implementing their provisions prompted stubborn, often violent, opposition.

At the University of Alabama a cadre of established and respected liberal professors encouraged inquiry and ferment. These included Ted Klitzke, head of the Art Department, John Ramsey in the History Department, Iredell Jenkins, the eloquently spoken head of the Philosophy Department, and his colleague, Billy McMinn who jokingly referred to Southern Baptists as "S.O.B's" in lectures rollicking with irreverent references to the religious pretenses extant throughout the Bible Belt. These senior academics supported hiring a cadre of young liberal professors like Hugh Ragsdale, who taught Russian history and a course titled, "Communist Movements," along with Ron Robel, a specialist in Chinese history. Liberal and younger faculty members allied with more academically inclined student leaders, many of them bound for law school as their entrée into state politics. Furthermore, from 1964 through 1967 and into 1968, the progressive impulse at the University of Alabama originated with SGA leaders, in many cases young men linked with the fraternity-dominated "Machine" that controlled campus politics.

Additionally, Alabama's administration consisted of progressives committed to moving the university in a new direction, albeit cautiously. They also understood the complex social, cultural, and economic factors that formed the warp and woof of Alabama's racial politics. At the University of Alabama, the administration, with the support of key faculty and student leaders, charted a liberal course alien to most white Alabamians and inimical to the Wallace administration.

While students at many universities turned against American involvement in Vietnam to rain enmity on the military and anything associated with it, support for the war effort and the armed forces stayed strong at the Capstone, at least for the time being. A number of factors contributed to this phenomenon.

Alabama's male students with a reasonable grade point average were less threatened by conscription than their counterparts in some parts of the country. One alternative to the draft was to volunteer for the Air Force or Army National Guard. Another was to enroll in the two-year advanced programs offered by the campus ROTC detachments. After 1966, when ROTC was no longer mandatory, these programs enjoyed an abundance of applicants anxious to sign up since participants received the same draft deferments provided cadets at the military academies. For academic high achievers, a reserve commission conferred at graduation might allow them to delay active military service long enough to pursue further education in law, medicine, or as a graduate student. With luck, the war might end before they were called to active duty.

There also was a large cohort of young men who had dropped out of school or for whom high school graduation marked the end of their formal education.[6] Additionally, if the draft loomed for a university student, as a high school graduate "with some college," he stood a good chance of avoiding combat by enlisting in the Air Force or the Navy. Consequently, it took the tumult of 1968, including the Tet Offensive in January and February, Johnson's withdrawal from the presidential campaign in March, the assassinations of Martin Luther King Jr. in April and Robert Kennedy in June, along with the upheaval at the Democratic National Convention in Chicago in August to bring the Vietnam War to the forefront of student activism at the Capstone.

Despite the bombing and buildup of US forces that surged past three hundred thousand by August 1966, the war devolved into a stalemate. While air attacks knocked down bridges and disrupted rail and highway traffic, the North Vietnamese increased the flow of troops and supplies into South Vietnam.[7]

Tranquility in T-Town in the Summer of '66

Frank Rose's apprehension concerning what four more years of a surrogate Wallace regime might mean for the university aside, prospects for the future looked good. During the past year the university had received fourteen million dollars from the state and twenty million dollars from Washington, DC, and Frank Rose expected federal aid to increase by at least five million dollars before the end of the year.[8]

The summer term brought more good news. Woods Hall, the ninety-eight-year-old classroom building and the first structure constructed after the Civil War, was removed from the list of potential sites for the new Alabama Union building. The Committee for the Preservation of Woods Hall, a group reflective of the Capstone's campus activism at that time, headed the campaign to save the historic structure. Across the Quadrangle, Kappa Alpha Theta and Alpha Omicron Pi established colonies on sorority row. In early September, the state legislature increased its appropriation for the university by 8 percent (compared to 4.1 percent for Auburn). The administration passed the financial windfall on to the faculty with generous salary increases ranging from one thousand to two thousand dollars per year.[9]

Frank Rose continued building his team throughout the fall semester. He asked Raymond F. McLain to fill the interim dean's position in the College of Arts and Sciences while also serving as dean of International Programs.[10] Additional human capital accrued to the faculty when noted historian Daniel J. Boorstin of the University of Chicago spent a week on campus in October as the first visiting professor in a program initiated by SGA. Herbert J. Muller, an English professor from Indiana University, accepted an invitation to teach for the entire spring semester as a distinguished scholar in residence.[11]

The tardiness of the 1966 *Corolla*, normally distributed at the end of the spring semester, prompted an investigation by the Board of Publications. It blamed Mac Cowden, the former editor, and praised his successor, Coleman Lollar, editor of the 1967 *Corolla*, for working through the summer to prepare the final 153 pages for publication.[12] At many universities, with discontent over the war mounting, a late yearbook might have gone unnoticed. Not so at Bama.

Elysian Fields and Fields of Play

Changing times threatened Alabama's Greeks. The percentage of students pledging fraternities declined from almost 37 percent during the early 1950s to 20 percent by 1960. The majority of undergraduates in 1966, 80 percent of males and 60 percent of females, remained unaffiliated. Many among the baby-boomer generation were the first in their families to pursue higher education and, therefore, had no family tradition involving fraternities and sororities. Additionally, even amid the prosperity of the postwar economic boom, numerous families found financing a college education burdensome, ruling out the extravagances associated with Greek life. Furthermore, some scholarship and loan programs prohibited such affiliations. Finally, the emphasis placed on education as the key to success fostered a new sense of purpose among studious undergraduates.

Even if they could afford the associated costs, some saw the Greek system as incompatible with scholarship. For them, Roman toga parties seemed incongruent with the changing world. Others thought "elitist" fraternities limited their members socially to the upper and middle classes and were filled with young men intent on going into business or politics. Furthermore, the academic demands of the engineering and premed curricula left little time for socializing. Increasingly, students in the liberal arts and fine arts, those studying history, languages, and philosophy, saw the Greek system as militating against individuality by restricting one's circle of friends to those who shared similar outlooks, values, and opinions.

Then there was the race issue. In the fall of 1966, Ernestine Austin, an eighteen-year-old African American freshman from Citronelle, tested the racial climate along sorority row. "It was exciting," Ernestine stated in a *Crimson-White* interview, "I didn't feel inferior . . . not even when I was dropped. I felt down at first, but nothing bad towards anybody."[13] Dean Sarah Healy attempted to ease Ernestine's pain by telling her many other rushees also didn't receive bids and that race played no part in their rejection. Dean Healy was correct since everyone else who failed to receive a bid was also white.[14]

Most fraternities and sororities avoided language in their membership rules specifically referencing race. For one thing, US government–insured loans used to build fraternity and sorority houses forbade racial discrimination in the use of those facilities. Additionally, the more liberal university administrations across the country pressed their Greeks on racial matters.

Sigma Nu, unlike most fraternities, abjured ambiguity. Its membership rules specifically banned pledging people of African or Asian descent. At the 1960 Sigma Nu national convention—known as the "grand national chapter meeting"—held in Portland, Oregon, delegates passed legislation allowing a "waiver with honor" to chapters required by their universities to drop such discriminatory practices. By 1966, while seventy chapters had requested such waivers, only one had pledged an African American.

At the 1966 grand national chapter meeting in Kansas City, legislation to remove discriminatory language failed by a narrow vote. In the aftermath, Herman B. Wells, a Sigma Nu and chancellor of Indiana University, wrote his friend Frank Rose to ask if Alabama's fraternities retained such discriminatory clauses. The Alabama chapter of Sigma Nu, as Wells knew, had not requested a waiver.[15]

In his reply, Frank Rose admitted he thought every fraternity and sorority discriminated and that some, like Sigma Nu, maintained race-based proscriptions. He added, however, that if any fraternity or sorority decided to pledge blacks, the university administration would support them. "Our decision has been made," Rose stated, adding that "our decision" was made by him as president and without consulting the trustees. That being the case, since three Alabama trustees were Sigma Nu's, Rose asked Wells to keep his response in the strictest confidence.[16]

Sigma Chi discriminated more adroitly. It used a "social acceptability" clause requiring its chapters to pledge only those candidates acceptable to chapters and members anywhere in the country. Obviously, "anywhere" included the affiliates in Dixie. This was no idle threat. In 1965, Sigma Chi's national headquarters suspended its Stanford University chapter after it pledged a black rushee. Universities in Colorado, Minnesota, and Wisconsin then warned their Sigma Chi chapters that unless they proved they did not discriminate based on race, they risked losing their local chapter charter. When the Sigma Chi house at the University of Colorado failed to provide such evidence, the administration made good on its threat.[17] During the 1960s, despite the downward trend in membership, the Capstone's fraternities pledged between 500 and 600 a year while sororities took in between 450 and 500.[18]

After rush and fall registration, it was time to "tee it up and kick it off." *Look* magazine, Street and Smith's *College Football Yearbook*, *Playboy*, and the *Birmingham News* all picked Alabama to win its fourth national championship of the decade. *Playboy* tapped Coach Bryant as their "Coach of the Year," predicting, "Look for Bear to field the best team of his career."[19] The Crimson Tide opened the season by thrashing Louisiana Tech 34–0 at Legion Field.[20]

The week before kickoff, both the Associated Press (AP) and the United Press International (UPI) polls ranked Alabama the top team in the land. In those days, northeastern and West Coast sports writers who voted in the AP poll generally held southern teams in low regard, especially those from schools like Louisiana Tech. After Michigan State and the University of California at Los Angeles (UCLA) posted impressive wins in their opening games, sports writers jumped them ahead of Alabama. On Monday, when the new polls came out, both the AP and the UPI polls, the latter being the coaches poll, ranked the Michigan State Spartans first, the UCLA Bruins second, and the Crimson Tide third. There the Tide remained despite winning every game on its schedule and then whipping Nebraska 34–7 in the Sugar Bowl. Alabama's 17–7 victory over Ole Miss in Oxford the second week of the season had no effect on the polls. Only a footnote to history noted that in sixteen meetings since 1910, Ole Miss had not defeated Alabama.[21]

Until the mid-1990s, Alabama split its home games, playing half of them in Birmingham and half in Tuscaloosa. When Coach Bryant returned to Alabama in 1958, Denny Stadium seated only twenty-three thousand spectators. Eight years later, construction enclosed both end zones creating a "bowl" in time for fifty-nine thousand fans to watch the Tide swamp Clemson 26–0 in the campus season opener the second week in October. It appeared Alabama was rolling toward another national championship.

Billie Blair vs. the Board of Publications

During the 1958 gubernatorial Democratic runoff between Attorney General John Patterson and the "Fightin' Judge from Barbour County," George Wallace, the *Crimson-White* endorsed the more progressive Wallace. After Patterson won the election, possibly anticipating repercussions, the university adopted a policy forbidding political endorsements. This corresponded with an Alabama statute forbidding state employees and state-funded publications from endorsing political candidates.

Nevertheless, across Dixie and around the nation student newspapers regularly issued political endorsements. In October 1966, *Crimson-White* editor Billie Blair challenged the policy. The ferment and inquiry she precipitated typified what constructive dissent can accomplish.

On October 10, Dean John Blackburn, chairman of the Board of Publications, alerted Frank Rose that "a potential conflict similar or greater in magnitude to the Louis Armstrong situation" was about to occur.[22] Blackburn offered several options for dealing with the crisis from standing firm, modifying, or abandoning the policy to appointing a committee to study the situation further, the latter being the bureaucratic remedy favored by university administrators. What really scared them was that Billie Blair might endorse one of the two candidates opposing Lurleen Wallace. Rose feared such an endorsement might exacerbate the already contentious relationship between the university and the governor.

Two days later, Billie Blair endorsed Senator John Sparkman's candidacy. Since his reelection was a foregone conclusion, Blair's endorsement was about as controversial as sweet tea served at a Baptist covered-dish dinner.[23] Her heroic act jeopardized her position as editor and, though unlikely, might have led to suspension or expulsion from the university.

President Rose, balancing his inclination toward academic freedom against political realities, moved with characteristic caution. He first asked David Mathews to compile a historical summary of major board decisions on academic freedom for the past fifteen years. Next, he requested a legal opinion from Rufus Bealle, the university's attorney. He also wrote federal district judge Frank M. Johnson Jr. knowing his contentious relationship with George Wallace rivaled his own, asking the judge's opinion on the matter.[24]

Billie Blair prepared her case well. She reasoned that a revision to the SGA constitution signed by President Rose the previous spring invalidated the 1958 nonendorsement policy because it prohibited university administrators from censoring student publications or taking punitive action against editors. Rufus Bealle, however, disagreed. He maintained that the amended SGA constitution did not change Title 46, Section 147, of the Alabama State Code forbidding state employees from using state property or resources to promote candidates for public office. Since the *Crimson-White* editor received a student worker's stipend, Blair was considered a state employee.[25]

The board summoned Billie Blair to present her case. Prim and proper, she epitomized the "young professional" in bearing, attitude, and demeanor. Before proceeding, Dean Blackburn informed Miss Blair of her right to legal counsel. She politely replied that she sought legal advice prior to writing the editorial. This was neither an inquisition nor a lynching. Everyone in the room knew and liked Billie Blair, and most of them sympathized with her. So did the SGA, which passed a supportive resolution. Numerous newspapers across the state rallied to her cause, including the *Birmingham Post-Herald*, its editorial written by the journalist who, as *Crimson-White* editor in 1958, endorsed Wallace.[26]

Miss Blair spoke confidently. Challenging board members to change the policy, Blair asked, "Where will the line be drawn?" She stated the current policy might be used to prevent criticism of the governor or to muzzle the SGA, AWS, IFC, and other student organizations. Blair may have pushed the right button by inquiring, "Does this policy apply to freedom of expression by professors in state-owned classrooms?" She also pointed to student newspapers at public universities in nearby states, all of which regularly issued political endorsements. Blair concluded her testimony with, "Concern yourselves with freedom not just from an idealistic point of view, but freedoms extended to students at other state universities. Are we just as free?"[27]

Board members wrestled with the issue for seven hours without reaching a decision. When they reconvened a week later, a proposal to allow political endorsements resulted in a 6–6 tie. This left the decision up to Dean Blackburn as ex officio chairman. Instead of casting the deciding ballot, he proposed commissioning an outside study. Accordingly, the board hired Ruth Wilder, whose husband, James C. Wilder, worked in the dean of men's office, to investigate how other publicly funded southern universities handled political endorsements.[28]

Meanwhile, believing she stood firmly on the side of the angels, Billie Blair endorsed Don Collins, the Republican nominee for state's attorney general.[29] As October turned into November, a sense of dread hung over administration officials who feared Blair might endorse a candidate opposing Lurleen Wallace.

On election eve, Billie Blair remained true both to her calling as a journalist and, most importantly, to herself. In an editorial titled, "And Now, the Governor," she considered each candidate in turn, starting with the former governor's wife. "Lurleen Wallace is a mouthpiece for her husband—a power hungry politician who traipses all over the country running a hopeless race for the presidency." Next, she dubbed Republican congressman Jim Martin "too inexperienced . . . and even if he were qualified he would be hard-put to put any ideas he might have into practice." Then came the third candidate, the independent Dr. Carl Robinson, whom she described as "an auto-gyro with two degrees and a head full of ideas and no chance of winning." As for her endorsement, "There are none."[30] Billie Blair struck a blow for academic freedom at a crucial juncture; just how crucial no one at the time knew.

Undefeated, Untied, and Proud to Be Number Three

The 1966 edition of the Crimson Tide was the best team Bryant had coached to that point in his career. During the regular season, the Alabama defense allowed a total of 37 points while the offense amassed 301 points over ten games. Playing Nebraska for the second straight year, this time in the Sugar Bowl, the Tide romped by a score of 34–7. The margin of victory didn't matter. At the end of December the two major polls gave the national championship to Notre Dame with Michigan State as the runner-up. Both teams ended the season with nine wins and a tie, their single blemish coming in a 10–10 tie when they played each other.

Neither of the teams rated higher than Alabama played in a postseason bowl that year. Big Ten Conference rules, since changed, prohibited two consecutive appearances in the Rose Bowl and also forbade conference teams from accepting bowl bids elsewhere. So the number-two ranked Spartans remained in East Lansing. The 1966 national champions, Notre Dame, in those days did not accept postseason bowl invitations. On the first day of January, their players, along with those from Michigan State, watched on television as the Crimson Tide, the team *Sports Illustrated* named as the best in the nation, walloped the Cornhuskers.[31]

Most Alabamians, however, believed they knew why the polls denied their undefeated, untied Crimson Tide the national championship: the prejudices of northern sports writers. The 1967 *Corolla* carried a photo of a banner displayed by students during the Auburn game, "Alabama plays football, Notre Dame plays politics: In your heart you know we're #1."[32]

Sports historian Keith Dunnavant, in *The Missing Ring: How Bear Bryant and the 1966 Crimson Tide Were Denied College Football's Most Elusive Prize*, argued that the sports writers focused their animus not so much on the Crimson Tide as on George Wallace and, by extension, on the state whose image problem resulted from racially motivated Klan brutality. It also did not help that in November, near the end of the football season, Alabama voters overwhelmingly elected George Wallace's wife as their surrogate governor.[33]

The majority of Alabama fans never watched a game at Denny Stadium, much less darkened a classroom door at the Capstone. Furthermore, in the 1960s, with television limited to three networks, fans rarely viewed more than two televised Alabama games in a season. Radio connected most fans to their beloved Crimson Tide, radio and the televised Sunday afternoon *Paul Bryant Show*.

Cohosted by University Sports information director Charlie Thornton and Coach Bryant, the most widely viewed weekly television show in Alabama started with Thornton opening and then emptying a bag of Golden Flake potato chips onto a platter while Bryant swigged from a bottle of Coca-Cola. Throughout the hour, Bryant narrated the slow-motion game film. It didn't matter that Bear, his voice thickened into a gritty rumble by too many unfiltered Chesterfields, described only a handful of plays and sometimes got the players mixed up. What people tuned in to hear was not what Coach Bryant said but the folksy way he said it. Fans waited for the big defensive hit, which sometimes elicited from Coach Bryant, "Bingo! That's puttin' the bee on the bonnet."

The 1966 Crimson Tide probably was the best team Bryant coached after answering mama's call in 1958. Better yet, the members of that great team represented a university they could be proud of. Before the homecoming game with South Carolina, in the annual "State of the University" address delivered to the trustees, President Rose reported that at last June's commencement, Alabama conferred 75 doctorates, three times the number awarded in 1961, and awarded 724 master's hoods, up from 397 just five years earlier.[34] He also noted that the faculty had increased from 402 members in 1958 to 544 in the fall of 1966 and that over half possessed terminal degrees, compared with one-third when Rose took command. That, Rose reported, was better than the national average for state-supported universities. Governor-elect Lurleen Wallace, the first woman ever to sit in on a University of Alabama Board of Trustees meeting, spoke briefly, concluding her remarks by turning to her husband and saying, "I might invite you to sit in on future meetings."[35] She did.

Belles of Freedom

While the four thousand Alabama coeds found it impossible to defy the dress code, given they could be seen doing so, they regularly disobeyed the proscription against women visiting men's apartments. In the fall of 1966, the university finally took steps to change the policy. Ironically, many coeds appreciated the protection provided by rules limiting social interaction with the opposite sex. After all, citing curfew regulations provided an easy out for any young woman stuck with an unpleasant date. Characteristic of the Rose years, change occurred slowly and cautiously.

At the start of the fall semester, Frank Rose asked David Mathews to explore how other southern universities handled the issue. As a result, the university adopted a policy similar to those used by Auburn and the University of Florida requiring signed parental consent coupled with a form specifying the host's name, address, and phone number. Anyone signed out for a male's apartment also had to be signed in thirty minutes before curfew.[36]

Diminishing in loco parentis rules contributed, at least in part, to the advent of the sexual revolution. While some parents (and grandparents) fretted over the safety of their daughters and granddaughters, a more ominous cloud floated across college and university campuses, one bearing the aroma of marijuana. For the time being, the drug culture remained small at Alabama. Ironically, a quarter century earlier Timothy Leary, the guru of LSD who urged young people to "tune in, turn on, and drop out," strolled the Quad and partied with his brothers at the Theta Chi house.[37] Most students at the Capstone probably didn't know that and, according to a poll conducted in early 1967, they also seemed unaware of recreational drug use at the Capstone.

That's not to say there were no drugs on campus. Many turned to amphetamines to pull all-nighters during midterm and final examination periods. Popular campus myths told of students who, high on Dexedrine, turned in blue books filled with doodles or absolute nonsense. For those skittish of "going schizoid" on Dex, the Supe Store carried caffeine pills with commercial names like "No Doz" and "Verv."[38]

For anyone intent on taking the chemical approach to higher education, pep pills were readily available. Some physicians prescribed them. Diet pills could also be purchased from students whose parents obtained them to lose weight but then gave them to their progeny for studying. The more entrepreneurially inclined sold the pills at inflated prices during finals week. Finding a "connection" was easy, even in Tuscaloosa.

A Stormy Spring

On Christmas Eve, President Johnson ordered a two-day bombing halt over North Vietnam. Johnson extended the halt indefinitely after assurances from the Soviet Union indicated it was encouraging North Vietnamese leaders to negotiate an end to the war. On January 31, 1967, with no evident progress toward negotiations, President Johnson ordered the resumption of Operation Rolling Thunder. The renewed bombing reinvigorated the antiwar movement.

In early February, representatives from the Students for a Democratic Society, the W. E. B. Dubois Clubs, the Young Socialist Alliance, and the Student Nonviolent Coordinating Committee convened at the University of Chicago where they decried America's war in Vietnam as "racist, illegal, and murderous." Delegates called for "direct actions" to include staging campus demonstrations, war-crimes tribunals, sit-ins at draft boards and military recruiting offices, and holding fund-raising drives to support the North Vietnamese war effort. Bettina Aptheker, a student at Berkeley and member of the American Communist Party, attended the meeting along with other antiwar luminaries. Alabamians learned of this meeting, including plans for disrupting the nation's college campuses, from an article published in the *Birmingham News*.[39]

The seniors that spring of 1967 were freshmen when George Wallace stood in the door of Foster Auditorium. Now there were nearly three hundred African Americans among the more than seventeen thousand students studying at the university and its extension centers, including ninety-three at the Capstone.[40]

While there was little friction between white and black students, neither was there much interaction inside or outside the classroom. One white student observed, "It's just that people realize that they're here to get an education, so they leave them alone."[41] Many students, black and white, found it difficult to relate to someone from a different ethnic background. Some whites, still clinging to familiar prejudices, avoided any contact with blacks. Even among the more progressive there lingered fears of ostracism that might result from public displays of friendliness. Additionally, there were no black fraternities or sororities on campus, further limiting the social scene for African Americans. Limited social interaction drove many black students to dances and parties at Stillman College.[42]

Nevertheless, what was beginning to happen on campus differed sharply from the racial climate extant throughout the state where George Wallace remained tremendously popular with white voters. Federal court orders and desegregation guidelines issued by the Department of Health, Education, and Welfare notwithstanding, the Wallace administration still adamantly opposed desegregating Alabama's public schools. State superintendent of education Austin R. Meadows, issued a news release in August 1966 in which he defended segregated schools as part of God's natural order. "Segregation has been practiced down through the ages with good results for the civilized world." He explained, "Birds of a feather truly flock together. Wild ducks fly together and not with other birds." Meadows concluded, "There can be segregation without immoral discrimination against anyone. . . . Integration of all animal life would destroy humanity and the animal kingdom."[43]

Alabama did not go gently out of its long night of racial intolerance. After Governor Lurleen Wallace continued to resist school desegregation as vigorously as had her husband, on March 22, 1967, Judge Frank M. Johnson Jr. and two other judges on the US Fifth District Court of Appeals imposed a desegregation decree on Governor Wallace and the Alabama Board of Education affecting all public schools in Alabama.[44]

Meanwhile, in November 1966, the Emphasis '67 committee selected "The World in Revolution" as their theme for the forthcoming spring conference scheduled for March 17–19, 1967. The committee also planned to publish a magazine titled *Revolutions* containing articles by prominent, if also potentially controversial, authors not on the program. These included Bettina Aptheker, a Berkeley black student activist, Stokely Carmichael of the Student Nonviolent Coordinating Committee, and Alabama's own Theodore Klitzke, whose essay castigated the university for its lack of academic freedom. Figurative red flags went up in the president's office.

Frank Rose considered vetoing these authors but feared a possible student backlash and unfavorable media attention. He also expressed concern that student delegates invited from Princeton, Harvard, Stillman, and Tuskegee might stage potentially embarrassing demonstrations. David Mathews suggested a meeting with program cochairmen Richard McGill and Bobby Feldman and other student leaders. Rose agreed.[45]

David Mathews arranged the meeting at which he and Jeff Bennett presided, one also attended by John Blackburn and Sarah Healy. In addition to the program cochairmen, SGA president Ralph Knowles attended along with Billie Blair, who as editor of the *Crimson-White* represented the student media. Mathews sought middle ground between the students' inclination toward inquiry and ferment and the university's responsibilities for maintaining decorum and order.

After Ralph Knowles offered to work with the visiting student delegates to encourage responsible behavior, the meeting turned to the concerns over *Revolutions*, specifically the articles by Aptheker, Carmichael, and Klitzke. McGill and Feldman agreed to use the term "position papers" rather than "articles" to describe pieces published in the magazine. They also agreed to lead with an article/position paper by Gen. Earl G. Wheeler, chairman of the Joint Chiefs of Staff, defending US policy in Vietnam as a counter to Aptheker's highly impassioned polemic. A reprinted article by Roy Wilkins of the NAACP on progress in race relations was inserted to balance Carmichael's piece on "Black Power." In a memorandum to President Rose, David Mathews observed anything negative Klitzke might write concerning academic freedom at the university would be diminished by the publication of the professor's own critical article.[46]

The meeting alleviated some of Frank Rose's concerns. Furthermore, the invited participants were hardly controversial. These included Secretary of State Dean Rusk and the Pulitzer Prize–winning associate editor of the *New York Times*, James B. Reston. Frank Rose's friend David Nevin, associate editor of *Life* magazine and Stephen Wright, president of the United Negro College Fund and former president of Fisk University, were also on the program.

Emphasis '67 came off well, despite stirrings of dissent still novel to the Capstone. On the first night, after Stephen Wright spoke on race relations in southern states, during the question-and-answer period, a Tuskegee student chastised him for smiling when he talked to white students in the audience.[47]

The highlight of the program was Secretary of State Rusk's talk on Friday night. A small number of demonstrators greeted his arrival at the local airport while twenty picketers awaited Rusk in a roped-off area adjacent to Foster. There they sat, chatting amiably while a portable phonograph played Bob Dylan protest songs. One sign quoting William Cowper read, "War's a game, which were their subjects wise, kings would not play at." Another signed warned, "Turn your back on sinful silly sins you've sown. Add your straw to the camel's load. Pray like hell when the world explodes."[48] The only pot among the twenty protestors produced hot coffee.[49]

Across the street from Foster, Ralph Knowles explained to demonstrators that university policies limited picketing to Alabama students and faculty. He told them that if they crossed the street onto university property, they would be arrested and charged with trespassing. Posey Lombard, daughter of the dean of the Harvard School of Business, was one of four demonstrators who thanked Ralph and then strolled across the street. After booking at the downtown jail, they were released on their own recognizance.[50]

Inside, Dean Rusk defended US policy in Vietnam. He explained that while America's commitment was firm, it extended only to defending South Vietnam from aggression and not to defeating or destroying the Communist regime in North Vietnam. During the question-and-answer period, a number of university students politely informed the secretary of state that while they appreciated the sincerity of his position, US policy in Vietnam was misguided. A Tuskegee student presented Rusk with a petition signed by 526 students charging that African Americans bore a disproportionate share of the fighting.[51]

Emphasis '67 provided the university with good press on a national scale. The next Sunday's edition of the *New York Times* carried James Reston's complementary article titled, "Tuscaloosa: Report from the University of Alabama." Reston lauded the convocation for being "as free and outspoken as anything ever presented at Berkeley or Cambridge, Massachusetts."[52] While Frank Rose and other administration officials welcomed Reston's praise, linking the Capstone with Berkeley and Harvard only bolstered suspicions harbored by many Alabamians, including powerful elements in Montgomery.

In a State Whose Governor Is Lurleen Wallace

In early May, Norman Cousins, editor of the *Saturday Review*, delivered the luncheon address at the university's first Honor's Day. Referring to the Emphasis '67 and the diversity of opinions expressed in *Revolutions*, Cousins began his remarks with, "All this in a state whose governor is Lurleen Wallace." The program itself was noncontroversial; it was the "position papers" by Aptheker and Carmichael in *Revolutions* that got Cousin's attention. It also got the attention of some in Montgomery where reactions to Emphasis '67 converged with Governor Wallace's determined resistance to increasing the pace of school desegregation to pose a new and potentially serious threat to academic free-dom at the university and also throughout the state.

In the days following the March 22 decree issued by Judge Johnson, George Wallace approached key members of the state legislature to secure their sup-port for his wife's planned defiant response. Two days before going on state-wide television to reveal the specifics of her plan, Governor Wallace invited President Rose, along with the presidents of other historically white, state-supported colleges and universities, to a meeting in her office where she asked them to sign a document of support. The only one to refuse was Frank A. Rose.[53]

Governor Wallace's plan was to transfer control of Alabama's public schools from their local school boards to the office of the state superintendent of edu-cation. Rose feared this attempt at consolidation of power might later be ex-tended to the state's colleges and universities. His opposition meant more to George and Lurleen Wallace than the acquiescence of all the other college and university presidents combined.

First, none of the other presidents possessed Frank Rose's national stature, nor did they have his influence with the Johnson administration. Second, the University of Alabama possessed considerable clout among the state's business and political elites, many of them Alabama alumni. Third, in most cases a call from the governor's office to any state college or university president brought instant acquiescence. Not so when the phone rang in Tuscaloosa.

In large part, the Capstone's independence flowed from the fact that while the governor appointed the boards of trustees at most state colleges and uni-versities, the boards at the University of Alabama, Auburn University, the Uni-versity of South Alabama, and Alabama College at Montevallo (now Monte-vallo College) enjoyed more autonomy because when a trustee died or resigned, that particular institution's board of trustees, rather than the governor, named the replacement.[54] That rankled both Governor Wallace and her number one assistant. That rancor increased after the university's SGA passed a resolution supporting President Rose and denouncing the governor's attempted takeover of the public schools.[55]

Rose's opponents in the state legislature seized the opportunity to revive the recently failed speaker ban bill. On Tuesday morning, April 4, speaking to Alabama lawmakers, Representative Ralph Slate of Morgan County de-nounced *Revolutions*, claiming the publication contained "articles by people who want to turn the University of Alabama over to students who want to run things like they do in Berkeley."[56] Representative Leland Childs representing Jefferson County and the only Republican member of the state legislature, quickly cobbled together a resolution creating a committee to investigate campus subversives.[57]

That evening Rose traveled to Birmingham to speak at a fund-raiser for the new law school building. After a few introductory remarks Rose, his voice cold with controlled anger, defended Emphasis '67 and the publication of *Revolutions*. "The University," Rose declared, "never has censored student publications and other than cautioning editors to avoid publishing anything libelous, seditious, or obscene, it never will, at least not while I'm President."

Rose grew more emphatic. "I'm not for sale!" he told the audience in an unwavering voice. "And as long as I am president, the University of Alabama is not for sale." After a long applause from the more than 150 lawyers present, Rose continued, "I want to sleep at night with a clear conscience. If this job demands any more than that, I guess I'll have to find another job." Rose then let loose on the people of Alabama, accusing them of suffering from "an inferiority complex, and cursing the damn earth by thinking everyone is against them."[58]

Reaction to the controversy overwhelmingly favored Frank Rose and the university. While students on campuses across the nation demonstrated against their administrations, at the Capstone they joined with liberal faculty to support their president. The day after Rose's "Here I Stand" declaration, students congregated on the lawn in front of the President's Mansion. Some carried hastily made signs that read, "A rose is a Rose" and "This is a free university. Thank you, Dr. Rose."[59]

Entire departments signed letters of support. Ted Klitzke, as department chair, wrote the letter of support from the Art Department. Luminaries like Iredell Jenkins and John Ramsey sent personal messages of encouragement. Letters and telegrams also poured in from scholars and alumni around the state and across the nation.

In that sea of conservatism surrounding the university's island of liberalism, Frank Rose's enemies smelled blood. The Citizen's Council chapter in the Birmingham suburb of Tarrant sent a condemnatory telegram. Another critic raised a familiar canard, "It seems from your recent explosion you would like to make another Berkeley out of Alabama."[60] A particularly nasty letter addressed to "President Tony Rose," dubbed him, "Phony Tony" and asked him to "once and for all settle the speculation as to whether or not you are of Semitic ancestry."[61] Rose consigned these to a file marked "crank letters."

The storm intensified in May when Gary Dickey, editor of the *Tropolitan*, the student newspaper at Troy State College (TSC), penned an editorial commending Rose. After George Wallace's close friend, TSC president Ralph W. Adams, prohibited its publication, Dickey published the title, "A Lament for Dr. Rose," over a blank space with a banner containing the word "censored" running diagonally across it. Troy State responded by charging Dickey with "insubordination" and not allowing him to register for fall classes. Although the state prohibited any student suspended or expelled from one state college or university from enrolling in another, Auburn University admitted Dickey pending the outcome of a lawsuit he had filed against Troy.[62]

On Friday, April 15, with the future of academic freedom at the university in jeopardy, the Board of Publications received a forty-page study compiled by Ruth Wilder. It found a majority of state-supported colleges and universities allowed school newspapers to endorse political candidates. During the board's deliberations, SGA president Ralph Knowles asked, "If we refuse the right to endorse, might this also lead to refusing them the right to criticize the government?" The vote came on a secret ballot. It favored Billie Blair by a margin of 8–1. The *Crimson-White* was free to issue political endorsements.[63]

Governor's Day took place two weeks later. As usual, the audience inside Foster auditorium consisted overwhelmingly of Army and Air Force ROTC cadets for whom the event was mandatory. The larger story was on the Quadrangle and outside Foster Auditorium.

While six people attempted to demonstrate the previous year, thrity-six demonstrators showed up for Governor's Day '67. They carried signs reading, "We Love Dr. Rose," "Can the Klan," and "Justice Now!" No one protested the war in Vietnam, indicating these demonstrators focused their ire at Governor Lurleen Wallace and her husband. After the parade, the protestors moved to an area designated for their use outside Foster, within sight of the spot where George Wallace, almost four years earlier, stood defiantly against the inevitability of change.

Inside, President Rose graciously introduced Alabama's first woman governor. In her address, Lurleen Wallace accused the university of embarking on a "collision course with state legislators" and defended state lawmakers who criticized the Emphasis '67 program, maintaining that they "were not challenging freedom of expression but the judgment of those who exercised this liberty."[64] The uniformed audience responded with polite, if subdued, applause.

Student Government Association president Ralph Knowles followed Governor Wallace at the podium to deliver the first SGA "State of the University" address. He said what President Rose couldn't. Knowles began by praising the recent establishment of the Alabama Association of Student Body Presidents (AASBP), noting that the group included representatives of all the state's public as well as private colleges and universities . . . including its historically all-black institutions. He then reviewed SGA's involvement with Head Start and the tutorial assistance initiatives, both of which he pointed out worked almost exclusively in Tuscaloosa's black community. He concluded by praising Emphasis '67 as "more exciting, stimulating, and informative than last year's program." At its conclusion, the audience gave Knowles a solid, if restrained, ovation, probably due to the fact that most of them were in military uniform and not all that happy about being there in the first place.[65] On the platform, President Rose stood to shake hands with the SGA president as he returned to his seat, the one to the right of the governor's spouse, where George C. Wallace sat, his eyes fixed on the doors at the far end of the auditorium where, four years earlier, he reveled in a political theater of his own creation.

A Different A-Day

The last week in March, 151 hopefuls showed up for spring football drills. Quarterback Kenny "Snake" Stabler, was looking forward to his senior year, but with spring drills drawing to a close, Coach Bryant announced the suspension of his first-string quarterback. Bryant claimed Stabler was "disregarding our regulations and conforming to those set by someone else."[66] New York Jets quarterback Joe Namath, having once been suspended by Bryant, sent Stabler a telegram consisting of just three words, "He means it."[67]

Something not widely noticed occurred at 1967's intersquad game. Dock Rone and Andrew Pernell, two African Americans, suited up. When spring drills began, five black students were among the fifty-two "walk-ons," hopefuls not recruited or on scholarship. Over the next three weeks, most of the walk-ons walked off, including three of the five African Americans. Rone and Pernell stuck it out to become the first blacks in crimson and white, albeit in an intersquad game. While neither player returned for fall practice, they eroded one of the remaining—and vitally important—barriers to racial equality at Alabama. Later Coach Bryant opined that had Rone returned in the fall, he might have made the team. Two years later, Andrew Pernell again walked-on and was offered a scholarship, which he was unable to accept because Southeastern Conference rules forbade players from holding any other forms of assistance and he was already the recipient of a more lucrative grant from the Presbyterian Church.[68] Otherwise, the Tide might have fielded its first integrated team in 1969 rather than 1971.

Developments in Student Government

By spring 1967, a struggle for the soul of SGA was under way. A rising faction of independents wanted to take control of student government and then move it in a more progressive direction. The politically dominant faction issued from the newly established University Party.

When the University Party met in early March, it endorsed Don Siegelman for SGA president. He was backed by Jack Drake, an independent in his first year in law school and well connected to the student power structure. Drake listed Siegelman's impressive qualifications. He had served as Arts and Sciences senator, chaired the SGA committee studying course evaluations, was a member of the Festival of Arts committee, represented Delta Kappa Epsilon fraternity on the IFC, and was a member of the Board of Publications. The handsome, well-spoken Siegelman got the nod and ran unopposed. The quintessential Machine candidate, Don Siegelman also was a determined political progressive.[69]

On Saturday morning immediately after the election, President-elect Siegelman joined Ralph Knowles in welcoming twelve student body presidents from around the state to campus. Later that morning, they founded the Alabama Association of Student Body Presidents (AASBP). After naming Don Siegelman as president, the AASBP passed three resolutions. The first criticized Governor Wallace for her defiance of the federally mandated desegregation of Alabama's public schools. The second supported Frank Rose in his struggle with the state legislature over the speaker ban bill. The third condemned Troy State College president Ralph Adams for censoring Gary Dickey's *Tropolitan* editorial.[70]

The formation of the AASBP, along with the resolutions it passed, constituted deliberate and concerted acts of defiance aimed not at the university but at the governor and her administration. Furthermore, the defiance originated with campus leaders who comprised the university's elites, students from good families, some with substantial Capstone pedigrees. Ralph Knowles and Don Siegelman were Greeks. Knowles was already enrolled in law school, while Siegelman would return to Alabama after graduating from Georgetown University's law school to serve as secretary of state, attorney general, lieutenant governor, and, from 1999 to 2003, as the governor.

Spring into Summer

While the struggle between the university and the Wallace administration developed into a kind of cold war as summer approached, campus life continued largely unaltered. In late February, students and a sprinkling of faculty filled Morgan Hall's auditorium where pop artist Andy Warhol, after an hour of showing excerpts from his underground films, most of them featuring his consort, Viva, confided, "I haven't really thought about whether what I do is art or not."[71]

The last Saturday in April, the annual Sigma Chi Derby took place. Five sororities battled through the usual contests, including water-soaked sisters plowing into mounds of flour in search of their sorority pins and a favorite called "the zip strip." The latter involved sisters dressed in white garments zipped into sleeping bags with the winner being the first to emerge dressed in black. Then came the chorus-line competition and, finally, the crowning of the new "Sweetheart of Sigma Chi," Linda White, a Pi Beta Phi.[72]

On the more serious side of the Capstone, on May Day, Michel Van De Veer, a student writing from his "headquarters" at 1202 Eighth Street, issued the "Founding Manifesto" of the University of Alabama Democratic Students Organization (DSO). "Our planet is bursting with existence," the manifesto began, and then lamented that the masses still lived in poverty while students languished in apathy. Van De Veer declared DSO intended to establish itself as "a new intellectual center for ferreting out social and political injustice."[73]

Students for a Democratic Society had not yet established a campus chapter. Given the strained relationship with state legislators determined to prevent Alabama from morphing into Berkeley, the last thing Frank Rose needed was anything resembling SDS at the university. Dean Blackburn ordered an investigation that identified Van De Veer as "a potential nuisance generally opposed to administration policy." Investigators discovered he had enticed Jack Drake, SGA member Mike Stambaugh, and *Corolla* editor Coleman Lollar into membership. Despite records of service in campus organizations, the investigator's report noted that these were students "suspected of harboring extreme viewpoints."[74]

Amid frolic and ferment the purposes of higher education continued. Earlier in the semester, the trustees approved the construction of a fourteen-story "wheel-like" dormitory to house four thousand female students. Work began in May with an estimated completion date of August 1968.[75] Looking to the future, President Rose asked Jeff Bennett to form a committee to oversee the implementation phase of construction on the new Alabama Union.[76]

John Edward Bratly, retired president of the Exploration and Drilling Corporation of Dallas, Texas, delivered the commencement address to the class that had entered just after the university desegregated.[77] This, the first class of the "third University of Alabama," joined the citizens of a state still struggling with issues attendant to racial justice.

As spring turned into summer, while dissidents on campuses from Boston to Berkeley raised questions (and occasionally some hell), students at the University of Alabama continued to discover a complex world of new possibilities swirling around them. For the present, Alabama's political activism remained sporadic and hardly apparent amid fraternity parties (raising more familiar forms of hell), football games, and beauty pageants. Nevertheless, the dissent among a handful of progressive students and faculty fed on the energy exuded by their determination to overcome the past and move toward a better tomorrow. It took a while, but the 1960s finally reached the Capstone.

On the day after Jack Drake graduated from the Alabama School of Law, he and Carol Self were married. (Photo courtesy of *Crimson-White*)

Students for a Democratic Society demonstrate on the steps of the Alabama Union, in fall 1969. (Hoole Special Collections Library, University of Alabama)

"Woods Hall Quads," Sunday afternoon rock concerts sponsored by New College sparked the first concerted rise of student dissent in fall 1969. (1970 *Corolla*, Hoole Special Collections Library, University of Alabama)

Capstone students participate in the October 15, 1969, nationwide moratorium to end the war in Vietnam. President Mathews approved events as long as they did not interfere with classes or disrupt normal campus activities. (1970 *Corolla*, Hoole Special Collections Library, University of Alabama)

History professor Hugh Ragsdale speaks as part of the October antiwar moratorium activities. (Hoole Special Collections Library, University of Alabama)

President David Mathews introduces dean of students Joab Thomas to student leaders in fall 1969. (Hoole Special Collections Library, University of Alabama)

Jerry Rubin smokes a joint during his address in
Foster Auditorium on Sunday afternoon, May 3,
1970. Efforts to determine who invited Rubin to
campus were soon overcome by events associated
with the shootings at Kent State University.
(Hoole Special Collections Library, University of
Alabama)

Wednesday night, May 6, 1970, candlelight vigil in honor of Kent State and Jackson State victims organized by Tuscaloosa Women's Movement. Carol Self, seated on the steps of Denny Chimes just beyond the female singer, watches over the proceedings. (Hoole Special Collections Library, University of Alabama)

Following the vigil at Denny Chimes, a thousand students walked from Denny Chimes to the Army ROTC building where they placed lighted candles on the steps. (Hoole Special Collections Library, University of Alabama)

"To the Mansion!" Students then moved to the President's Mansion to "See David." President Mathews and his family were secluded elsewhere for the night. From there students briefly blocked traffic on University Boulevard and then moved on to occupy the Supe Store in the Student Union Building. (1971 Corolla, Hoole Special Collections Library, University of Alabama)

Many students opposed the tumult on campus in May 1970. Phi Delta Theta brothers raised a sign outside their fraternity house to show their support for the administration. (Hoole Special Collections Library, University of Alabama)

Dressler Hall goes up in flames at two o'clock in the morning on May 7, 1970. Circumstances surrounding the burning were never resolved. (Hoole Special Collections Library, University of Alabama)

In the aftermath of the May 1970 tumult, newly hired special assistant for campus security, *Tuscaloosa News* publisher James Boone, the son of Buford Boone, and President Mathews confer as they look toward the future. (Hoole Special Collections Library, University of Alabama)

6

A Regional Center for Academic Excellence

Between Tuscaloosa and Montgomery

George Wallace continued his quixotic pursuit of the presidency throughout the summer of 1967. Meanwhile, in Montgomery, state legislators intent on punishing President Rose for opposing Lurleen Wallace's attempted preemption of integration of Alabama's public schools asked Rose and other college presidents to explain how they vetted speakers invited to campus.[1]

Frank Rose exuded confidence, at least in public. Not yet fifty years of age, his black hair, parted in the middle, grayed at the temples. Tall of stature and always dressed in a dark suit, white shirt, and dark necktie, he looked like a university president. In photographs, even those with George and Lurleen Wallace, Frank Rose's eyes twinkled in concert with his broad smile combining grace with charm.

Rose's demeanor belied a seething frustration with George and Lurleen Wallace. In a letter to McGeorge Bundy, formerly a member of President Kennedy's inner circle who had since moved on to the presidency of the Ford Foundation, Rose noted relentless harassment from the Wallace administration had driven him into the job market. "Last month I was offered the presidency of a large corporation in New York," Rose wrote, "I wanted to accept the offer, but at the insistence of Douglass Cater, the trustees, and faculty, I decided to remain at the University of Alabama."[2]

In June, as the battle with state legislators over Emphasis '67 and the limits of academic freedom continued to threaten the university's financial stability and, more importantly, its academic credibility, Frank Rose dispatched David Mathews to Montgomery to monitor developments on the speaker ban bill and rally support among lawmakers. While Mathews thought the university was making progress in obtaining greater financial support from the legislature, he also thought most legislators were oblivious to the relationship between academic freedom and educational excellence.[3]

In July, President Rose explained his opposition to the proposed speaker ban bill to the House Judiciary Committee. He stated that the university never invited speakers to campus because they were controversial and always sought to balance points of view. Rose outlined procedures for vetting potential speakers and asked lawmakers to trust the university.[4] Back on campus, an editorial in the *Crimson-White* accused the bill's author, Senator Leland Childs, of "fanning a fire that doesn't exist, especially since the University has never invited a Communist to speak on campus."[5]

The university had its supporters. Presidents Harry M. Philpot of Auburn and D. P. Culp of Alabama College joined Frank Rose in opposing the bill. So did representatives of the Alabama Bar Association, the Alabama Press Association, the Alabama Education Association, the Alabama Federation of Labor, the United Farm Workers, and the Association of University Women.[6] A vote by the committee resulted in a 9–9 tie, one short of postponing the bill indefinitely and thereby killing it. A compromise motion asking college and university presidents to submit letters outlining their speaker policies passed by a narrow margin. Since President Rose detailed the university's policies in person, submitting the letter amounted to a formality.[7]

Senator Childs, unsatisfied with President Rose's statements to the committee, wanted every state college and university, as a matter of "operational procedure," to ban Communist speakers from their campuses.[8] On August 1, Childs moved that the Senate Education Committee report favorably on the bill, a procedural step for bringing legislation to the senate floor for consideration. While Childs was distracted in conversation with colleagues, a Rose ally called for a vote. The committee subsequently voted not to report the bill out of committee. Child's angry accusations of "railroading" aside, Rose's allies, many of them Alabama alumni marshaled by Mathews, had aborted the bill.[9]

Rose's enemies, however, got a measure of revenge by passing Joint House Resolution 50, something Mathews thought was aimed specifically at the University of Alabama.[10] It resolved that the Alabama state flag and the Confederate battle flag be raised alongside the American flag before the homecoming games at both Alabama and Auburn, and during the pregame ceremonies at the annual Alabama-Auburn game, accompanied by their respective bands playing "Dixie." The resolution passed by a unanimous voice vote. Although not legally binding, the unanimity behind Resolution 50 carried clout. Perhaps legislators didn't consider how a national television audience might react to "Dixie" and the flag of rebellion waving alongside Old Glory. Perhaps they did but didn't care.

Poorly conceived as the resolution was, the state legislature controlled the purse. Despite increased spending on education, much of it supporting George Wallace's fiefdom of junior colleges, community colleges, and trade schools, the state still ranked forty-eighth out of fifty in per capita expenditures on education.[11] Frank Rose's efforts in Washington, DC, obtained funds exceeding allocations by the state legislature. Furthermore, the growing number of alumni chapters provided a structured network for further fund raising. Despite the mood in the legislature, the university ended up receiving an 8.14 percent increase in its budget for the 1967–69 biennium, representing a hike from $17,816,847 to $19,375,992 with a conditional appropriation of $2,500,000 allocated for the extension center in Huntsville.[12]

Frank Rose was only partially satisfied. He knew the funding increase was not enough to enable the university to compete with its counterparts throughout most of the South. In addition to grants received from foundations and the federal government, in September Rose initiated planning for a very ambitious capital campaign to be unveiled at the end of the spring semester. The goal remained: make the University of Alabama a regional center for academic excellence.

Rising Dissent Elsewhere

In 1968, student unrest intensified on campuses in much of the country, especially at progressive bastions in the Ivy League and throughout the northeast the University of Wisconsin and the University of Minnesota, and also along the Pacific Coast. Southern campuses, with a few exceptions in Virginia, North Carolina, and Florida, remained relatively peaceful. At the University of Alabama, threats to academic freedom were predominantly external, emanating from hostile elements in the Wallace administration and state legislature.

Suppressing dissent, in addition to being inconsistent with the nature of higher education, risked exacerbating or worsening it. On the other hand, simply defending the principle of dissent, or pointing out the virtues of youthful idealism, rarely countered the harsh realities manifesting on many campuses. In the early 1960s, student dissent centered on freedom of speech and extending civil rights to all Americans. Between 1965 and 1966, the nature of protest morphed into student rights, with the war in Vietnam gaining steadily in importance. Beginning in the fall of 1967 and continuing into the following year, US policy in Vietnam, and more pointedly, the amount and tenor of student control over the academy, increasingly dominated a more radical agenda.

Academic tradition and the liberal conscience demanded that colleges and universities remain open to divergent and unpopular points of view, peaceful protests, and respect for the rights and dignity of students. But the rising tide of irrational disorder and growing demands for "student power" tested the mettle of many university administrators. The challenge for faculty, students, and administrators was to identify issues that might prompt crises before they unfolded, and then to address those issues before the respective positions of the various constituencies became entrenched and inflexible.

Problems facing colleges and universities were similar in many regards. At the University of Alabama, issues involved the role of students in selecting and inviting speakers to campus, input into curriculum development, rights in appealing grades and disciplinary actions, and the freedom to print and publish opinions in school publications. These involved the relative powers delegated to the administration and to the students.

For the time being, the center held at the Capstone because a comparatively liberal administration and moderately progressive SGA leaders remained united in their alliance against the state legislature and Governor Wallace. Angst over the speaker ban bill resided with top administrators, the faculty, SGA leaders, and the *Crimson-White* editorial staff. Most students, away on summer break, were unaware of the controversy.

Meanwhile, the bombing of North Vietnam continued amid rapidly rising consternation over its military effectiveness and moral efficacy. In May 1967, a Louis Harris poll found 45 percent of Americans favored total military victory in Vietnam while 41 percent inclined toward withdrawal provided the North Vietnamese did as well. The same poll showed 81 percent of Americans expected a long war.[13] Moral issues attendant to the world's leading superpower pounding the agrarian countries of Southeast Asia with the weight of more bombs than fell during all of World War II drove part of the antiwar movement. The uncertainty generated by conscription, however, heightened anxiety among draft-age males.

As the war in Southeast Asia escalated, so did the size and militancy of the antiwar movement. What frightened many Alabamians—and others throughout the land—was the increasing number of antiwar protestors seemingly allied with America's enemies. Buttons and posters proclaiming "Victory to the National Liberation Front" and shouts of "Ho, Ho, Ho Chi Minh, the NLF is gonna win" fed the notion that antiwar protestors were subversives in cahoots with Communists, both foreign and domestic. It also jeopardized support among Americans who questioned the moral and strategic justifications for the war but were unwilling to forsake their patriotism. Even if they thought the war unwise, they wanted nothing to do with protestors sympathetic to Communists.[14]

The war on the other side of the world seemed far away to most Alabama students. For many, the big news in the summer of 1967 was that Sylvia Hitchcock, an art major from Miami entering her senior year, was selected as Miss USA in the Miss Universe Contest. When the twenty-one-year-old brunette left campus for home in May, she departed the Chi Omega house draped with a sign reading, "Congrats Sylvia: Miss USA."[15] Later that summer, Sylvia was named Miss Universe.

An Autumn of Portents

Humid warmth engulfed Legion Field in Birmingham for the Tide's opening game with the Florida State Seminoles on Saturday evening, September 23, 1967. Since the University of Houston had thumped FSU 33–13 the previous week, the Bama faithful expected their team to extend its winning streak to eighteen games.[16] Late-arriving fans walking toward the stadium assumed the two roars they heard heralded Bama's first two scores. After entering and looking at the scoreboard, they saw the unbelievable: the Tide trailed by two touchdowns.

Kenny Stabler, who had worked his way back onto the team following his suspension during spring training, brought Alabama back. Still, the Tide ebbed and flowed and in the end, Florida State came away with a 37–37 tie. After the game Bryant graciously admitted, "They out-toughed us and they whipped us. The way those kids played us, it would have been a shame for them to lose."[17] A tie with Florida State portended an autumn of changes.

Up to a point, Frank Rose sided with students when it came to allowing dissent. Certainly, David Mathews could not have alluded to the inevitability of dissent in his address to student leaders in 1965 without Rose's approval. Additionally, it was Rose who placed students on many of the university's standing committees and also secretly committed his administration to backing any fraternity or sorority willing to lower its racial barriers. Additionally, he gained enormous capital with students by standing behind Emphasis '67 when it came under fire, an episode that reflected the gap between the university and student leaders on the one hand and the Wallace administration and the state's more conservative elements on the other. But caution bounded Rose's progressive impulse, as demonstrated when he canceled Louis Armstrong's performance.

During the autumn of 1967, the Alabama SGA probed those limits. Rose also believed too much academic license might beg educational anarchy, just as too much administrative control could lead to tyranny.[18]

Don Siegelman was the most politically astute SGA president between 1963 and 1970. Understanding that financial autonomy underwrote political power, he sought greater authority in directing how student funds might be spent. He also saw the SGA as a defender of student rights, a concept gaining currency within the activist community. Dean John Blackburn sensed the urgency of a developing challenge.

In his position paper written in late September, Blackburn urged university administrators to rein in the SGA. "The autonomy of student government in terms of finances is not, in my judgment, something which can be determined by compromise or collective bargaining. It must be decided on the basis of the institution's educational philosophy." The dean warned against letting the SGA become a bargaining agency for students at large. Blackburn thought its proper role was to provide students with opportunities for "meaningful experiences which might, in turn, impact their fellow students."[19] Don Siegelman soon validated the dean's prescience.

A few days later, at the first meeting with a joint session of the SGA legislature, President Siegelman laid out his agenda. He proposed a four-day academic week, the end of midterm grades, the introduction of a pass-fail grading system, and the inauguration of a student-sponsored honors program. "We should make ourselves aware of University policies and obey them but also question and even oppose them when they jeopardize students' rights."[20] Siegelman needed an opportunity worthy of tossing down the gauntlet.

Don Siegelman created that opportunity by hitchhiking on an issue arising from last spring's eruption over Emphasis '67. At his behest, SGA passed two bills. The first established a committee to enter an amicus curiae or "friend of the court" brief on behalf of Gary Dickey in his lawsuit against Troy State College. It did not matter to Siegelman that the Fifth Circuit Court of Appeals had already found in Dickey's favor and ordered TSC to readmit him.[21] Siegelman wanted more than justice for Gary Dickey. He wanted to expand and exert the rights of students. A popular button of the day read, "Students are people too."

By a vote of 20–5, SGA approved the second bill establishing a "Committee for Responsible Approach to the Defense of Student Rights." That bill proposed a court consisting of SGA officers, with Siegelman as chairman, to defend rights not only at the Capstone but also "on other campuses where actions have a significant relation to student rights at the University of Alabama."[22] These two bills, if signed by President Rose, would have greatly expanded the role of SGA and diminished the administration's authority.

Rose moved cautiously and deliberately. First, he asked David Mathews to establish a liaison to SGA's newly formed and approved Committee on Academic Matters, asking Joseph T. Sutton, the executive director of institutional analysis, and Richard Thigpen from the dean of men's office to serve as members. Thus, having demonstrated he understood and appreciated SGA's wish for a larger role in academic matters, and after receiving a legal opinion against filing the friend of the court brief, Rose responded to Siegelman.

President Rose first praised the idealism behind SGA's actions, especially concerning students' rights and freedoms. Then he slammed the door. "The Board of Trustees has invested me with the responsibility for directing affairs of the University and of exercising final authority over the actions of any branch thereof. . . . The Student Government Association is a subdivision of the University and, its actions cannot be disassociated from the institution." Stating that any court action by SGA could not be accomplished separate from the university, he returned the two bills unsigned, recommending that SGA seek avenues for clarifying student freedoms that did not involve the use of the SGA's name or funds.[23]

Siegelman was just getting started. The Alabama-Auburn Better Relations Committee, established earlier in the decade to promote sportsmanship during the annual football showdown in Birmingham, met as usual a few weeks before the big game. The Auburn delegation suggested that the prayer prior to kickoff be excluded since they felt "football games are not conducive to invocations." The two delegations then drafted a joint resolution to that effect and submitted it to their respective presidents for approval. The committee also took on Resolution 50. Siegelman sent President Rose a letter stating they had also decided the combined bands would not play "Dixie," nor would the Confederate flag be raised.[24]

President Rose responded politely, firmly, and immediately. Rose informed Siegelman that, after consulting with President Philpot of Auburn, their decision was that the pregame ceremonies would proceed as planned, including the raising of the Confederate flag while the two bands played "Dixie." Furthermore, an ordained minister would bless the event.[25]

Rose probably shared Siegelman's disdain for raising the Confederate battle flag and playing "Dixie." But he also understood some fights aren't worth the effort. Frank Rose tempered his idealism with a wisdom born of maturity and experience: two qualities lacking in most twenty-year-olds.

Elsewhere, the antiwar movement gained momentum. In October 1967, Yale University chaplain William Sloane Coffin allied with Yale alumnus Benjamin Spock to oppose the war. On Friday, October 20, at the beginning of a mammoth Washington, DC, rally at the conclusion of "Stop the Draft Week," Coffin and Spock hauled a battered briefcase purportedly filled with draft cards they had collected to the Department of Justice to be turned over to Attorney General Ramsey Clark.[26]

The following day, a crowd estimated at one hundred thousand gathered at the Lincoln Memorial to hear speeches and sing protest songs. Speaking to the protestors thronged around the reflecting pool, pediatrician Benjamin Spock declared Lyndon Johnson, not Ho Chi Minh, was "America's true enemy." Then William Sloane Coffin addressed the crowd before turning the microphone over to civil rights icon John Lewis who led the crowd in chanting what became the mantra of the antiwar movement, "Hell no! We won't go!" As the chanting subsided, Lewis called for a moment of silence for Che Guevara, the Argentine-born revolutionary recently killed by counterguerrilla forces in Bolivia. On the platform, William Sloane Coffin bowed his head in silence.[27]

Hundreds of miles to the south, seventy thousand fans assembled at Legion Field to watch Alabama, which had not faltered since the tie with Florida State, take on the Tennessee Volunteers. Among the spectators was Alabama's own Miss Universe, Sylvia Hitchcock, who flew into Tuscaloosa on Thursday to spend time with her sorority sisters and other friends prior to the big game on Saturday.[28] The Vols triumphed by a score of 24–13. With a tie and a loss at the halfway point of the season, the worried faithful began to taste the bitter fruits of humility even as campus life proceeded much as it had in the past.

The Cotillion Club kicked off is season in late September with Anthony and the Imperials singing their rendition of Little Anthony's 1958 hit, "Tears on My Pillow."[29] In October, the Board of Publications selected Ed Still, a senior majoring in political science and member of the SGA, to edit *Farrago*, the new campus feature magazine. The word "Farrago," according to Still, meant "hodge podge" in French or, perhaps, "elephant fodder." Given Still's increasingly progressive bent, it was not surprising that the first *Farrago* contained an article on the fiftieth anniversary of the Bolshevik ascent to power.[30]

The 1967 homecoming slogan, "Bulldogs Become Bama Believers" or "BBBB," testified to the hard-core faith of Tide true believers. The Friday night pep rally on the Quad included a bonfire and fireworks display. On Saturday morning, eight floats and fifty convertibles carrying campus beauties followed the Million Dollar Band up University Boulevard and into downtown Tuscaloosa.

The *Crimson-White* described the Tide's 13–0 win over Mississippi State as a "mistake filled defensive battle" due, in large part, to a "sputtering offense." Words like "mistake filled" and "sputtering" had not been used to describe a Bryant-coached team since his first year back in 1958.[31]

The Tide won the rest of its regular season games, not impressively, but posting wins nonetheless. A 7–3 victory over Auburn completed the 8–1–1 campaign and garnered an invitation to play Texas A&M in the Cotton Bowl. Gene Stallings, the Aggies' coach, played on Bryant's Southwestern Conference championship team ten years earlier. He also was one of the survivors of the infamous Junction City, Texas, training camp of 1954 when Bryant took his team to an isolated field in south Texas for ten days of horrific preseason preparations meant to condition the players and winnow the chaff. Stallings was among the few who didn't quit.[32]

The year 1968, later recognized by historians as a "watershed" in American history, began poorly for the Crimson Tide, Alabama fans, and students. On New Year's Day, Texas A&M defeated Alabama 20–16. A photograph forever etched into Tide lore showed Coach Bryant lifting a smiling Stallings aloft as the mentor carried his victorious protégé off the field.

From Portents to Reality

In October, Frank Rose received and accepted an invitation to join the Citizen's Committee on Peace with Freedom in Vietnam. The committee's three cochairs included the former US senator from Illinois Paul H. Douglas, retired General of the Army Omar N. Bradley, and Archbishop Robert E. Lucy. The group's brochure stated that it sought "to make sure that the majority voice of America is heard—loud and clear—so that Peking and Hanoi will not mistake the strident voices of some dissenters for American discouragement and a weakening of will."[33]

Meanwhile, life at the Capstone continued still largely unaffected by events swirling beyond campus. In early November, Ray Charles, whose engagement two years earlier was canceled due to a drug arrest, performed in Foster Auditorium. The program accompanied the selection of the "Top Corolla Beauty." Miss Lynne Epsman took the prize. Lynne also served as head of the Crimson Girls, a group of young women who acted as official hostesses at university events, commander of the Army ROTC's sponsors, and as secretary of the upcoming Emphasis '68 committee.[34]

On the last day of November, Eugene McCarthy, the senior senator from Minnesota, announced he was challenging President Johnson for their party's nomination in the upcoming election. He promised to restore the faith of America's youth in the processes of the nation's politics.[35]

Cynicism among America's youth increased toward the end of the year. Despite October's "Stop the Draft Week" and sporadic demonstrations at recruiting stations across America, the machinery of war ground along. Recruits, whether volunteers or draftees, were inducted, trained, and then dispatched to Southeast Asia. Furthermore, a Louis Harris poll conducted just after Christmas indicated almost 60 percent of respondents favored escalating the war if doing so would secure a satisfactory conclusion. That same week, SDS leaders convened at Indiana University, where they faced the reality that the ineffectiveness of their movement resulted from the lack of control over its campus chapters.[36]

As 1968 got under way, unrest among Alabama's small contingent of dissidents focused on students' rights and Frank Rose's supposed intractability in dealing with SGA. Only those males flirting with academic disaster worried about the draft. The largely apathetic student body seemed more concerned with the vicissitudes of college life and what came after: jobs, marriage, or continuing their education in law, medical, dental, or graduate school.

In late January 1968, the Viet Cong, supported by North Vietnamese forces, launched a massive attack inside South Vietnam, striking in thirty-six of forty-four provinces. Coming in the aftermath of optimistic predictions, images of dead Viet Cong inside the compound of the US embassy in Saigon, a month-long bitter fight to retake the ancient imperial capital at Hue in northern South Vietnam, and the photo of Saigon's police chief summarily executing a Viet Cong prisoner, burned into America's consciousness. In the aftermath, US policy changed from escalation to deescalation.

On March 13, Eugene McCarthy startled the nation with a strong showing in the New Hampshire Democratic primary, losing to President Johnson by only 230 votes. Three days later, Senator Robert Kennedy announced his candidacy for the Democratic nomination. Kennedy posed a more formidable threat to President Johnson.[37]

In February, President Johnson replaced Secretary of Defense Robert S. McNamara with a trusted friend, Clark Clifford. The new secretary, after speaking to a range of midlevel officers with recent combat experience in Vietnam, became convinced no level of escalation could succeed. A memorandum written by Secretary of the Air Force Harold Brown also bothered Clifford. Brown detailed three proposals he thought would win the war, each involving increased bombing of North Vietnam, Laos, and South Vietnam.[38]

A deeply troubled and conflicted president faced reality. On the evening of March 31, 1968, Lyndon Johnson announced on national television that he was limiting the bombing of North Vietnam. He ended by stating he would not run for another term.

At the Capstone, on Friday night, March 1, the Air Force ROTC held its annual military ball, the theme of which was "Tomorrow the Stars." Against the backdrop of a giant cardboard, chicken wire, and crepe paper rocket, cadet officers presented the twelve members of the Angel Flight as sabers of the drill team flashed above their heads.[39] Junior and senior cadets, having already been sworn into the Air Force Reserve, didn't worry on Monday when the Selective Service announced that higher draft quotas necessitated curtailing most graduate school deferments.[40]

Two weeks later, at noon on Friday, March 15, the Democratic Student Organization organized what cochairman Jack Drake said would be a weekly event lasting until the war in Vietnam ended. An estimated ninety-five students joined Jack Drake and Michael Van De Veer, professors Hugh Ragsdale and Ron Robel, and Reverend Keever as they stood silently for fifteen minutes on the steps of the Alabama Union. A crowd twice that size watched from the sidewalk. A few jeered. The second protest took place the following week during Emphasis '68.[41] The war lasted seven more years.

Emphasis '68

In November, the Emphasis '68 committee informed Frank Rose of the selected topic, "Directions: American Society at the Crossroads," and assured him of their commitment to working with the university. Headed by Redding Pitt, the committee was balanced with student and faculty advisors representing conservative, moderate, and progressive viewpoints. Pitt was a member of Kappa Alpha fraternity. Lynne Epsman, a Sigma Delta Tau sorority member and recently elected "Top Corolla Beauty," served as committee secretary. Dag Rowe, a junior majoring in political science and member of the Sigma Chi fraternity, also served on the committee. These were "establishment" students with Machine connections. On the more progressive side, along with Ed Still, stood Coleman Lollar and Sondra Nesmith. Advisors included John Ramsey, Victor

Gibean, David McElroy, Ted Klitzke, and Bob Keever.[42] David Mathews sent the committee a memo reminding members that President Rose must approve speakers before invitations were issued.[43]

Yale chaplain William Sloane Coffin had been duly vetted and then was sent an invitation signed by President Rose. But because Coffin had since joined Spock in opposing the war and had also played a prominent role in "Stop the Draft Week," one might assume Rose, who strongly supported President Johnson's Vietnam policies, might have developed second thoughts. Perhaps Rose also wanted to avoid another controversy and potential conflict with Montgomery generated by Emphasis.

With Emphasis only four weeks away, Rose called the committee to his office. He did not tell them to rescind Coffin's invitation. Instead, Rose suggested Coffin's presence on the program might exacerbate the university's strained relationship with the state legislature. He appealed to their loyalty, reminding them of their offer to cooperate with the administration.

Following the meeting, the committee reconvened at the Emphasis office. Ed Still argued for canceling Emphasis rather than knuckling under to the administration. The committee voted not to do that. After further discussion, they acceded to Rose's request and rescinded Coffin's invitation. Coleman Lollar resigned in protest.[44]

The committee had invited Massachusetts senator Ted Kennedy to deliver the keynote address. On Thursday, two days after the New Hampshire primary, Ted Kennedy phoned Redding Pitt to tell him his brother might soon get into the presidential race. In that case, he asked if Emphasis would be willing to invite Senator Robert Kennedy to speak in his place. Pitt agreed enthusiastically.[45]

Redding Pitt didn't coordinate that possible change with the president's office partly because he felt Rose would not object since Robert Kennedy addressed Emphasis '66. Pitt also wanted him to speak because of his personal support for Robert Kennedy's candidacy. On Monday, the Kennedy campaign confirmed that the candidate would be available and Pitt extended the invitation.

Frank Rose was not happy. In addition to violating the university's protocols on inviting speakers, this invitation put him in a difficult position. Rose's friendship with Robert Kennedy served the university well during desegregation in 1963, but Rose had since developed a close relationship with President Johnson, based in part on his unwavering support for administration policies in Vietnam. Additionally, given Frank Rose's recent clashes with the Wallaces and the state legislature, he may have anticipated joining President Johnson's cabinet in his second term. The awkwardness of this situation notwithstanding, Rose could not rescind an invitation extended to—and accepted by—a US senator.

Otherwise, a balanced Emphasis '68 program included Roy Wilkins of the NAACP, noted lawyer Melvin Belli, Ferenc Nagy, prime minister of Hungary until the Communists took over in 1947, and Harvard economist and Kennedy administration insider John Kenneth Galbraith. South Carolina senator Strom Thurmond was asked to close the proceedings with an address on Saturday morning.[46]

Two hundred cars packed with students and faculty made their way across the river to Northport to greet Kennedy who arrived two hours late. The Young Democrats (YD) and the Democratic Students Organization arranged the airport welcome, one that included a large sign that read, "Bama Backs Bobby." DSO also positioned protestors in front of Coleman Coliseum to distribute pamphlets announcing Friday's noontime antiwar vigil. The crowd, though smaller than hoped for, accorded Kennedy a warm welcome.

Kennedy opened with a joke. "Today, I come to you with both good news and bad news. The bad news is that Bear Bryant will not run as my vice president." A short pause let the audience chuckle, then Kennedy rebounded, "The good news is that Coach Bryant is willing to let me run as his vice president!"[47] After the applause and cheering subsided, Kennedy delivered his standard campaign speech.

Kennedy drew a crowd of ten thousand, by far the largest for Emphasis '68. No other session or speaker attracted audiences larger than nine hundred. When the symposium ended on Saturday morning, fewer than three hundred were on hand to hear Strom Thurmond defend the war in Vietnam. A *Crimson-White* editorial commenting on Emphasis '68 facetiously suggested that scheduling the program earlier in the week would have avoided conflicts with weekend fraternity parties.[48]

On Friday morning after Kennedy spoke, Ted Klitzke submitted his letter of resignation effective at the end of the semester. He was leaving to become dean at the Maryland Institute's College of Art. Given that Klitzke had been the proverbial horsefly on the administration's rump ever since he marched in Selma three years earlier, one doubts any tears fell in the president's office.[49] Later that day, forty to fifty protestors held the second peace vigil on the steps of the Alabama Union.

Although President Rose deflected some of Don Siegelman's progressive agenda, he shared SGA's progressive inclinations. In October, Rose appointed a liaison committee to improve contact with SGA and other student organizations, the purpose being to help students define their problems and assist them in finding the most appropriate administrative office for addressing their concerns. President Rose asked David Mathews to chair the Academic Liaison Committee (ALC).[50]

During the spring, with student unrest increasing across the nation and DSO initiating events like the weekly noontime peace vigils at the Capstone, the ALC arranged a series of informal meetings for faculty, administrators, and students to explore matters of mutual interest. These meetings, involving various deans, student leaders representing a wide range of organizations, and faculty members normally occurred over dinner.[51]

Tom's Place

Since the Human Rights Forum's inception in 1965, it had morphed into an informal group known as the "political science forum" or simply "the forum." There were no elected officers, charter, or constitution, and no dues. Meetings were held in student apartments or, occasionally, a faculty member's home. By the fall of 1967, these meetings involved political networking, lively conversations, and a lot of beer drinking.

A forum "get together" occurred every other Thursday night. In the fall of 1967, the most common venue was a small, two-story wood frame house located at the edge of campus and rented by Tom Hall, a senior majoring in history. Tom's place also served as a safe haven for the university's gays and lesbians. Don Siegelman, Coleman Lollar, Ed Still, Sondra Nesmith, and Jack Drake often attended forum meetings. Hugh and Kate Ragsdale, Jay and Alberta Murphy, Ron Robel, Bob Keever, John Ramsey, and Victor Gibean represented the faculty. Beer flowed freely, cigarette smoke hung in the air, and the stereo blared "Lucy in the Sky with Diamonds," from the Beatles' latest album, *Sergeant Pepper's Lonely Hearts Club Band*, while a revolving lantern rotated red, blue, yellow, and green lights through the living room to provide a psychedelic effect. On the wall hung a poster that read, "War is not healthy for children and other living things."

Many forum participants, including Tom, were regulars at the Friday antiwar vigils. Tom, a tall, lanky fellow whose acne scars accentuated his swarthy complexion, kept the apartment open while he studied at the library, providing a safe place for students alienated by the buttoned-down fraternity and cashmere-sweater sorority types who dominated the Capstone's social agenda. For those who dared to be different, including Bama's still-in-the-closet gay community, Tom's place provided sanctuary.

The Machine and the Turning of Campus Politics

On a chilly evening in late February, 150 students gathered on the columned porch at the Kappa Sigma house to hear Joe Espy announce his candidacy for SGA president. "If I'm elected, I will establish better communications with the administration. I will work through them, not against them."[52] Espy promised a more conservative SGA.

The opponent, Ed Still, the bespectacled editor of *Farrago* and member of the SGA House of Representatives, was too serious and far too liberal to have ever joined a fraternity. Espy, by contrast, belonged to a top fraternity and touted his conservative views. Two weeks earlier, when Still announced his candidacy, he stated, "I believe that we must preserve the philosophy that student government has followed over the last couple of years, to see restrictions on students' behavior—both academic and personal—removed."[53]

While no one gave Still's candidacy much of a chance, some saw the election as significant. Coleman Lollar, his activist voice increasingly heard among the small cadre of campus radicals, asserted, "Ed Still's candidacy will force the election to be decided on platforms rather than fraternity 'basement deals.'"[54] Lollar's reference to "basement deals" alluded to the Machine.

The fix was in. Influenced by SGA president Don Siegelman, the Machine ran Joe Espy because they thought he had the best chance of winning, his good looks appealing to female voters. They also decided to support Paul Clark, a conservative Kappa Alpha and fellow Machinist, for vice president. Despite increasingly liberal views on civil rights and the war in Vietnam, the Machine allowed Newman Strawbridge to run for secretary-treasurer but without its endorsement. Despite the progressive inclinations of past Machine leaders, keeping power outweighed ideological considerations. An exposé published two weeks before the election bared the Machine's inner workings.

Under the banner headline, "Secret Group Exposed," the *Crimson-White* ran two articles revealing the current iteration of the Machine, along with a reprint of a 1961 exposé written by then *Crimson-White* editor Jo Anne Singley, an editorial condemning the machinations of the Machine, whose roots extended back to the 1870s and the founding of the Theta Nu Epsilon (TNE) fraternity at Wesleyan University. At its peak, TNE maintained eighty-three known chapters along with an unknown number of groups bearing exotic names like "Iron Mask" and "Society of the Yellow Rose."[55]

TNE appeared at Alabama in 1909, morphed into the "Society of Friends," was known in 1930s as "The Group," and then disappeared during the war. In the 1950s, it reemerged as the Machine with thirty to thirty-five members. Singley maintained that the largest and most prestigious fraternities provide one to three members. While its membership included a handful of independents, albeit in a second-tier status, the Machine excluded female members.[56]

Singley's exposé drove the Machine underground, where its influence waned, opening the door for people like Don Stewart and Zach Higgs, the last non-Machine SGA presidents of the decade. In 1965, the Machine resurfaced as a tightly run, nearly all-Greek organization. When reexposed in March 1968, the Machine consisted of representatives from eleven top fraternities as well as Theta Tau, the professional society from the College of Engineering; included because few engineering students went Greek due to the academic rigors of their curriculum.[57] A sidebar listed Joe Espy, Don Siegelman, Redding Pitt, Paul Clark, Newman Strawbridge, Eddie Friend, and Ralph Knowles as members, the latter being "inactive" since he was in law school. A Machine member went inactive upon graduating and was replaced with someone generated by the membership.

According to the article, the Machine delivered one thousand votes from fraternities and looked to sororities for an additional one thousand votes, secured through the influence of boyfriends or "pin-mates." Machinists invited sorority members, usually their girlfriends, to dinner at the University Club where student leaders addressed issues attendant to campus politics. The boyfriends then told their dates that they had attended a Machine meeting and that they were now part of the elite group. They were not, but the ploy enabled the manipulation of sorority votes.[58] Since only 3,000 to 3,500 students voted in campus elections—in part because most students thought they were fixed—the 2,000 votes delivered by the Machine provided a comfortable margin of victory.

Machine tentacles extended into almost every corner of campus politics. A look through any *Corolla* from 1965 through 1970 shows the same people in leadership positions across the range of campus organizations. The Machine influenced who was inducted into Omicron Delta Kappa, tapped for the Jasons, and who presided over the Cotillion Club. It also decided who chaired the homecoming, Emphasis, and Bama Day committees.[59] Less than two weeks after the Machine was exposed, 2,878 students voted, fewer than the normal turnout of 3,000 to 3,500. Joe Espy tallied 2,240 votes to Ed Still's 638.[60]

Elsewhere on election night, the newly chartered Afro-American Association (AAA) drew up a list of grievances to be presented to Frank Rose the following morning. These included hiring a black faculty member and campus police officer, adding a course on African American history, equal opportunity for blacks in student employment, opening off-campus housing to African American students, and equal representation in the SGA.[61]

Turnings

After graduating from Nathan Bedford Forrest High School in Jacksonville, Florida, Bud Silvis enrolled at the Capstone in 1964 to study chemistry. As was the case with most freshmen males, Bud faced choosing between Air Force and Army ROTC. He selected the Air Force and discovered he liked it. Indeed, Bud's blond crew cut seemed out of place among cadets inclined to fudge regulations on hair length. While his gung-ho attitude irritated fellow cadets, the AFROTC faculty pegged Silvis as "officer material."[62]

In the fall of 1966, Silvis entered the precommissioning, advanced program where he rose rapidly from cadet second lieutenant to cadet major. Silvis also completed a flight-training program designed to prepare pilot-qualified students for the air force's fifty-three-week flight school. By May 1967, summer camp and one final year of academics lay between Bud and the wild blue yonder.

In September Bud returned from summer camp as a cadet lieutenant colonel on track for commissioning. The experience, which included a ride in the backseat of a jet trainer, usually pumped up returning cadets. Bud, however, seemed to have experienced an epiphany.

Bud's blond hair spilled over the collar of his summer tan uniform. His beard looked to be at least a month along. He wanted out of ROTC but the air force was reluctant to release him after having completed the preflight program. Rumor held that after returning to campus from summer camp, Bud used his knowledge of chemistry to whip up a batch of LSD. After dropping acid, dropping bombs lost all its appeal. The air force released Bud but not without penalty. The ten hours of ROTC academic credit he lost delayed graduation until after the fall semester in 1968. For Bud Silvis, the summer of '67 was a summer of turning.[63]

Through the 1960s, Alabama was a "football school" and basketball suf-

fered for it. During Coach Hayden Riley's eight-year tenure as head basketball coach, Tide cagers won 102 games while losing 104. Consequently, support
for the sport lagged. For example, in February 1968 attendance at a basketball
game in Coleman Coliseum broke an SEC record when 15,014 fans showed
up to watch Alabama play Louisiana State University. The fans didn't come
to watch the Tide play so much as they did to see LSU's phenomenal Peter P.
"Pistol Pete" Maravich score 59 points to defeat Alabama 99–89. Three weeks
later, Coach Riley resigned.[64]

Coach Charles M. Newton, head basketball coach at Transylvania College,
replaced Riley. Newton, who came to Transylvania the same year Frank Rose
assumed its presidency, compiled 169 wins against 137 losses in a state where
basketball, not football, reigned supreme. Additionally, Rose developed an almost fatherly affinity for Newton. While still coaching at Transylvania, Newton
took a one-year leave of absence to work on a doctorate in physical education
at Alabama, during which he coached freshman basketball. In the summer of
1967, Newton lived in the President's Mansion with the Rose family.[65]

Frank Rose set up a job interview between Coach Bryant and Coach Newton. During that interview, Newton asked if he would be free to recruit black
players. Bryant told him he could recruit anyone who qualified academically.
Newton also asked for a four-year contract thinking it would take that long to
turn the tide of Alabama basketball. Bryant agreed and offered him the job.[66]

Coach Newton integrated Alabama athletics in 1969 with the recruitment
of Wendell Hudson, the first African American to accept a sport's scholarship
at Alabama. Not only did Newton play a key role in breaking down racial barriers at the Capstone, during the 1970s, Alabama won three conference titles.
Newton's hiring, like others during Frank Rose's tenure, was essential to Alabama's comprehensive commitment to turning both the Tide and the university.

To Freely Speak, Inquire, and Learn

As the spring semester drew to a close, former SGA president Ralph Knowles,
by then a second-year law student, delivered the address at the annual Omicron Delta Kappa banquet. President Rose sat in the audience along with Don
Siegelman, the immediate past SGA president, and Joe Espy, Siegelman's successor. Before starting his address, Knowles apologized to anyone who might
be offended by his remarks, stating he considered everyone in the room his
friend and that he meant to offend no one.

Following a brief discussion of campus activism across the nation, Knowles asserted that while large-scale dissent had yet to reach the Capstone, the number of frustrated student progressives was increasing. He acknowledged that the current quiet on campus resulted from administrators and student leaders working toward common goals. He also noted that SGA had changed from being "a government of petty politics and carnivals into a meaningful, relevant and effective tool."[67] He praised SGA for its role in past Emphasis programs and thanked President Rose for his strong stand in support of Emphasis '67.

Knowles then turned his attention to the most recent SGA elections. He characterized students who voted for Joe Espy as "people who have not yet broken from the bonds of the decadent traditions of the Deep South" and accused new student leaders of wanting to undo the progress made by SGA since 1965. Then he opened up on the administration. Knowles accused the university of lacking respect for students' rights, for not allowing SGA to file a friend of the court brief in the Dickey case, and for rescinding Coffin's invitation to speak at Emphasis '68. He demanded an immediate end to all in loco parentis regulations and concluded by predicting an explosion of dissent within six months.[68]

The *Crimson-White* carried the full text of Knowles' remarks. It also penned an editorial titled "Open your eyes." While disagreeing that an explosion was imminent, the writer thought increased unrest likely and then lightly admonished Knowles for his references to southern decadence. "There is, the *Crimson-White* believes, today more of the new South than the Deep South on campus, though we too grow desperate over the state of Alabama politics. But politics is not the whole game." Despite disagreeing with some of Knowles' comments, the editorial concluded, "Ol' Ralph told it pretty much like it is."[69]

The game soon changed. Just after midnight on May 7, Lurleen Wallace lost her two-year battle with cancer and was succeeded by Lieutenant Governor Albert Brewer. After a month in mourning, George Wallace returned to the presidential campaign trail.[70]

Reorganizing for a Stride into the Future

During the spring, the Rose administration completed a studied redistribution of responsibilities among principal administrative officers designed to streamline the organizational structure and improve coordination between the university and its extension centers in Birmingham and Huntsville. Accordingly, Jeff Bennett assumed the newly created position of provost with responsibility for coordinating operations between Tuscaloosa, Huntsville, and Birmingham.[71]

Within the new organization, David Mathews assumed the position of executive vice president, working directly for Frank Rose and charged with matters attendant to the daily operation of the university. The deans of all the colleges reported to Vice President for Academic Affairs Raymond F. McLain who reported through David Mathews to President Rose. John Blackburn became dean for Student Development with Sarah Healy assisting as associate dean. Rounding out the new organization was an Office of University Relations under Larry T. McGehee.[72]

Executive Vice President Mathews assumed massive new responsibilities. Although it appeared Jeff Bennett held a higher position as provost, his duties mostly involved coordinating activities between Tuscaloosa and the extension centers in Huntsville and Birmingham. Mathews, on the other hand, was responsible for over 1,800 faculty and staff members and overseeing the annual operating budget of $27,500,000 and $12,000,000 slated for construction.[73] President Rose defined Mathews' duties as analogous to a presidency of a single university within a multicampus system. In a letter Frank Rose wrote nominating Mathews as one of the Jaycees' Ten Outstanding Men of 1968 he noted, "This young man will be president of a major university in a very short while."[74]

On May 10, the university welcomed four hundred guests from across Alabama and the South to inaugurate a four-hundred-million-dollar capital campaign dubbed "A-STRIDE," an acronym for "Alabama's Statement of Trust: Responsible, Intellectual, Dedication to Excellence." This initiative towered over previous fund-raising efforts by endeavoring to raise forty million dollars each year over the next decade. This was the most ambitious program of private philanthropy in the history of the state of Alabama and the second largest ever undertaken by a state university anywhere at any time.[75]

After a reception at Indian Hills Country Club and a buffet dinner in the Martha Parham Hall cafeteria, buses carried the guests to Coleman Coliseum for a program produced by ABC Television. Five thousand local guests, in addition to the four hundred special alumni and friends flown in for the event, viewed a program that included an address by Frank Rose, music by the Million Dollar Band, the University Symphony and Choral Union, and a performance by the Alabama State Ballet. There was a film presentation narrated by Alabama alumnus Jim Nabors in which senior editor at *Newsweek* James M. Cannon, Coach Paul W. Bryant, and Alabama Supreme Court associate justice Thomas W. Lawson testified to what their alma mater meant to them. Others appearing in the production included Werner von Braun, director of the Marshall Space Flight Center in Huntsville, and Luther Terry, former surgeon general of the United States. Frank Rose wrapped up, "The University of Alabama shall stride toward excellence by paying the price of excellence. We accept the challenge to make this, the boldest step forward in our history." Buses then returned out of town guests to the airport where chartered airliners waited to ferry them back to Mobile, Montgomery, Gadsden, Huntsville, and Atlanta.[76]

When the class of '68 arrived in the summer of 1964, Klansmen were picketing theaters and restaurants in Tuscaloosa. Their tenure at the Capstone encompassed a time of both physical change and academic growth both for the university and for themselves. On Sunday, May 26, after a commencement address by philanthropist Kemmons Wilson, founder and chairman of the board of Holiday Inns of America, the class of 1968 embarked on a journey into what some hoped was the best of times and others feared might be the worst.[77] Despite the turmoil and confusion of that world, many of those new Alabama alumni were determined to make a difference. And some of them did.

7
Campus Militancy Grows
A Past Still Present

The past hangs like a perpetual present over the Capstone with the Woods Hall Quadrangle providing a majestic reminder of what was—and is—the University of Alabama. In addition to Woods, three other historic buildings bound the Quad: Clark, Manly, and Garland Halls. These four structures represent the rebirth of the university in the post–Civil War era, their presence reflecting tradition.

Across a broad street, nestled next to the Amelia Gayle Gorgas Library, is the small, white roundhouse armory where, during a thunderstorm late on the night of April 3, 1865, cadets picked up muskets for an expected encounter with Yankee raiders, one that resulted in a brief skirmish before President Garland withdrew the cadets, avoiding a needless bloodletting at the war's end. Today, every few minutes one of several "Crimson Ride" buses pulls up to the library, ferrying students to and from dormitories at the northern edge of campus and parking lots nearly a mile to the east.

The campus was smaller in the summer of 1968 when most Alabama students abjured political and social activism, whether from apathy or concentration on educational and professional goals. While a few students focused on issues like the war in Vietnam and the struggle at home for racial justice, most took advantage of a few years of relatively carefree living, doing enough to get by while still "doing their own thing" by partying, dating, or watching TV. An adventurous handful, taking Timothy Leary's advice, turned on, tuned in, and dropped out. The majority, however, disapproved of campus disruptions and avoided demonstrations. Over the next two years, as unrest spread across the country, mounting tensions between a growing number of Alabama's dissidents and the administration prompted a series of increasingly contentious confrontations.

Bama's band of activists consisted of students disillusioned with a system they thought incapable of changing itself. At the higher level, the system included both the federal and state governments. From the student dissidents' perspective, the university's power structure and its policies were things they could confront and possibly alter. In the fall of 1968, they became more determined and, when confrontation failed to bring about change, frustration led to disruption.

Conservative elements in the state—especially the legislature—attached the label of "Communists" to the small cadre of campus radicals. Outlandish attire and making heroes of revolutionaries like Che Guevara and murderous despots like Ho Chi Minh and Mao Tse Tung fed suspicions among older Alabamians and also alienated dissenters from the majority reluctant to abandon established symbols of middle-class orthodoxy.[1] In the spring of 1968, while Students for a Democratic Society claimed seven thousand members and thirty-five thousand supporters on campuses across the nation, it had yet to establish a chapter at Alabama.[2]

A Handful of Troublemakers

In late April, a thousand miles north of Tuscaloosa, Columbia University erupted into SDS-inspired mayhem. There, in the middle of New York City, a red flag flapped atop Columbia's administration building while a huge portrait of Karl Marx dominated the entrance to a nearby classroom building. A banner erected by the Black Panthers proclaimed, "Power to the People!"[3]

Grayson Kirk, Columbia's sixty-four-year-old president, handled his campus crisis the way many other presidents did theirs: the wrong way. He let the demonstrators seize the initiative in a confrontation designed to diminish the administration's authority. Columbia's uninvolved students were the primary target of the two hundred or so members of SDS and their sympathizers. After a week of negotiations resulted only in increased demands from SDS, Kirk finally sent in hundreds of police to do what a squad might have done on the first day. It was theater staged to win uninterested and apathetic students over to SDS. The administration fell into their trap.[4]

Although SDS didn't have a chapter at Alabama in the summer of 1968, the Democratic Student Organization (DSO) did. According to Jack Drake, DSO coordinated its activities not only with SDS but also with the Southern Student Organizing Committee (SSOC), a group that grew from fifteen chapters in ten southern states in 1964 to thirty chapters four years later.[5]

Despite Ralph Knowles's predictions of an imminent explosion of campus unrest, Frank Rose clung to the notion that dissent emanated from a "handful of troublemakers" whose discontent was "directed as much against the apathy of their own age group as against the 'system' of society in general."[6] Rose saw this handful as consisting of no more than fifteen to twenty malcontents.[7] Other university administrators viewed the situation differently.

Vice President Mathews and Dean Blackburn collected and shared articles on campus unrest with staffers in the Office of Student Development. Their primary concern in 1968 focused on efforts by some associated with past Emphasis committees to fashion programs that provoked controversy. This led Richard Thigpen, the director of men activities within Dean Blackburn's office, to recommend administrators exert more leadership in the area of student-invited speakers.[8]

New Opportunities and Uncertainties in the Summer of 1968

In David Mathews' capacity as executive vice president, he sent Frank Rose a weekly memorandum detailing his activities. These memoranda kept Rose abreast of what was going on and what might be anticipated in terms of policy formulation and implementation. David Mathews, whose duties made him in effect the chief operating officer at the Capstone, was taking hold of the reins of power and some who remembered him from his student days resented it.

In June, the university, as a part of its initiatives with Stillman College, added Joffre T. Whisenton to the vice president's staff. He was both the first African American to earn a doctorate from Alabama and the first to join the administration.[9] Whisenton was a welcome addition: an articulate, experienced alumnus and a southerner who understood the challenges facing higher education in Alabama along with the subtleties of southern culture.

The financial picture turned ominous during the summer. President Rose was unsure if the university would receive the $158 million requested from the legislature to undertake a ten-year building program. Additionally, university costs rose at an annual rate of 5 percent. While Rose hoped A-STRIDE would generate forty million dollars a year to offset federal dollars siphoned off by the rising costs of the war in Vietnam, six months into the campaign it had yet to render a single substantial contribution.[10]

More uncertainty emerged in June when, after a month as provost, Jeff Bennett accepted the position of director of legislative liaison for the National Health Services and Medical Health Administration in Bethesda, Maryland. Except for four years spent as a marine during World War II, Bennett's association with the university went back to his student days in the 1930s. In a *Crimson-White* interview, Bennett stated he was most proud of the role he played in desegregation.[11]

His departure came at a difficult time. The University of Alabama needed to hire 175 new faculty members to meet minimum accreditation standards attendant to faculty-student ratios. This wasn't going to be easy since it would have taken an estimated 15 percent increase in faculty compensation to extricate the university from the lower third of southern institutions of higher education. Library holdings, another area considered by accrediting agencies, numbered 1,179,600 books and documents in the Capstone's ten libraries; an average of 59 holdings per student. This compared poorly with Duke University's 260 and the University of Virginia's 180, but stacked up better against Mississippi State University's paltry 36 volumes per student.[12]

Stepping Out Innovatively

In the spring of 1967, SGA and the administration approved the establishment of the Experimental College, a student-run institution resembling "free universities" forming on other campuses. It was up and running by September 1968. Experimental College attempted to lift the burden of grades, foster informal interaction with faculty, and move students from being "passive receivers" of facts into a more interactive learning experience. Over five hundred students registered for noncredit courses on topics ranging from the ethics of existentialism to the black arts. Typically, classes met an hour or two a week, usually convening in the evening in dormitory lounges, off-campus apartments, or private homes. Bill Moody was named student chairman and a faculty board of advisors was established to oversee courses and programs.[13]

David Mathews proposed a bolder and more academically respectable innovation: New College. Early in the fall semester, he routed a document titled, "A New College for the University of Alabama" through the various deans to Vice President for Academic Affairs McLain. Mathews' concerns over the growing impersonal nature of large universities prompted the New College concept to meet the needs of interested students and innovative professors who might otherwise be stifled in a megauniversity structure. Mathews envisioned New College as a way to overcome what he characterized as a mediocrity endemic to the "'follow the leader syndrome at Alabama.'"[14]

Innovation of this sort was new to the university's tradition-bound deans and senior faculty. It likely would have gone nowhere had its author not been the executive vice president. That being the case, McLain formed a committee to study the proposal. At their initial meeting, members raised a plethora of objections. Some argued existing honors programs met the needs of highly motivated students. Others worried New College might divert funds needed to support current programs. Content with the status quo, they wanted to forestall change. McLain, whose experience in higher education exceeded that of Frank Rose and David Mathews combined, knew the special relationship Mathews enjoyed with the president compelled serious consideration leading to almost inevitable implementation. That being the case, he wanted New College to succeed.[15]

Jack Drake's Challenge

Jack Drake dressed differently from other students, usually wearing slacks with a shirt buttoned to the collar. His blond hair, while not long, also was not stylish. Jack's rumpled, unselfconscious appearance belied an incisively sharp intellect coupled to determined idealism.

As a freshman, Jack watched US marshals escort Vivian Malone to class. Violence in Selma during his sophomore year pushed Drake toward the fringe of campus dissidents. During this time, he roomed with Ed Still in Mallet Hall, a dorm reserved for the more studious. Drake and Still formed a critical mass intent on progressive change. Through SGA they met Ralph Knowles and other campus progressives. In the spring of 1968, Still, Van De Veer, and Drake, along with a handful of others, founded DSO.

Like George Wallace nearly a generation earlier, Jack enrolled in a program side-stepping the baccalaureate and leading straight to a law degree. By 1968, Drake and the administration had been elbowing one another for some time. Drake was more than a troublemaking dissident. As a top performer specializing in cross-examination on Alabama's nationally acclaimed debate squad, he had brought honor to the university.[16]

In April 1968, after the Emphasis committee succumbed to pressure and withdrew William Sloane Coffin's invitation, the Young Democrats attempted to challenge the university's speaker-vetting policy by inviting Julian Bond, the only African American then serving in the Georgia legislature, to speak on campus. Knowing the policy required a potential speaker's name be submitted for approval two weeks prior to the engagement, they purposely delayed asking permission until days before the event. Upon receiving the late request, Dean Blackburn admonished the YDs but also approved the invitation. When

Julian Bond spoke, John Blackburn was there to hear and to meet him. A reception followed at Tom Hall's place.

Thwarted but undaunted, a few days later the Young Democrats repeated the gambit by inviting black comedian Dick Gregory to campus without providing the requisite two weeks' notice. This time Blackburn used much stronger language in his admonishment and also denied the request.[17] But then he relented. That Gregory turned down the invitation due to other commitments was irrelevant to the Young Democrats who used the stratagem to raise an issue.

William Sloane Coffin aside, the university approved nearly all requests for speakers. From the DSO's perspective, the issue was students' rights and not whether a particular voice was heard on campus. This coincided with the general tenor of dissent on other campuses, focused as it was on expanding students' rights while diminishing the authority of administrators.

At the start of the fall semester Jack Drake, as speaker chairman for DSO, submitted four names Frank Rose could not approve without putting the university in a perilous position and also jeopardizing his job: Eldridge Cleaver, a Black Panther and convicted felon; yippie Jerry Rubin; Herbert Aptheker, ideologue for the Communist Party, U.S.A.; and Tom Hayden, a founding member of SDS.[18] On Thursday, September 27, in accordance with the policy, Drake submitted the list to Dean Blackburn who turned it over to the Student Life and Learning Committee.

A still warm early autumn dusk settled over the Quadrangle as Drake walked up the steps of the Alabama Union toward the Office of Student Development. Inside, Assistant Dean Glenn Stillion and members of the Student Life and Learning Committee awaited. Dean Sarah Healy represented the administration. Victor Gibean, Dale Cramer, and Leon J. Weinberger were there on behalf of the faculty. SGA president Joe Espy, Associated Women Students (AWS) president Jerrianne Hammock, and Dana Clay, editor of the *Crimson-White*, represented the student body.

Stillion called the meeting to order, introduced DSO's request, and then turned the floor over to Drake, who went straight to the point. "I came here tonight to see if you had any questions. DSO will ask these speakers to campus. Our purpose is to get the University to remove its present policy. We will go to court if this request is refused."[19] When Drake finished presenting his case, Stillion informed him that unless DSO heard otherwise, it could proceed with the invitations.

After Drake left, the discussion indicated every member of the committee understood DSO's invitation request for what it was: a challenge to the university's authority. The committee also understood granting this request would bring down the wrath of Montgomery and, quite possibly, end Frank Rose's presidency. In the end, the committee unanimously rejected DSO's request.

Incident at the Haight Hut

Twenty-two year-old Bud Silvis, a year after being released from Air Force ROTC, looked forward to graduation and then entering the medical school at the National University of Mexico. During the fall semester, in addition to working as a chemistry lab instructor, Silvis had joined in a business venture with a man named Bob Ford and his wife. Their enterprise, the Haight Hut, involved a "head shop" located at 1420 University Boulevard.

Head shops, a fixture of the counterculture, sold psychedelic posters, love beads, incense, water pipes, and, in the minds of Tuscaloosa law enforcement, a lot more. Accordingly, around four o'clock in the afternoon on the Friday before the Ole Miss game, Tuscaloosa police, sheriff's deputies, and agents of the Federal Bureau of Narcotics and Dangerous Drugs descended on the Haight Hut. They arrested nine university student shoppers on vagrancy charges, a ploy the Tuscaloosa police used on students who, after all, had no visible means of support. They also arrested Silvis for possessing and trafficking in LSD. Bob Ford, co-owner of the Haight Hut, and his wife, who worked there, were arrested on lesser charges. Bond was set for Silvis at ten thousand dollars and one thousand dollars each for Bob Ford and his wife.[20]

The following day, Saturday, October 5, Ole Miss defeated the Crimson Tide by a score of 10–8. Alabama's only touchdown came on a fumble recovery in the Ole Miss end zone with eight seconds left in the game.[21]

Rose Responds to Drake

On Saturday, October 12, Frank Rose sent Jack Drake a letter denying DSO's request. "Never before has the issue been placed in such a clear-cut manner before this institution." Rose noted that although the university almost never denied requests for speakers, no organization ever questioned its prerogative for doing so. "That Constitutional rights are so all inclusive as to prohibit the institution from being able to control its own destiny . . . raises questions concerning the institution's ability to influence the quality and shape of its educational product." He concluded, "I do not believe the University of Alabama is prepared to give such recognition at this time."[22]

An ad hoc Faculty Committee on the Role of the Student at the University of Alabama, chaired by E. Roger Sayers, a biology professor, sent a letter to President Rose supporting DSO. The committee contended the administration should not deny any chartered organization the right to invite whomever they pleased to campus.[23]

Rose had his backers. Professor Howard Wilson, a professor from the College of Engineering expressed "wholehearted agreement" with Rose and added that he spoke for the majority of his colleagues. Senator Leland Childs sent a telegram reminding Rose that if the speaker ban bill had passed, this incident never would have arisen.[24] In addition to hundreds of approving letters pouring in from all over the state, the Alabama Press Association also passed a resolution of support.[25]

Frank Rose stood firm on potentially treacherous ground. He faced the challenge of moving the university in a more progressive direction while also placating the conservative state legislature. And, although his relationship with Montgomery eased after Albert Brewer became governor, Rose expected George Wallace to enter the Democratic primary in 1970 and knew he thrived on bashing "Communists on campus."

In early November, the American Civil Liberties Union filed DSO's suit against Frank Rose and the University of Alabama in the US District Court for Northern Alabama, charging the defendants with violating students' rights under the first and fourteenth amendments to the US Constitution. The suit wound its way through the federal court system before finally being dismissed.[26]

Tragedy at 1420 University Boulevard

On Friday, October 18, the county grand jury indicted Bud Silvis for possessing and trafficking in LSD. While his attorney arranged bail, the prosecutor informed Silvis that he was drawing up a warrant on marijuana charges and that he would be back in custody within hours. A tide of despair rolled over Bud Silvis.

It took Bud's lawyer nearly three hours to arrange the ten-thousand-dollar bail. That done, Bob Ford and his wife drove the despondent young man from the courthouse to his room above the Haight Hut, where they also lived. Opposite the Haight Hut, looking eastward along University Boulevard toward a line of eateries and other small businesses catering to students, Ford stopped briefly to let Silvis open the back door and step onto the sidewalk. While Bud crossed the street to the Haight Hut, the Fords drove a few yards, turned left onto Reed Street and then made an immediate left into an alley. As they pulled into a parking space by the back door, a loud crack split the crisp air of a mid-October late afternoon. The couple rushed in. Bob bounded up the stairs, his wife hurrying behind him. They opened the door to Bud's room to find him face down on his bed, blood pooling around his head and matting into his sandy blond hair, a 22-caliber pistol in his hand. Nearby was a short note, its contents since lost.

Within minutes, police cars and an ambulance pulled up in front of the Haight Hut, snarling Friday evening traffic and frustrating students headed downtown for drinks and dinner and then to the Bama Theater to check out Jane Fonda starring in *Barbarella.* The ambulance rushed Silvis two miles east along University Boulevard to Druid City Hospital. His mother, in town for the hearing, and his lawyer were at his side along with Dean Healy when, an hour later, Bud Silvis left this life. A Tuscaloosa police officer waited in the hallway ready to arrest Bud Silvis on marijuana charges should he survive, and of course, inform him of his right to remain silent. Bud did.[27]

Crimson Pride

The 1968 edition of the Crimson Tide, less fearsome than in years past, remained formidable enough to carry seven wins against two losses—at the hands of conference rivals Ole Miss and Tennessee—into the season's finale against archrival Auburn. The game was made poignant by the presence of Dr. Pat Trammel, the quarterback of the 1961 national championship team, who had recently finished medical school.

Throughout the decade, Trammel often returned to the Capstone for homecoming to help lead the pregame pep rally. Earlier in the season, during the half-time ceremonies at the Vanderbilt game, Governor Brewer presented him with the first "Pat Trammel Award" to be given annually to the Tide player who best combined athletic leadership with scholarship. A sense of urgency lingered around the award. Testicular sarcoma, a virulent form of cancer, had a blitz on the former quarterback.[28] A few weeks later, with cancer closing in on Pat Trammel, Coach Bryant invited him and his young son to sit on the team bench during the Auburn game. After the Tide bested the Tigers 24–16, team captain Mike Hall presented the game ball to the ailing former quarterback who wept openly as he handed it to his son. Ten days later, cancer sacked Pat Trammel.

Something else made this year's homecoming and the Auburn game notable. A year earlier, when Don Siegelman attempted to end the hoisting of the Confederate flag before the Auburn game, Rose slapped down the initiative to avoid aggravating the more fractious elements in the legislature. Starting with homecoming, the Confederate flag no longer flew alongside Old Glory and the state flag.[29]

DSO Responds

The Monday after Bud Silvis committed suicide, DSO held a noontime rally on the steps of the Alabama Union. Originally planned as a rally to draw attention to the university's speaker's policies and partly as an antiwar demonstration, the tragedy at the Haight Hut infused the event with new energy and urgency.

In accordance with ground rules agreed to by the administration and DSO, demonstrators stood silently on the steps of the Union for fifteen minutes and then walked along the sidewalk on University Boulevard, past the President's Mansion and Denny Chimes, to Canterbury Chapel on Hackberry Lane. There they broke into seminars to discuss issues stemming from the recent arrests by Tuscaloosa police and ways to promote activism on campus and in the community.[30]

During negotiations, Dean Blackburn expressed reservations concerning outsiders that DSO had invited to participate. He also was concerned over DSO's claim that the demonstration was being cosponsored by Students for a Democratic Society, the Southern Students Organizing Committee, and Student Nonviolent Coordinating Committee. Blackburn cautioned that the university would enforce its policy limiting on-campus demonstrations to Alabama students, faculty, and staff. Both Blackburn and Drake knew the university had no authority over activities at Canterbury Chapel since it was located off campus, even if the separation was the width of Hackberry Lane.

In 1958, Frank Rose hired Col. Beverly Leigh, another of his boyhood friends from Meridian, when he retired from the air force following an ROTC assignment at Georgia Tech. Despite the limited nature of his duties, mostly involving seeing that campus air-raid shelters were stocked with food and water, giving talks to local service clubs, and maintaining communications with local law enforcement, Leigh sometimes acted as if he possessed broad, if also unspecified, powers when dealing with campus unrest, as was the case at Governor's Day 1966 when his intervention resulted in two demonstrators being arrested. Accordingly, Leigh led a small contingent of university police who escorted the students during their walk from the Alabama Union.

When the marchers turned onto Hackberry Lane they spotted Tuscaloosa police cruisers and officers, some in uniform and others in plain clothes, in front of Canterbury Chapel. While the university police stood on campus property outside Foster auditorium, Colonel Leigh crossed Hackberry Lane to Canterbury where he mingled with the Tuscaloosa police, shaking hands and slapping backs. He also seemed to be pointing out various student demonstrators to an officer scribbling in a notebook.

Benjamin T. Phillips, a reporter for the *Southern Courier*, a liberal Birmingham weekly, snapped photos. Suddenly, two undercover officers jumped him. One snatched away Phillips's camera and exposed his film while the other handcuffed the reporter. When his wife rushed over to ask why he was being arrested, she was told it was for disorderly conduct and that if she didn't move away, she'd be joining her husband.

James Bains, a twenty-five-year-old activist from Oneonta, Alabama, and a declared congressional candidate on the National Democratic Party of Alabama ticket, was also arrested and charged with vagrancy. The two men were then driven to jail and booked. Although bail for disorderly conduct and vagrancy usually amounted to three hundred dollars and one hundred dollars respectively, Judge Joe "Burn 'em" Burns set their bail at five thousand dollars each.[31]

At the end of the month, DSO used a mimeograph to run off a one-page flyer, the first issue of its newsletter titled, "Impressions." Beneath a peace symbol, the words "POLICE HARASSMENT" caught the readers' eyes. The flyer noted the suicide of Bud Silvis and the arrests at Canterbury. It also announced a vigil to be held on the steps of the Alabama Union at noon the following day, October 30.[32]

Over one hundred demonstrators congregated on the Union steps. Tommy Thompson, a student activist, repeatedly asked a crowd of several hundred onlookers to join them. A few did. Feeling his oats, Thompson then offered, "You members of the University police, if you are being harassed by the Tuscaloosa police, come join us." A few smiled. At Canterbury just ten days earlier, when a university officer crossed Hackberry Lane to ask the Tuscaloosa police why they were arresting Phillips and Bains, they threatened to arrest him for interfering with their arrest.[33]

Meanwhile, down at the courthouse, Judge Burns showed his true colors. At the hearing to set a trial date for Phillips and Bains, Burns announced a two-week delay to await the arrival of FBI reports. Burns added, "If you are not students, we want to find out why you are here. We are not going to tolerate anyone coming into this community to tear it down." Burns then lit his burners, "I used to be president of this university [student body president, he meant to say] and I don't like to see people come in and try to tear it down. I killed Japs who meant less harm than some people in this country."[34] The judge set bail at five thousand dollars each, explaining that he did so in order that "we can find out who your fellow travelers are." An actor portraying a Hollywood B-movie caricature of a southern judge could not have played it better than Burn 'em Burns.

Other Voices

There were other, less strident but increasingly vehement, voices of dissent. For years, most students viewed the Associated Women Students organization as an extension of the Dean of Women's Office. Until 1968, the Machine-dominated SGA saw AWS as something akin to cowgirls and female detectives, the weaker sex dabbling in manly business. In Alabama, Lurleen Wallace's brief political career aside, politics was exclusively a male franchise. The Machine and law school, the former totally a male domain and the latter only slightly less so, could provide contacts useful to anyone seeking political office.

In April 1968, AWS president Marsha Griffin and president-elect Jerrianne Hammock united to support a resolution vowing, "AWS will keep pace with the times in assuming leadership in political, moral, and social issues by setting the tone for others."[35] Another resolution held students should be allowed to invite any speakers to campus who might "further the educational process." AWS also urged changes in policies on curfews and women living off campus.

Vice President Lois Cobb proved ardently committed to transforming AWS into a viable women's advocacy tool. As a freshman, she attended the International Associated Women Students (IAWS) seminar at West Virginia University. The following year, Lois served as a delegate to the IAWS convention at Southern Methodist University where she lobbied to have the next year's convention at the Capstone. In 1969, the University of Alabama became the first Deep South University to host an IAWS convention.[36]

By the summer of 1968, Sondra Nesmith, a founding member of DSO, had gone well beyond AWS. In August, she engaged in a *Crimson-White* "Forum 68" exchange with Pan-Hellenic president Beth Caldwell over the female students' rights at the university. The exchange pitted a budding feminist against a traditional Bama coed.

"The University treats its students like small children. Let's lay it on the line;

at this institution, STUDENTS ARE NIGGERS!" (Emphasis in the text) Sondra Nesmith went on to accuse the university of maintaining a "separate but equal policy of discrimination against women students." Her complaints focused on the vestiges of in loco parentis policies attendant to curfews and proscriptions against women living off campus.

Beth Caldwell countered. "Rules are made for the protection of students. Like parents, the University's administration must have certain controls over us." She admonished students for their "rebellion, protests and demanding of so-called rights," and asked what part these behaviors played in the educational process.[37]

In 1968, despite the conservative presidency of Joe Espy, SGA embraced AWS initiatives because Jerrianne Hammock, while more liberal than her predecessors, was not a radical feminist. Early in the first semester, Larry Auerbach and Jeff Bayer joined freshman AWS representative Cathy Johnson to introduce a resolution calling for self-regulated hours for all female students with copies sent to Frank Rose, Sarah Healy, AWS, and the *Crimson-White*.[38]

Had AWS been more radical, it may well have alienated itself from the student body, especially the Machine and SGA leadership. Likewise, the university's small number of African American students did not engage in the kind of militancy associated with black power movements on other campuses, even the South's more elite institutions like Vanderbilt and Tulane. But the specter of the Klan didn't hover over Nashville and New Orleans like it did Tuscaloosa.

The Afro-American Association (AAA) received its charter on March 28, 1968. The following month their first set of demands called for hiring full-time black faculty members and a black officer for the campus police, offering courses in African American history and culture, and fair representation on committees appointed by SGA and AWS.[39]

Over the summer, professor John Pancake attended a black history seminar at Duke University to help him prepare a fall course titled, "The Negro in the United States." A follow-on course, offered during the spring semester, would focus on the civil rights movement. Edward Nall, first president of AAA, criticized the approach for its "lack of sociological bearings to show how conditions developed."[40]

There were other issues affecting the 117 African American students at the Capstone in the fall of 1968. Tuscaloosa's landlords resisted renting apartments to black students. Although the university bore no legal obligation to help students find suitable off-campus housing, Dean Blackburn understood the potential consequences should the university's AAA chapter file suit against a local real estate company, particularly the prominent Pritchett-Moore Agency. Blackburn suggested Frank Rose ask Harry Pritchett to open rentals to black students and urge his friends in other Tuscaloosa agencies to do likewise.[41]

Given that Henry Pritchett helped mobilize local business leaders behind desegregation in 1963, one might assume he would be helpful on this sensitive issue. Five years earlier, Tuscaloosa's elite feared the adverse effects racial strife might have on business. The local white establishment consisted of realists whose acceptance of desegregation did not include endorsement of integration. Realtors feared that whites, even white students, would be reluctant to rent apartments previously occupied by blacks, especially if these were furnished. Although it was 1968 and not 1956, Tuscaloosa was still in Alabama.

In August, with their impatience increasing, the AAA followed up with two more demands, the first of which urged President Rose to prevail on faculty and staff to use the word "Negro" rather than "nigra" when referring to African Americans. The other called on Coach Bryant to integrate the football team.[42]

Bureaucratic imperatives and the university's propensity for referring difficult issues to committees impeded rapid decision making. Nevertheless, Alabama tried. In addition to the two courses in African American history, the university dispatched an English professor to a seminar at Cazenovia College in New York to help him put together a black literature course. It also compiled a list of African American professors who might be interested in teaching at Alabama.

By August it was getting late to recruit faculty, regardless of race, for the fall semester. With courses set in catalogues, most professors wouldn't switch jobs knowing the impact it would have on the losing institution. Furthermore, in 1968, with George Wallace strutting on the national political stage and almost certain to return to Alabama politics, enticing black scholars to Tuscaloosa would have been challenging.

The issue that most rankled Bama's African American students, however, involved recruiting black athletes. In August, AAA president Edward Nall figuratively climbed Mount Sinai to voice their concerns directly to Coach Bryant. The Bear spoke, not from a burning bush, but ex cathedra nonetheless. The assistant David Mathews dispatched to observe the encounter reported, "Coach Bryant went on the offensive. He made the entire conversation a one-sided affair." Bryant spoke kindly as he assured Nall of his commitment to recruiting outstanding athletes regardless of race. He told him that in the spring they offered basketball scholarships to two black prospects but were turned down.[43]

At the end of the semester, during the first week in December, the AAA held a conference focused on the theme, "Black Unity Is Black Strength." Chairman John Cashin of the National Democratic Party of Alabama addressed the need to establish "black identity." Johnny Parham, director of youth activities for the National Urban League, suggested roles African American students might play within the University of Alabama.[44]

Turning Tides at Home and in Vietnam

The semester ended on a down note for the Crimson Tide. Its 8–2 record wasn't good enough to secure a top ten poll standing, therefore the twelfth-ranked Tide headed to the Gator Bowl, what many Bama fans considered a second-tier bid. There Alabama faced the Missouri Tigers, the Big Eight Conference runner-up and, as such, disdained by the Bama faithful as an "also-ran" from a lesser conference and unworthy of playing a team that lost only two games by a total of three points. On the last afternoon of 1968, the also-ran Tigers ran over the Crimson Tide by a score of 31–10.[45]

At the end of 1968, American troop levels in Vietnam climbed toward 550,000. In November, Richard Nixon defeated Vice President Hubert H. Humphrey to win the White House by the thinnest of margins, doing so in part by intimating he had a "secret plan" to end the war. President Nixon promised "peace with honor" and also vowed to bring the troops home by January 1973, the end of his first term.

The strategy turned to air power to cover the withdrawal. Another Tet-style offensive, if it occurred, might slow down troop reductions by making it politically unpalatable. To prevent such an attack, the plan called for bombing the infiltration corridors running through Laos and Cambodia and then into South Vietnam. Before it was over, American aircraft dropped nearly three million tons of bombs on the Ho Chi Minh Trail, while B-52s bombed supply caches and troop concentrations along the border between South Vietnam and Cambodia. Because Laos and Cambodia were neutral countries, the bombing was classified "Top Secret." Bombing on such a scale could not be concealed and when revealed it reinvigorated the antiwar movement when dwindling draft quotas and troop withdrawals threatened to detract from its urgency.

From Cheerleader to Radical

Carol Ann Self served as the 1964 band sponsor as a sophomore and was a cheerleader during her junior and senior years. She was easily recognizable because while the smallest of four female cheerleaders, she jumped higher. Also during her sophomore year, the Pi Kappa Phi's selected Carol as their "Star," their fraternity sweetheart. Additionally, as a junior and senior, she represented her sorority as a member of the Army ROTC sponsor squad. In the minds of many, Carol Self epitomized the ideal Capstone coed.

In the fall of 1964, deeply disturbed over the humiliation heaped on rush candidates, Carol and her roommate, Ann Brownback, refused to participate in rush-associated activities. The following spring, when Carol and Ann talked about joining the protests in Selma, their sorority threatened to lift their pins. When, after graduating in 1967, she arranged a date for a younger sorority sister with an African American student, the sorority threatened the sister with expulsion.

Carol and Ann Brownback spent the summer of 1967 in Ann's Volkswagen bus touring the United States and Mexico. Upon returning to Tuscaloosa, Carol entered graduate school to study speech pathology. Ann's dating Ralph Knowles drew Carol into Bama's small group of campus activists, where she met and befriended Ralph's little sister, Cheryl. In November 1967, Carol joined the McCarthy for President campaign where she met Jack Drake, whose intelligence and independence attracted her. Attraction turned to fascination and then to love. Shortly after Jack returned from the 1968 Democratic convention in Chicago, the former cheerleader became engaged to the leading campus radical. They married on May 31, 1969, the day after Jack Drake graduated from law school. Miss Alabama was going rogue.[46]

Frank Rose Resigns

In September 1968, a member of the national board of the Urban League wrote Frank Rose to commend him for his moral courage and for "Making Alabama a place of mutual respect and progress for the citizens of the South." Rose responded, "This week I am beginning my twelfth year at the University of Alabama, and in some ways it seems as if it has been a hundred years. While I have grown weary of having to fight so much, I still feel that I cannot leave at the present time."[47]

The summer of 1968 was not good for American college and university presidents. According to the *Chronicle of Higher Education*, an estimated three hundred institutions of higher education were seeking new presidents, eighty of them major universities. Presidents exiting the halls of academe often cited difficulties dealing with campus disturbances as a primary reason.[48]

On January 27, 1969, President Rose joined them by submitting his letter of resignation to Governor Brewer and the University of Alabama Board of Trustees. "I am resigning to become Chairman of the Board of General Computing Corporation and President of the Education, Health and Research Foundation." Rose asked that his resignation become effective on September 5, 1969, marking twelve years to the day since he accepted the job at Alabama.[49] Of the twenty-two presidents that had headed the university since 1831, Rose's tenure ranked third in length.

Frank Rose prepared the university for his departure by building a solid corps of leaders and administrators to carry on. He had recruited Paul Bryant and C. M. Newton, who turned around the Capstone's two major athletic teams and brought in Raymond McLain as vice president for academic affairs. He also groomed, mentored, and positioned David Mathews as a possible successor. President Rose concluded his letter of resignation, "If I were not satisfied that the transition to new leadership can be a smooth one, I could not in conscience leave."[50]

Rose's resignation came as no surprise to associates and friends who knew how heavily the demands of the presidency weighed upon him. His struggles with George Wallace and the legislature burdened Rose most, the former more than the latter. While at many universities it was student discord that drove presidents from office, Frank Rose did not consider the university's small cadre of dissidents particularly troublesome. "They have had their heyday," he told the *Tuscaloosa News*, "The majority of students are aware that this trouble is the work of a handful, and the faculty members are aware of the dangers of anarchy."[51]

The overwhelming preponderance of personal correspondence indicates the primary source of Frank Rose's discontent, starting in 1963 and deepening for five years, was George Wallace and his supporters. Rose viewed campus dissenters through "rose-tinted glasses," insisting, as per the quote above, that they were few in number and not very influential. His strategy of caution and accommodation frustrated progressive-minded students and faculty alike. Rose's willingness to stand up for academic freedom, as in the two threats posed by speaker ban bill advocates and his refusal to endorse Lurleen Wallace's effort to take over Alabama's public school boards irritated more conservative—and potentially powerful—elements in the state. After the second speaker ban showdown, Rose's caution increased as evidenced by the decidedly tough stand he took in resisting DSO's effort to bring in a group of truly radical speakers, as well as the not so subtle pressure he placed on the Emphasis '68 committee to withdraw their invitation to William Sloane Coffin. While Rose had his supporters among alumni and in other quarters, he had critics both from a growing number of frustrated elements within the institution on one side and the troublesome conservative elements on the other. Additionally, there was the likelihood of another George Wallace administration.

"Om" with a Southern Lilt

The search for a new president provided an opportunity for campus activists to extend their power. In February, Bill Moody, student director of the Experimental College, drew up handbills announcing a meeting to form a committee to explore ways to participate in the upcoming presidential search. Accordingly, Jack Drake and Ralph Knowles took the proposal to John Blackburn who approached the trustees. Drake and Knowles were both surprised and pleased when the board agreed to their request. The devil was in the details.

Experimental College students selected Drake and Knowles as delegates. The Afro-American Association weighed in, making the case for a black representative. SGA produced its own plan, one that didn't include Drake, Knowles, or a black student. Instead, Joe Espy and AWS president Jerrianne Hammock would serve as primary delegates with two SGA members as alternates. Students from the Experimental College rejected SGA's plan, formed the "Concerned Students" (CS) group, and then passed a resolution demanding SGA accept their delegates.

On Monday, February 17, SGA met behind closed and locked doors in their offices at the Alabama Union to hear representatives of various student groups voice concerns and offer suggestions. After fifty or more CS members poured through an unlocked side door into the meeting room, someone phoned the campus police. Demonstrators greeted Chief Rayfield, Colonel Leigh, and four officers with, "Who called the pigs?" and "It's the Gestapo!" They then began humming "om," a supposedly mystical word able to put the soul at ease. Colonel Leigh had other ideas for achieving contentment when he barked, "Okay kids. Let's wrap this up. I have a basketball game to attend."[52] The humming protestors left peacefully, their om floating on a distinctly southern lilt.

The following night Drake held a meeting to consolidate the Concerned Students into the "Union of Students" or "US," to work on the delegation to the presidential search. New constituencies weighed in. The unchartered Students for a Democratic Society joined AAA in demanding representation. Dissent was spreading.

President Rose, meanwhile, instructed Joe Espy to coordinate with SGA presidents at the Huntsville and Birmingham extensions in selecting four primary and four alternate representatives: two from Tuscaloosa and one from each of the extensions, along with a like number of alternates. Rose also knew that the trustees had limited student participation to the initial screening of candidates with further deliberations, interviews, and the selection conducted solely by trustees. When that news reached Jack Drake, he launched a petition drive that accumulated 2,600 signatures, which Joe Espy refused to validate, claiming some signatures appeared several times. Drake admitted that was true but also unavoidable.[53] In the end, the students' role in the search was limited to reviewing resumes. This increased the growing level of frustration.

Final Scenes

In late March, Jack Drake turned his attention to the SGA elections. Four decades later, Drake admitted, "I knew I wouldn't win. . . . I ran for the hell of it."[54] After he used the word "shit" in a *Crimson-White* interview, the paper's editor published an apology and affirmed her commitment to the university's policy against publishing obscenities. Sarah Healy expressed her regrets as well. "We hope Jack Drake is aware his choice of words clouded the merit of whatever he had to say."[55]

Warren Herlong and Mike Williams rounded out the top of the ticket. On April 1, Herlong garnered 1,481 votes to Williams's 1,429 and Drake's 674, eliminating Drake and leading to a runoff that Herlong won handily. The top spot at SGA passed back into liberal hands.[56]

In April, Frank Rose received a letter from the University of Denver asking him to suggest a candidate for vice chancellor for student affairs. Rose recommended John Blackburn, who after earning his masters at the University of Colorado briefly taught at the air force's intelligence officer training school located at Lowry Air Force Base near Denver and enjoyed living there.[57] In his strong endorsement, Rose noted the role Blackburn's "wise counsel" played in bringing about peaceful desegregation.[58]

On the morning of April 22, 1969, David Mathews escorted Governor Albert Brewer from the airport in Northport to the President's Mansion, where Frank Rose welcomed him and his party to Governor's Day. At ten o'clock, a nineteen-gun salute greeted the governor's arrival at the reviewing stand on the Quadrangle. After the parade, cadets gathered in Memorial Coliseum, where, following Governor Brewer's remarks, outgoing SGA president Joe Espy introduced his successor, Warren Herlong.

A few days later, Carleton K. Butler retired as director of the Million Dollar Band. In September, majorettes supplanted Miss Alabama, the lone band sponsor cradling a bouquet of chrysanthemums as she strutted alongside the drum major at the head of the band. Some Alabama alumni sensed another tradition floating away on the winds of change.[59]

Late on the afternoon of June 1, 1969, President Frank Rose led the faculty procession into Memorial Coliseum. The Reverend George M. Murray, Bishop of the Diocese of Alabama of the Protestant Episcopal Church, delivered the invocation. Executive Vice President F. David Mathews then introduced Judge Thomas S. Lawson, chairman of the board of trustees. He, in turn, introduced the commencement speaker, Dr. Frank Anthony Rose.[60]

8
In Defense of Reason

A New President

Starting in June 1969, the mood on campus shifted. When women's fashions became less conventional, the Capstone's female students, led by AWS, called for an end to dress regulations. The administration responded by allowing women to wear slacks and jeans to class. Their new look, at times bizarre and eccentric, echoed rumblings of rebellion among a student body caught between the rhythmic sounds of the Supremes and the psychedelic musings of Jefferson Airplane.

It would take more than a change in the women's dress code to toss the mantle of tradition that rested over the Capstone. Despite relative youth, David Mathews, who projected the aura of the quintessential southern gentleman, understood the compelling force of tradition; how it made people do the necessary, even when it was difficult or unpopular. He also appreciated how tradition sustained institutions and their leaders through tribulation and turmoil.

On Thursday, June 5, 1969, the university trustees gathered in a recessed meeting of the board called by President Pro tempore Thomas S. Lawson. A major university had offered its presidency to David Mathews and was pressuring him for a decision. Mathews already had turned down several offers, including one the previous year to become vice president for academic affairs at Elmira College in New York.

First, the board discussed various plans for restructuring the state system and adopted what they called the "Arizona model" with presidents at the campus in Huntsville and Birmingham as well as one in Tuscaloosa. Mathews, by then the leading candidate to succeed Rose, stated his agreement with the plan and then excused himself while the board turned their attention to the primary reason for the meeting. While some expressed reservations concerning

Mathews' relative youth, none doubted his capabilities or intelligence. Additionally, Frank Rose had made known his support for the Mathews' candidacy. After trustee Ernest Stone, the state superintendent of education, described Mathews as "the brightest star on the educational horizon in the entire Southland," trustee Dan McCall moved he be named president. Trustee Stone seconded the motion, which the board unanimously adopted. After Mathews accepted the offer, the board agreed not to make their decision public until presidents could be selected for the other campuses and related administrative matters resolved.[1]

On Monday, June 16, when Governor Brewer announced the appointment, David Mathews and his wife Mary were at his side. He also stated that while the trustees had not yet decided on a president for the Huntsville extension, Joseph Volker was their choice for the Birmingham campus. Under the Arizona model, the new system provided independence for each institution.[2] Additionally, the three presidents formed a "Council of Presidents" that was to meet monthly, with the chairmanship rotating annually.[3]

At thirty-three, David Mathews was the youngest of the twenty-three presidents in the university's 138-year history. Mathews not only radiated youthful exuberance, he embraced youth by elevating Larry T. McGehee, a graduate of Transylvania College with a doctorate in religion from Yale University, to the executive vice presidency. McGehee was six months younger than Mathews. James Wilder, the director of University Relations, was twenty-nine years old.[4]

Students welcomed David Mathews. They identified with his youth and believed he sympathized with their idealism. Even Bama's student activists seemed ready to give the new president a chance. After all, hadn't he encouraged youthful dissent at the meeting of student leaders four years earlier? Hadn't Mathews worked with supportive elements in Montgomery to thwart the most recent speaker ban bill initiative? Furthermore, students who took Mathews' American history course knew he was an inspiring, if also demanding, teacher. While Frank Rose urged the pursuit of academic excellence, David Mathews required it.

The faculty divided over the selection. Professors who remembered David Mathews as a student recalled his intelligence. Some felt uneasy about innovations he pushed as executive vice president, especially New College. Others saw Mathews as Rose's protégé and may have presumed sycophancy. There were faculty members who questioned his credentials, as if a PhD from Columbia University's Teachers College was not quite up to a doctorate earned in history or the hard sciences. Younger professors either resented his rapid rise or anticipated the dawning of the Age of Aquarius.

Generally, expectations for the young man from Grove Hill, Alabama, ran high. Nevertheless, as students inclined to push dissent too far soon discovered, limits bounded the new president's tolerance. His foremost responsibilities included protecting the interests of the university and the safety of its students. Like his predecessor, President Mathews answered to several constituencies: trustees, alumni, the state legislature, and the people of Alabama who looked to the university to educate and prepare future citizens. He also bore the mantle of tradition. Some thought he did so imperiously.

Poised for a New Era

The university's construction program totaled thirty million dollars million in projects under way or planned. Over thirteen thousand students were expected to enroll in September. Academic initiatives included a Master of Arts in Latin American studies, an African American studies course, and expanded cooperation in graduate programs with Auburn. Additionally, the School of Social Work received accreditation in the spring, allowing the university to confer twenty-three Master of Social Work degrees at the May commencement.[5]

Building projects included an eight-story addition to the Amelia Gayle Gorgas Library, scheduled for completion in the winter of 1970. President Mathews and other administrators looked forward to moving into the Rose Administration Building at the end of the fall semester. Married students had a new thirteen-story residence housing three hundred families. In March 1970, bids would go out for the new student union building containing a variety of offices, dining facilities, meeting rooms, game rooms, a ballroom, post office, and bookstore. Bama's Greeks were building as well, with housing starts for three fraternities and three sororities.[6]

In September, 13,034 students enrolled at the Capstone, 5,029 females and 8,005 males, a 7 percent increase over the previous year. The total included 10,772 undergraduates, 1,937 graduate students, and 325 men and women enrolled in law school. Blacks made up less than 2 percent of the student body.[7]

There's a Storm Coming

As David Mathews settled into the president's office, across the campus a storm was brewing even with the promise of a new day. Integrating the small number of black students into the university community proved difficult. Although most white students accepted desegregation, few embraced integration. Black students' complaints about some faculty using terms like "nigra" rather than "Negro" indicated the problem extended beyond the student body. Racial distinctions mattered more than class differences since white students like Jack Drake and Don Siegelman, young men from working-class backgrounds, became campus leaders. Most students found racial interaction novel and awkward. Additionally, some black students had to overcome legacies associated with attending segregated public schools that were far more separate than equal.

The color barrier cracked by desegregation remained unchipped in Crimson Tide athletic programs, including that of its vaunted football team. Andrew Pernell, one of two blacks who participated in the A-Day Game in 1967, tried out again in the spring of 1969. He was offered a scholarship, but could not accept it since he already had a grant totaling $2,070 from the United Presbyterian Church. Southeastern Conference regulations forbade students on athletic scholarships from receiving other grants. Furthermore, had he remained on the squad, National Collegiate Athletic Assoiciation (NCAA) rules would have counted the church scholarship against the number allowed for the team, thus depriving another player of aid. Andrew dropped off the team. When in the summer of 1969, acute funding problems compelled the denomination to cut its grant to Andrew Pernell, by then, no more football scholarships were available.[8]

Presbyterian Life, the denomination's magazine, published an article detailing Pernell's plight. The author, Wilmina M. Roland, wrote, "Andy was academically eligible for the team; he was a good athlete. But a varsity football player who was black could be regarded as an embarrassment to the University of Alabama. Whether this had anything to do with Andy being told he could not be on the team because he had received another scholarship is a matter of speculation."[9]

Professor Willard F. Gray, chairman of the Faculty Committee on Intercollegiate Athletics wrote Richard J. Cadigan, editor of *Presbyterian Life*, pointing out that Andy's problem was not that the university was unwilling to provide a football scholarship, but that the Presbyterian Church's program foundered.[10] Rowland's article may have been an attempt to shift blame, or perhaps revive the scholarship program through increased donations. Unfortunately, Andrew Pernell suffered.

The first African American to accept a varsity scholarship, Wendell Hudson, a star basketball player from Parker High School in Birmingham, enrolled in September 1969 and moved into Paul W. Bryant Hall, the athletic dormitory reserved for football and basketball players. Until the autumn of 1971, freshmen were excluded from varsity competition, so Hudson spent the 1969–70 season on the freshman team.[11] The University of Alabama desegregated its athletic programs cautiously. In part, this was because many Alabama fans were not as accepting of desegregation as the faculty and students at the Capstone. Additionally, top black athletes received offers from northern, midwestern, or western institutions where black athletes were already accepted.

Such deliberation frustrated black students. On July 3, 1969, the Afro-American Association sued Coach Bryant, President Mathews, the University of Alabama Board of Trustees, and, for good measure, Robert Finch, the secretary of Health, Education, and Welfare. The suit charged that not offering black athletes scholarships violated the thirteenth and fourteenth amendments to the US Constitution.[12] Athletic Department records indicated that five scholarships were offered to black athletes in 1968, but none accepted. In 1969, Wendell Hudson was the only player to accept one of six scholarships offered to black athletes. After the 1969 high school football season, Alabama extended ten offers to black prospects. Only one, Wilbur Jackson, accepted. John Mitchell, after two years at Eastern Arizona Junior College, also received a scholarship to play on the 1971 team.[13]

Although the AAA dropped the lawsuit, their willingness to seek legal recourse kept the university's Athletic Department's feet to the fire on integrating sports, especially football. The slump in gridiron fortunes between 1968 and 1970 also added urgency to the process. Coach Bryant needed—and wanted—talented players regardless of color.

Starting in September, the *Crimson-White* gave voice to African American students with a weekly feature titled, "On the Black Front," written by R. Edward Brown. He started his first piece with, "Members of the Afro-American Association are black students who were unsuccessfully weaved into the main fabric of the University community. They have experienced multi-forms of racial injustice. . . . To quote Eldridge Cleaver . . . 'there's a storm coming.'"[14]

Women's Issues

For years, President Rose dealt with in loco parentis rules by talking with AWS representatives and then referring their concerns to committees for further study. Female students impatient for change knew this for what it was: stalling. President Mathews moved rapidly by comparison, although not quickly enough for AWS leaders.

David Mathews shared many of Frank Rose's reservations. He feared that drastically modifying curfew hours posed major challenges to sexual mores extant in Alabama's households and also might affect support in the legislature. Furthermore, curfews did not rank as high as other issues on his list of desired reforms. In a handwritten note titled, "Evaluation of Critical Steps in the Curfew Crisis," Mathews suggested meeting with alumni and parents in Alabama's major cities and during homecoming weekend to explain possible changes to curfew polices.[15] Mathews spent his limited reform capital judiciously.

The administration used the September "Parents Newsletter" to explain that beginning in October, female students twenty-one years of age or older would be granted self-regulated hours. Females under twenty-one with senior standing could participate with parental consent, something that applied to about one hundred women. Eligible women could check out nonduplicable keys, which they could use to enter their places of residence at any hour and would be due back at their dormitories or sorority houses by noon the next day.

Interviewed in the *Crimson-White*, AWS president Lois Cobb, an advocate for ending all curfew regulations, called the changes "a step in the right direction." An editorial in the same issue dubbed the concessions "a pittance," and accused the administration of "putting students off with pats on the back."[16] In late October, the Social Rules Committee of the AWS House of Representatives passed a bill extending self-regulated hours to all senior, junior, sophomore, and second-semester freshmen women without parental consent and to first-semester freshmen coeds with their parents' approval.[17]

An AWS poll taken among sorority houses and dormitories found 2,403 coeds favored ending all curfews and 296 against, with 96 abstentions. The vote in sorority houses was closer than in dorms, although only two sororities voted against abolishing curfews. In November, the university made another concession by extending Sunday through Thursday curfew from eleven o'clock to midnight.[18] According to the self-regulated hours plan, juniors with parental consent could participate starting in the spring semester.

Developments in the Antiwar Movement

The Federal Bureau of Investigation reported that by late 1969, campus antiwar groups had become more committed to violence. According to the FBI, the threat focused on disrupting ROTC and impeding defense-related research. The bureau further noted that in 1968, antiwar demonstrations took place on 225 campuses and that 61 involved arson or bombing. Two hundred buildings were seized or occupied, with damages totaling more than three million dollars. Over 4,000 people were arrested, most of them students. There were 125 serious injuries reported and one death.[19]

The University Coalition (UC) for the October 15 Vietnam War Moratorium presented the Mathews administration with its first concerted challenge. A group consisting of the American Civil Liberties Union (ACLU), the Afro-American Association, National Democratic Party of Alabama, Experimental College, Democratic Students Organization, the Southern Legal Action Movement, and the local chapter of the AAUP asked the administration to dismiss classes for the moratorium. The Arts and Sciences Faculty Senate lobbied the administration to allow individual professors to decide whether to hold classes on October 15. The UC, meanwhile, lined up a series of lectures and panel discussions to be held throughout the day.[20]

The moratorium failed to gain traction with most Alabama students. One told a *Crimson-White* reporter he thought classes should continue because many students supported the war. Another opined, "The art people will be the only demonstrators." Jenny Osterman, a junior majoring in psychology, stated, "The moratorium won't have any effect on this campus because of the general apathy toward the war in Vietnam."[21] After a long debate, SGA voted to endorse the moratorium and asked that all classes be dismissed.[22]

The administration did not cancel classes but it approved moratorium activities as long as they did not interfere with normal activities or endanger the safety of students. Speakers on the morning of October 15 included Democratic senator Joe Tydings of Maryland and James Martin, a member of the Alabama National Republican Committee. At an afternoon session held in Foster Auditorium, history professors Russell Bryant, Hugh Ragsdale, and Ron Robel spoke, along with Jay Murphy from the law school.[23]

Life among the Nondissenters

Dissent, new to the Capstone, constituted only a part of the cultural landscape in the fall of 1969. At the early September conclave of student leaders Mathews, who four years earlier told their predecessors to expect, welcome, and embrace dissent, cautioned that many Alabamians had an unfavorable impression of the university. He urged them to "take the battle to the public" by meeting with parents and groups to explain from their perspective what was happening at the state's flagship academic institution.[24] David Mathews knew that campus unrest put administrators on the defensive. He also understood universities, being halls of reason where questioning is fundamental to academic freedom, were disadvantaged when dealing with dissent.

President Mathews had other issues he needed to address. In early October, he scrapped A-STRIDE because it had failed to produce one major contribution. Mathews shifted the fund-raising focus to sustained giving from corporations and wealthy individuals, coupled with expanding the number of alumni making smaller annual contributions. Mathews believed contributing alumni felt invested in the university.[25]

With Mathews as president, the New College concept moved rapidly to fruition and, after the president secured financial support, McLain started recruiting faculty and students. New College attempted to foster intellectual growth through the realization of individual potential. Mathews believed students should learn by thinking about and dealing with principles and concepts rather than by memorizing data, the norm in traditional approaches to undergraduate education. He envisioned a small, flexible structure employing highly individualized study and learning programs drawn from scholars across the faculty. While regular classes accounted for 70 to 75 percent of a student's total academic experience, the New College concept supplemented the curriculum by providing individually tailored courses along with internships and apprenticeships.[26]

Critics who dubbed New College "another honors program," were wrong. Unlike traditional honors programs, New College sought students with varying degrees of academic achievement. Applicants took an entrance examination, participated in an interview, and then submitted a resume detailing their educational history and academic goals. Only a relatively small number opted for New College, most sticking with the existing curriculum. All, however, were to a degree affected by the cultural shift increasingly apparent on campus.

The counterculture, especially music and drugs, affected Greeks and independents alike. The Greek section of the 1970 *Corolla* differed from earlier editions. Every sorority and fraternity featured group photos rather than the individual portraits of sisters and brothers, the young women in look-alike blouses and the young men in sports coats and ties. By 1970, boys wore their hair longer in the style of the day, but none were unkempt and there were no beards among these Greeks. Most fraternities and some sororities posed according to themes. Sigma Alpha Epsilon's theme was "men at leisure." A couple of brothers reclined on beach blankets. One, dressed as a yachtsman stood in a rubber boat while another, sporting an Australian bush hat, posed with a hunting rifle. The brothers of Delta Kappa Epsilon, dressed in sports coats and suits, turned their backs to face the house while a lone African American in work clothes faced the camera. The Kappa Delta sisters posed in costumes as they stood on or in front of a railroad trestle. One sister wore a football uniform, another dressed like a soldier, there was a southern belle and several donned hippie garb.[27] In April 1970, the IFC passed a resolution condemning the Machine.[28]

The Receding Tide

The 35–10 shellacking Missouri administered in the Gator Bowl started a two-year slump for the Crimson Tide that rendered 12 wins against 10 losses and a tie. In the 1969 season opener, Alabama struggled to post a 17–14 victory over Virginia Tech, a team considered a lesser opponent. For Bama fans, it was an unsettling start to an unsatisfying couple of seasons.

In October, the Tide lost back-to-back games, first falling to lowly Vanderbilt 14–10 and then to Tennessee 41–10. The next month, LSU beat Alabama at Legion Field by a score of 20–15. Auburn made it an unsatisfactory six wins and four-loss season by thrashing Alabama 49–26. For Tide faithful who thought the Gator Bowl was a step down, going to the Liberty Bowl in Memphis must have seemed like a tumble from the porch, one made all the more painful when the Colorado Buffalos prevailed 47–33. Six wins against five losses underscored a new reality for Tide fans: mediocrity.

College football celebrated its one hundredth anniversary in 1969. To mark the occasion, *Sporting News* asked one hundred prominent figures involved with the game to name its ten greatest coaches. Notre Dame's Knute Rockne ranked at the top. Coach Bryant, the only coach still active among the top ten, placed sixth. At the end of the 1969 season, his peers named Bryant "College Football's Coach of the Decade." With a record of eighty-five wins, twelve losses and six ties, he deserved the honor. Five of the twelve losses came in the last season of the decade.[29]

In the 1975 autobiography titled *Bear*, Coach Bryant reflected on those lean seasons with self-effacing modesty. "Everything that's bad with Alabama football is my fault. . . . I made a mistake with Kenny Stabler. I should have disciplined him but I didn't. Things went downhill from there. . . . I could feel control slipping away."[30] More was involved, some of it attributable to Bryant's inflexibility toward cultural changes and, for that matter, changes in college football. Bryant won with small, fast, tough players when other teams fielded big, tough, but slow players. By the end of the decade there were a lot of big, tough, fast players, and few played for Alabama. Furthermore, many were black.

While the presence of an imposing figure like Paul Bryant made the football program seem like an independent fiefdom, it was very much a part of the university. Although Rose, Mathews, and Blackburn attempted to work blacks into campus life, a challenge in itself, Coach Bryant's interest remained focused on winning football games. His approach had been to emphasize teamwork over individual performance. Fitting into the mold was essential and the occasional "odd ball," like Joe Willie Namath from Beaver Falls, Pennsylvania, found assimilation difficult. From Bryant's perspective, winning took precedence over affecting social progress. Even after it became evident Alabama was missing a pool of talented players, the time had to be right. Two mediocre seasons hastened the inevitable. Was it soon enough? In Alabama of the 1960s, historical legacies complicated and bedeviled progress. Perceived or real, there were limits to what could be done.

Additionally, the desire to coach in the National Football League distracted Bryant throughout the 1969 season while he and Miami Dolphin owner Joe Robbie negotiated a contract, which Bryant signed. In January 1970, Bryant changed his mind. Robbie let him off the hook because he was considering the young coach of the Baltimore Colts, Don Shula. The headline in the *Tuscaloosa News* read, "Bryant to Stay at Bama."[31]

Historian John David Briley, in his 2006 book, *Career in Crisis*, interviewed Bryant assistant coaches Clem Gryska, Dude Hennessey, and Pat Dye, all of whom believed recruiting players from outside Alabama and its neighboring states backfired. They felt recruits from states beyond the South were more likely to quit than those from Alabama or the surrounding states. Perhaps it was the unrelenting heat that lingers into October, making practices that start in August hot and hellish, the university's conservative social culture, or Bryant's "it's my way or the highway" attitude.

As Briley indicated, it was easier for a youngster from outside Alabama, or the neighboring states, to quit than it was for a local player. In places like Iowa, California, or New Jersey, where Bryant lacked iconic stature, friends and neighbors might ask, "What did you expect in a racist place like Alabama where the coach is named for a fearsome animal?" Down home, however, quitting on the Bear was not likely to be forgotten or forgiven.

After a decade of victories, despite grumbling over the losses, Alabama football rested on a solid fan base. Homecoming, held the first week in October, pitted the Tide against the Miami Hurricanes. The three finalists for homecoming queen included Diane Kirksey, a candidate sponsored by the Afro-

American Association. Although she didn't win, her presence on the home-coming court represented another breach in the color barrier.[32]

Dissent Builds, Student Power Grows

In September, the Alabama News Bureau published an article contending Alabama students were "selecting the route of 'responsible student power.'" It quoted SGA president Herlong who boasted students at the Capstone abjured "the trail of violence," while AWS president Cobb stated that while she and other coeds wanted all curfews eliminated, they were working with the administration to resolve the issue.[33] In September 1969, there was an air of cooperation between students and the administration. Events in October changed the climate, by November it turned nasty.

During the summer, the administration invited Warren Herlong, Lois Cobb, and Diane Kirksey to join a screening committee to help select John Blackburn's replacement. In November, when the administration announced that Joab Thomas, the interim dean, had been promoted into the job, Lois Cobb organized a petition drive in protest. Campus leaders, including Bill Kilgore, editor of the *Crimson-White*; Ed Still, *Crimson-White* managing editor; Ella Solomon, president of Pan-Hellenic; and Jim Zeigler of the SGA senate all supported the petition accusing the administration of ignoring students in the selection process. An editorial in the *Crimson-White* claimed Thomas, a biology professor, lacked the experience of someone like Glenn Stillion and opined Stillion should have been selected instead. Sarah Healy, whose tenure as dean of women antedated Blackburn's arrival as assistant dean by three years, also applied for the job and was passed over. Deeply disappointed, Healy soldiered on for another year as associate dean for student development and then retired.[34]

Assaults on Reason

In the second year of operation, in addition to offering courses titled "The Body as a Religious Symbol," and "The Homosexual Revolution," Experimental College also provided draft counseling and scheduled Sunday afternoon rock concerts on the Quadrangle. Thinking it had strayed from its original purpose, every faculty advisor cut their ties, leaving Experimental College in the hands of its student chairman, Bill Moody. He envisioned Experimental College as an instrument for pushing an extremely liberal social and educational agenda.[35] At the start of the fall semester, Experimental College held its rock concerts on the Quadrangle in front of the main library but then moved subsequent concerts to the smaller Woods Hall Quad. At a meeting in early October, SGA president Warren Herlong assured the administration all "Woods Hall Quads," as they were dubbed, would be conducted in conformity with university regulations.[36] The first three conformed.

On the last Sunday in October, Glenn Stillion played the role of "duty dean" at the fourth Quad billed as a "Do Your Own Thing Jam Session." The agreed-upon time for ending the concert was five o'clock in the afternoon. At midafternoon, Stillion called in campus police to remove tables set up for selling leather goods and other hand-made items in violation of university regulations covering vendors. He also noticed students roasting hotdogs over small campfires while others removed chairs and tables from classrooms. Promptly at five o'clock, Stillion ordered the power lines feeding electric guitars and amplifiers shut down. Minutes later, students hauled in a generator, hooked it up, and continued to rock.

When the campus police arrived, determined rockers formed a protective cordon around the generator. Stillion called off the cops, averting what might have devolved into a much nastier situation. With the concert continuing into the night, Stillion located Bill Moody and told him what had transpired jeopardized future concerts. On Monday, the *Crimson-White* published Moody's defiant response, "Students may have defied the University, but they have defied only an arbitrary rule. . . . There will be more Quads, whether permitted by the University or not."[37]

On Monday evening, Moody led fifty or more protestors to the President's Mansion to speak with David Mathews. They lingered for half an hour until Mary Mathews told them her husband was working in Carmichael Hall. The group moved there only to find the door to the presidential suite locked. They then staged an impromptu sit-in by squatting in the hallway. Larry McGehee emerged, talked with students, and then conveyed their demand for a meeting to David Mathews. Determined not to be intimidated, Mathews refused to speak with the demonstrators that night but suggested a meeting the next afternoon in the Alabama Union.[38]

Anticipating a large turnout, the administration moved the venue to Morgan Hall's auditorium where, at four o'clock, more than five hundred students and a sprinkling of faculty gathered. Warren Herlong opened by asking that questions be confined to the issue at hand. Bill Moody, after declaring rock concerts a "basic human right," recounted his version of Monday night's events at the President's Mansion and in the hallway outside the presidential suite. He claimed only twenty-five or thirty were involved and that they were not expecting to find Mrs. Mathews and the children at home alone. He added, "When we saw them, they kind of frightened us."[39]

Warren Herlong then introduced President Mathews who began his remarks with an attempt at levity. "First, I'd like to apologize to Mr. Moody and others. I can assure you my wife and children didn't mean to frighten you." After allowing for a few seconds of subdued laughter, the president got to the point. David Mathews spoke forcefully rather than loudly, and with what his admirers might call "graceful deliberation" and his detractors saw as condescension. First, Mathews offered that no reasonable person could object to students gathering on the Quad to listen to music. He then listed his concerns, including the use of campfires as posing a fire hazard and the noise that disturbed students in the library. After he pronounced the removal of furniture from classrooms "unacceptable," students responded with groans of "Aw, come on!" and "That didn't happen!"

Mathews continued, his voice calm, as if instructing students that term papers must be handed in on time. "While I believe you had no malicious intent, . . . what your actions said was, 'There are more of us than there are of you.'" Shouts of "Come on!" and "Not true!" interrupted the president, who continued to focus on their supposed intent to intimidate. One student moaned in response, "We were going to burn down the University with flowers." President Mathews then invited questions.

Someone asked if Quads might be held on Saturday afternoons and nights, asserting that rock concerts made no more noise than football games or fraternity parties. Moody responded that bands donated services on Sunday but played for pay at fraternity gigs on Friday and Saturday nights. When a student asked who decided to cut off the power at five o'clock, an exasperated Mathews replied, "We are off the fundamental point." He then left by a side entrance. Bill Moody ended the meeting by declaring the issue a symptom of greater problems.

Two generations, separated not so much by years as by expectations, talked past one another. Students wanted music on Sunday afternoons and assurances that they could have it because it was "their right." President Mathews was less concerned with the concerts than he was the disregard for rules and their attempts to intimidate. On Monday evening and Tuesday afternoon, students had Woodstock on their minds. David Mathews had February 1956 on his. President Mathews agreed to continue the Quads provided participants observed the rules. He made SGA responsible for ensuring no drugs or alcoholic beverages were involved.

This confrontation marked the first major student challenge to the new president and many beyond the Quadrangle watched his response. Most Alabamians welcomed his strong stand. Tuscaloosa's mayor offered to put city police at the university's disposal during any future campus disorder.[40] The Chamber of Commerce and Rotary Club passed resolutions of support, the latter asked Buford Boone to deliver theirs in person. Given that Boone and Mathews both experienced campus riots in 1956, it must have gratified the young president to receive a resolution of support from the hands of the man who won a Pulitzer condemning disorder and submission to mob rule.[41] The Arts and Science Faculty Senate also passed a supportive resolution to which Iredell Jenkins attached a letter commending David Mathews on his "low-key approach."[42]

Not every student supported the dissidents. Several complained that music from the Woods Hall Quad could be heard in the library. Three coeds wrote, "To permit it to go on all afternoon and all night is an infringement to us as students."[43] A freshman from New York noted that he came to Alabama to avoid the disruptions plaguing campuses in his state. He urged firmness in dealing with students, adding, "I guarantee these 'Quad people' won't stop. They have gained one victory and they will look forward to others."[44] His warning proved prescient.

The day following the Morgan Hall confrontation, Bill Moody formed the "Steering Committee of the Peoples' Movement for Free Quad Concerts" and called a press conference. Over one hundred people attended, including reporters from three Birmingham television stations and one from the *Tuscaloosa News*. Chip Letson, the Peoples' Committee "commander of tactical forces," wore a World War II German army helmet. Buddy Hallman, self-proclaimed spiritual leader, donned a feathered Indian headdress. Doug Newby, the committee's designated "president" of the University of Alabama, dressed for the occasion in sport coat with a large paper flower poking through the lapel complemented by a flowery tie. Campus yippie leader Ernest Hallford chaired the meeting.

Hallford, a graduate student in English, proclaimed a "victory celebration" in the Union ballroom. Commander Letson declared that the university "now belongs to the students," and Newby added it would be sold to the lowest bidder. They also announced Newby's forthcoming presidential inauguration at the next Wood's Hall Quad.[45]

When President Mathews met with students in Morgan Hall, he assumed reason would prevail. SGA took a balanced view, citing "overreaction" by the administration and a segment of the student population. Attempting to provide perspective, Mathews told the media, "We have had some students express concerns about the use of the Quadrangle for rock music gatherings—we have had no Berkeley uprising." He continued, "We are very open to conversation, but we cannot allow mass action to be substituted for reason. We will be reasonable and fair, but we will also be firm in the defense of reason."[46]

As autumn continued into early November, the campus briefly quieted. Iredell Jenkins, who attended the next concert, reported the noise at Woods Hall was "almost terrifying" but hardly audible a few hundred yards away.[47] There was more to dissent than music.

On Tuesday, November 17, Ernest Hallford led thirty demonstrators intent on disrupting Army ROTC drill. The protestors carried signs and yelled, "One, two, three four, Tricky Dick end the war!" and "Two, four, six, eight, fornicate and smash the state." A few days later, Hallford and his cohorts attempted to serve eviction notices to the ROTC detachments. The deputy commander at the army detachment met the would-be evictors as they approached Tuomey Hall, accepted the notice, and then withdrew into the building. On the other side of the library, the air force detachment's deputy commander listened to the reading of the notice, turned around, and walked back inside Barnard Hall, "saluting" the yippies with a dismissive wave of his hand. Hallford taped the notice to the building's outer door. It claimed ROTC was being evicted because its instructors were academically unqualified, the military's presence threatened intellectual freedom, and that "war is not a pleasant thing."[48] It was signed by "Dr. W. Douglas Newby, PhD, LLD, DD, and LSD; President of the University of Alabama."

The next week, David Mathews declared procedures for dealing with student demonstrations inadequate and instructed Larry McGehee and Richard Thigpen to devise new ones. A few days later, early Sunday morning, November 30, vandals sprayed obscenities on fourteen campus structures. The messages varied from "Free UA" to "Students are Niggers at UA" to "Fuck UA" and "Get out ROTC." Some personal comments referenced David Mathews. Buildings defaced included Martin ten Hoor Hall, the Amelia Gayle Gorgas Library, both ROTC buildings, the new and yet-to-be occupied Rose Administration Building, Denny Chimes, and the President's Mansion. Most of the damage was removed or covered up by midmorning. The graffiti on Denny Chimes, however, required sand blasting.[49]

Other Forms of Student Engagement

Bill Mills, a student from Mobile, presided over the "U.S.A. Group." Shortly after the Woods Hall controversy subsided, the U.S.A. Group circulated a petition supporting Nixon administration policies in Vietnam. Mills planned to deliver it to Vice President Spiro Agnew when he visited Montgomery in November. According to a University News Bureau announcement, the petition gathered over five thousand signatures.[50] Bill Mills gave it to Alabama republican Jim Martin who promised to pass it on to Vice President Agnew. The number of students signing the petition more than doubled the number present at most Woods Hall Quads.

Meanwhile, Emphasis morphed from a single annual conference into a series of events, with speakers invited to campus throughout the year. In October, the new format consisted of a panel made up of three prominent African Americans: Mayor Charles Evers of Fayette, Mississippi, the brother of slain civil rights leader Medgar Evers; comedian Dick Gregory; and Sam Bradley, a politician from San Francisco.[51]

On the first Wednesday night in December, Janis Joplin performed in Memorial Coliseum. SGA program chairman Al Kitchens paid off-duty campus police time-and-a-half to provide security, hoping they would prevent nonpaying students from sneaking in. Instead of guarding entrances, the police stationed themselves near the stage, intent on arresting Janis Joplin if she said or did anything they deemed obscene. Sure enough, after spotting her boozing it up with the band in the dressing room, they threatened to arrest them all. When the officer in charge stated the university had rules prohibiting alcoholic beverages in the dressing room, Kitchens asked if the same rules applied to the presidential suite where guests routinely imbibed.

Janis Joplin opened with a rendition of "Bo Diddley." Before plunging into her second number, she yelled, "I can't help it if God made me illegal," a reference to her recent arrest in Tampa for shouting obscenities from the stage. Janis closed the show with "Piece of my Heart."[52]

Meanwhile, Emphasis chairman Tom Gordon planned to invite Abbie Hoffman to campus. In December, he contacted Hoffman's agent to start the process for a March appearance. Hoffman, convicted of instigating riots in Chicago during the 1968 Democratic Party convention, was free on bond pending appeal. The concept involved a debate between Hoffman, Senator Wayne Morse of Oregon, and George Wallace. On December 7, Warren Herlong and Tom Gordon informed Mathews that Hoffman might be speaking at the March

Emphasis program. Three days later the committee submitted Hoffman's name to the Student Life and Learning Committee, the first step in gaining approval for inviting him to campus.[53]

A New Decade

The Louisiana State University (LSU) basketball team visited Tuscaloosa on Saturday, February 7, 1970, filling Memorial Coliseum with fans eager to watch Pistol Pete Maravich and the team coached by his father, Petar "Press" Maravich. Alabama basketball reached its nadir at midseason after losing twenty-two straight SEC games. Then, on the last day of January, the Tide bested Mississippi State 95–75, sending hopes high, perhaps unreasonably so given the next opponent was LSU.

At half-time, the A Club, consisting of students who distinguished themselves in varsity athletics, inducted its new members, giving the game a celebratory note. Club members, seated near the LSU bench, reportedly heckled the visiting team even as Pistol Pete poured in a record sixty-nine points.

Despite Maravich's scoring binge, the game was close when referees ejected an LSU player for unsportsmanlike conduct. Adding to the tension, Pistol Pete and his father each received a technical foul associated with the incident. In the end, the Tide prevailed 106–104. As the LSU team walked toward their dressing room, fans pelted them with paper cups, many still containing ice and soda. When a university photographer snapped a photo of Pistol Pete and then called him a "high school player," Maravich responded with a fist to the jaw. Fans poured onto the floor. An LSU player decked a male Bama cheerleader. No one was hurt severely, but the spring semester was off to a raucous start.[54]

In February, six students entered the race for SGA president, an indication of growing interest in campus politics. John Wymer, Tony Davis, and Jim Zeigler were favored. Among the other candidates, Rich Isaacson, who boasted that he was the first person of Irish-Jewish descent to seek the office, attacked the Machine along with "drug-crazed hippies." Nolan Hatcher claimed to be an "unapologetic, pie-loving, flag-waving, clean-cut heterosexual." Mike O'Bannon touted support from the Neo-Immolationist Party, a political entity lost to history.

The Machine backed Davis, a Kappa Alpha, and Wymer, also a Greek. Zeigler ran on support for the rights of female students, better race relations, improved academics, and integrating independents into the social life of the university. Zeigler defeated Davis in a run-off.[55]

The Abbie Hoffman Affair

At the end of February, Abbie Hoffman was set to speak at Emphasis '70. On March 3, the *Tuscaloosa News* reported Hoffman would debate Senator Morse, and George Wallace, who refused to debate Hoffman, would speak immediately after the debate. The following day, Senator Morse's office phoned to say an unavoidable commitment had arisen in Oregon on March 16. Hoffman would have the stage all to himself.

That same day, David Mathews discussed the Hoffman invitation with his staff. Afterward, he phoned Governor Brewer to inform him that he was canceling Hoffman's appearance following reports of violence on campuses where Hoffman, or his associates, had spoken. Mathews warned Brewer that he might be included in a suit almost certain to be filed by ACLU on behalf of Emphasis '70. The governor said he believed the matter should be settled in the courts.[56] Mathews then announced his decision. When he did, Emphasis chairman Tom Gordon declared the committee would sue the university. Accordingly, the ACLU filed suit in the US district court asking for an injunction.[57]

The sides formed. Attorneys for the ACLU, C. Erskine Smith, Ralph Knowles, and Morris Dees, represented Emphasis. Warren Herlong, still president of SGA, cosigned the suit with Tom Gordon. They were hopeful, if only because a federal judge recently ruled in favor of Auburn students who sued after President Harry Philpot banned Yale chaplain William Sloane Coffin from campus.[58]

On the afternoon of March 5, Morris Dees met with David Mathews while he was in Montgomery on university business. Each stood firm, their friendship, going back to their student days when they taught a Sunday School class together at the First Baptist Church, notwithstanding. Dees knew Mathews would be meeting with students the next afternoon. Perhaps not so confident federal district judge Frank M. Johnson Jr. would impose the injunction, Dees sent a telegram to Warren Herlong urging him to implore students to avoid any disruptions that might prove detrimental to the ACLU's case.[59]

On Friday afternoon, students and faculty filled Morgan Hall's auditorium. Mathews took the stage and, after the noise subsided, reminded everyone of his efforts to defeat the speaker ban bill in 1967 as indicative of his past support for bringing in speakers with different points of view. Then, speaking more cautiously, Mathews declared, "I'm afraid the public feels we want to hear what is sensational rather than what is sound."[60]

Mathews explained he canceled Hoffman's invitation based on campus disturbances that followed talks by him or others associated with the Chicago Seven. A student noted that since riots had occurred at several universities after George Wallace spoke, consistency demanded his invitation also be rescinded. Mathews replied that because Wallace had spoken many times at Alabama without inciting riots, it was reasonable to expect his presence at Emphasis '70 posed no threat. At that point, Ernest Hallford brought the meeting to a culminating point by declaring, "I guarantee you that if George Wallace comes to this campus on March 16, there is going to be violence." Several students shouted support.

After the shouting quieted, a shaken Mathews replied, "I am astounded by your willingness to say we will have violence. Frankly, I have no answers." He then left the stage. Warren Herlong urged students to let the courts decide the matter and avoid disturbances that might lessen the chances for gaining an injunction.[61]

On Monday, March 9, Judge Johnson refused to issue a temporary restraining order. He did, however, leave open the possibility he might do so if new evidence arose. Meanwhile, the Faculty Senate of Arts and Sciences passed a resolution expressing its concern that the president acted without consulting them. SGA weighed in on the side of students and the Graduate Students Association urged Mathews to rescind Wallace's invitation.[62]

On Monday, March 16, 1970, as George Wallace prepared to speak, Judge Frank Johnson sent the case to the next highest court, ending any prospect Abbie Hoffman might be speaking.[63] The greeting accorded Wallace resembled a hootenanny in a hornet's nest. Students, many wearing ratty jeans or multicolored pants, congregated in the seats at the front of the stage. Some dressed in Indian garb, with feathered headdresses and leather vests. A few pasted Wallace bumper stickers to their foreheads or chests. A crudely drawn poster read, "Weirdoes for Wallace!" They gave the past and would-be future "Guvnor" an environment he relished, one feeding his most caustic rhetorical flourishes.

George Wallace and Albert Brewer were locked in a heated campaign in the Democratic primary scheduled for June. Given the law-and-order mood among the electorate, the disorder at Emphasis '70 favored Wallace, playing to his strengths. When he mentioned his record on education, hecklers chanted, "We're number fifty," referring to the state's low ranking in public education. When a student ran on stage to present Wallace with a pair of dirty socks, Wallace kissed the socks along with the presenter's hand. He ended his talk with, "You activists here tonight helped me get a lot of votes in Alabama. I'll take my money and go home."[64]

Following Emphasis, a tenuous peace returned to campus. President Mathews explained to trustees why he cancelled Hoffman's appearance, telling them he considered the violence on other campuses visited by Chicago Seven defendants, and also noted the courts had backed universities that banned speakers who posed a threat of inciting violence. Mathews also cited the behavior of students at the press conference conducted after the Woods Hall controversy, the attempts to disrupt ROTC, and the vandalism over Thanksgiving break. He said that before making his decision, he also weighed the marches on the President's Mansion and the sit-in outside his office in October. Ernest Hallford's threats of violence intensified Mathews' determination to stick by his decision. The trustees unanimously passed a resolution supporting President Mathews.

Turmoil, in whatever form, receives the immediate attention of journalists. Later, historians, from the perspective of time, conduct their analyses. At the University of Alabama, where the past intertwines with the present, even as dissent grew along with elements of counterculture extravagances, certain traditions persevered.

Sustaining Traditions

Bama Day went on as in past years. There was the ROTC drill competition followed by the Million Dollar Band marching along University Boulevard, this time with majorettes leading the way. Then came Masons in fezzes tossing bubble gum to children while clowns danced. Over on the Quadrangle, a crowd clustered around Denny Chimes to watch Danny Ford and Alvin Samples, cocaptains of the 1969 football team, place their hand- and cleat prints into wet cement.

On Thursday, April 23, the Army and Air Force ROTC celebrated President's Day. The Monday edition of the *Crimson-White* featured a full-page photograph of a university policeman dragging yippie leader Ernest Hallford off the Quadrangle by his hair. The incident occurred near the reviewing stand where Mathews stood as cadets marched past. Witnesses testified that during the playing of the national anthem, Hallford, standing in a cordoned-off area near the reviewing stand, raised his fist in defiance. After the anthem, he and a student named Mike Golomb ran toward the reviewing stand until tackled by police officers; one then pulled Hallford by the hair for several yards before cuffing him. The police stuffed the duo into a squad car and drove them to Dean Thomas's office. After Hallford explained that they rushed the stand to display the yippie flag, Thomas scolded and then released them.

The caption beneath a *Crimson-White* photograph showing Mathews riding in a jeep stated, "President Mathews greets student protestors with a smirk." It is impossible to tell from the photo if Mathews was smirking, smiling, or, for that matter, doing anything other than looking at the protestors.[65] The wording of the caption and the full-page photograph of Hallford being dragged by his hair revealed a growing separation between a portion of the student body and the administration.

On Tuesday, April 28, President Nixon authorized US combat forces to enter Cambodia to join South Vietnamese units that had been operating there for several weeks. At the Capstone, final exams, less than a month away, marked the approaching end of a year during which unprecedented acts of student defiance and dissent had occurred. So far, the Capstone's bastions in defense of reason had withstood the assaults of dissent and disruption, but a new storm was about to break.

9
May 1970
Days of Rage and Reason

Jerry Rubin Comes to Campus

On Wednesday, April 29, rumors percolated around campus that Chicago Seven member Jerry Rubin, out on bail pending appeal of his conviction for instigating riots at the 1968 Democratic convention, might be headed for the university. By Friday, May 1, the administration was preparing for Rubin's pending appearance at a Woods Hall concert dubbed "The Festival of Life." The Experimental College properly registered the event but did not request permission for a speaker.[1]

With David Mathews out of town for the weekend, the administration made decisions based on rumors, albeit substantial ones. Dean Joab Thomas changed the concert venue from the Woods Hall Quad to Foster Auditorium, reasoning that if things got out of hand, it would be easier to control the crowd within a confined area. Administrators focused on containment rather than preemption after attorneys told them they could not prevent Rubin, or anyone else, from visiting the university and that they could act only after he violated regulations pertinent to speaking or picketing on campus. As part of the containment strategy, officials alerted the Tuscaloosa police and local office of the Federal Bureau of Investigation. The FBI assured the university that Rubin was under surveillance and they would revoke his bail if he instigated violence.[2]

Bill Moody, who graduated in January and was working in Washington, DC, claimed private individuals, not the Experimental College, arranged for Rubin's visit. He accused Mathews of leaving town to avoid dealing with the issue and advised students to "just do it."[3]

On Sunday afternoon a crowd that university officials estimated at between 400 and 800 and students calculated at closer to 1,500 gathered in Foster Auditorium. While student bodyguards clustered at the edges of the stage, Jerry Rubin walked out dressed in red velveteen trousers and a tie-dyed T-shirt. To prevent provoking the crowd, the university limited the number of uniformed officers present. Meanwhile, Tuscaloosa police in mufti and FBI agents mingled among the audience.

Rubin, his flailing arms framing his unkempt hair, rambled from topic to topic. "Long haired people are the new niggers—white niggers. Everything George Wallace says about us is true. . . . I haven't taken a bath in over six months. . . . I'll never get another hair cut." Observations on personal hygiene covered, the shaggy sage of Chicago turned to international relations. "The American people have been conditioned to salivate upon hearing the word 'communism.' I say 'Right on communism!' Communism is Che Guevara, Ho Chi Minh, and the Viet Cong! They are our brothers!" He peppered his tirades on the war in Vietnam with interjections like, "Free all prisoners and imprison all judges."[4]

During his talk, Rubin unfurled what he described as a new yippie flag; a red marijuana leaf superimposed on a black background, and then flung the pot-spangled banner into the audience. A student seated at the edge of the stage handed Rubin what appeared to be a marijuana cigarette, from which he took a hit, passed the joint back to his new-found friend, and then invited the audience to meet him on the Washington Mall for an Independence Day "smoke in." For his finale, Rubin declared God a yippie. His talk completed, student bodyguards escorted Rubin out the door and into a van for the short drive to an off-campus apartment where he held court for admirers and the press. Once there, Rubin boasted, "We really out-witted them this time. . . . Next week I might be back and I will bring Abbie Hoffman and Timothy Leary with me."[5]

The next morning, a *Crimson-White* editorial praised Experimental College for doing what Emphasis '70 failed to do: bring a truly controversial speaker to campus. It claimed that any rules that were broken made up for Mathews barring Abbie Hoffman's appearance at Emphasis and concluded, "The Rubin incident reveals speaker rules should be done away with forever."[6] While students read *Crimson-White* accounts of Sunday's supposed coup, inside the Rose Administration Building, David Mathews and his staff set about identifying who invited Rubin and what, if anything, to do about it. Events unfolding hundreds of miles to the north in Kent, Ohio, soon swept aside concerns about Jerry Rubin's visit.

Setup

Relations with the governor's office improved significantly during the two years since Albert Brewer succeeded Lurleen Wallace. In May 1970, polls indicated

Governor Brewer still held a slight lead over George Wallace in the Democratic primary scheduled for early June. Brewer and Wallace both stood on tough law-and-order platforms, with Wallace constantly harping on "hippies and pointy-headed professors running the nation's campuses." The rowdy reception accorded Wallace at Emphasis '70 bolstered his standing among many Alabama voters—as he predicted it would. With the election looming in June, Rubin's appearance played to Wallace's advantage.

Over the weekend of May 2 and 3, while the university's small but growing cadre of dissidents reveled in anticipation of their Sunday visitor, students on other campuses demonstrated against US forces fighting in Cambodia. Across the nation, campus strikes abounded, creating chaos with end-of-semester routines like administering and grading final exams and preparing for commencement. On Saturday, May 2, National Guardsmen wounded a student while dealing with disorders at Ohio State University.[7] At nearby Kent State University, when Friday's demonstrations spilled over into the town of Kent, its mayor asked the National Guard to restore order. The next day, following an antiwar rally, demonstrators burned the Army ROTC building. On Sunday, the Ohio National Guard moved onto the Kent State campus. The guard answered protests with tear gas.

At noon on Monday, May 4, when two thousand Kent State students rallied, guardsmen equipped with gas masks and loaded M-1 rifles, lobbed tear gas canisters into the crowd. After that failed to disperse the demonstrators, the guard positioned itself on a small rise known as Blanket Hill while protestors formed in a parking lot facing them. At 12:25 P.M., the guardsmen opened fire. Their sixty-one-round fusillade lasted thirteen seconds and killed four people, two of them bystanders.[8] Reaction at the University of Alabama came slowly. Some focused on finishing term papers and preparing for final exams, while others enjoyed the warm spring days creek banking on Hurricane Creek.

On Tuesday, the Democratic Students Organization, Students for a Democratic Society, and the Tuscaloosa Women's Movement met to organize their responses. Cheryl Knowles and Carol Self handed out flyers for a memorial service scheduled for Wednesday evening. In addition to commemorating the deaths at Kent State, Carol and the group wanted to honor four black students killed when police fired on demonstrators protesting a segregated bowling alley in Orangeburg two years earlier at South Carolina State University.[9]

On Wednesday morning, students passed out handbills that read, "Strike." At noon, 150 to 200 protesters gathered on the steps in front of the Alabama Union to hear speeches by Bob Keever, Leon Weinberger, and Iredell Jenkins, who, along with Cheryl Knowles, focused more on the tragedy at Kent State than on the fighting in Cambodia. Morris Simon, who worked for Dean Thomas in the Office of Student Development, reported that Gina Twitty, a sophomore from Homewood, spoke so eloquently he assumed a communications professor named Michael G. McGee composed her speech. Cheryl Knowles encouraged everyone to gather at Denny Chimes at seven thirty that evening for the Tuscaloosa Women's Movement's candlelight memorial service.[10]

To the Colors

Following the rally, which attracted more than the usual number of onlookers and hecklers, two groups confronted each other in front of the Alabama Union. One group, led by Doug Newby, wanted the flag lowered to half-mast. The other insisted the flag remain as it was. Earlier that morning, President Mathews phoned the Union post office to ask the postmaster to lower the flag. Since the pole belonged to the postal service and not the university, the postmaster called his superiors in Memphis who informed him that unless they received a written request from President Mathews, the flag must remain at full staff. Therefore, the flag flew high as tensions around the flagstaff mounted.

Hoping to quell the dispute, the postmaster lowered the flag, folded it, and carried it into his office. At that point, a student removed his white T-shirt, upon which was stenciled the word, "Strike," and then attached it to the halyard, raising it to half-mast. Just as someone from the opposing group started to remove the makeshift banner, Joab Thomas and a small contingent of campus police arrived.

Thomas spoke at length with both groups before their attention turned to the flag flying two hundred yards away in front of the Amelia Gayle Gorgas Library. That flag was raised and lowered each day by Air Force ROTC cadets. Thomas instructed a university police officer to follow him as he set off for the library, demonstrators from both factions in trail. Before they reached the flagpole, air force officers emerged from Barnard Hall to haul down the flag.[11]

At four o'clock, an ad hoc faculty meeting convened in the first floor auditorium at Martin ten Hoor Hall. At the start of the meeting, some faculty members objected to the presence of students and reporters from the local NBC television affiliate. Following a lengthy debate, they excluded the press but allowed students to remain. After three hours, the assembly passed a resolution expressing sympathy for the deaths at Kent State.[12] That same afternoon,

President Mathews issued a statement stating his deep concern over the killings and urged respect for all points of view, stating, "It is especially important that the houses of reason continue to function."[13]

Wednesday Night, May 6

Cheryl Knowles and Carol Self hoped Wednesday night's candlelight service might attract two hundred to three hundred participants. More than two thousand showed up. Lighted candles flickered as students and faculty made brief, sympathetic statements. Respectful voices sang "Where Have All the Flowers Gone?" and "Blowin' in the Wind." Then the crowd formed a line, some walked side-by-side while others moved alone across the Quad to the Army ROTC detachment at Tuomey Hall.

Inside Tuomey, officers and noncommissioned officers waited, ready to defend the building if necessary. Some wanted weapons distributed, but cooler heads prevailed. When the procession arrived, Captain Robert Gray and Sergeant Major Curtis Duco emerged. Gray, in an effort to keep the situation cool, took a low-key approach. "I know half y'all," Gray said in greeting. He pointed to his neighbor, Ed Still; then to his brother-in-law; recognized a first cousin; and greeted several classmates from graduate courses in which he was enrolled. Captain Gray asked the crowd to stay calm and ended with, "Y'all please, please be careful."[14] The captain and the sergeant then withdrew behind locked doors. Demonstrators quietly placed lighted candles on the sidewalk and steps leading up to Tuomey Hall.

Hostile onlookers gathered across the street in front of Garland Hall. During the placing of candles, they sang "Happy Birthday." The situation grew tense, with only a thin cordon of university police separating the groups. Carol Self recalled, "We didn't think about how to end the demonstration. I was shouting something like, 'Okay, y'all, that's it—it's over—time to go!'"[15]

Stoney Johnson, a leader among campus yippies, yelled, "To the Mansion." Shouts of "Strike! Strike! Strike!" And cries of "To the Mansion," accompanied by rhythmic clapping, propelled the crowd back to and around Denny Chimes and across University Boulevard to the President's Mansion's sprawling lawn. Stoney Johnson climbed the elegant curving stairs to the second story above the portico and then rapped on the twin glass doors. No one answered. The Mathews family had moved to an undisclosed location.[16] The university police arrived, followed shortly thereafter by SGA leaders, including the new president, Jim Zeigler. Glenn Stillion joined Morris Simon from the Student Development Office. Up on the balcony, Stillion, Zeigler, and others tried to address the crowd, but to no avail.

Someone suggested blocking traffic in front of the mansion might prompt a rapid response. After a contingent sat down in the middle of the street, Stillion and Simon hurried over to warn them that what they were doing was dangerous and likely to bring a very strong reaction from the Tuscaloosa police. Then someone shouted, "To the Union!" Perhaps relieved to have discovered a less risky alternative, they jumped up and headed for the Alabama Union. At that point, many called it a night.

A reduced crowd of around six hundred gathered at the Alabama Union, where they sat on the steps or headed for the Supe Store snack bar, open to serve a few late-night coffee drinkers stocking up for all-night study sessions. Clerks continued selling until the room full of demonstrators intimidated them into closing. After the clerks retreated, newly installed SGA president Jim Zeigler served up ice cream while other students helped themselves to snacks.[17]

The crowd thinned as the evening crept toward midnight. Stalwarts urged females to defy their curfew and suggested that those who returned to their dorms set off fire alarms. Meanwhile, Hank Hawkins and Mark Mandell encouraged the remnants to devise a list of demands to be presented to President Mathews. Stoney Johnson urged that the list include amnesty; Jack Drake wanted it to address political prisoners and collective bargaining. Caucuses gathered in corners where discussion continued into the early morning hours. Carol Self, who wanted to sleep in her own bed, persuaded her husband to come with her.[18] Jack dutifully followed.

The crowd dwindled as the night wore on. Representatives from the dean's office stayed with the group. Perhaps that is why there were no significant acts of vandalism or mischief beyond pilfering snacks and ice cream. By one o'clock in the morning fewer than fifty students remained inside the Alabama Union. They racked out on sofas and chairs in the upstairs lounges or made themselves as comfortable as possible on the floor.[19]

At 2:02 fire alarms sounded in Dressler Hall, a World War II–vintage wood frame structure most recently used as a gymnasium for intramural sports and scheduled for demolition to make way for the new student union complex. Young men poured out of nearby residence halls to watch the flames consume more than half the building. President Mathews, awakened thirteen minutes later, first phoned Governor Brewer and then called Floyd Mann, state director of public safety.

Floyd Mann dispatched a contingent of Alabama State Troopers to Tuscaloosa, officers trained in riot control. The next morning, Governor Brewer sternly warned that campus lawlessness and violence would be dealt with severely.[20] By dawn, 100 state troopers had converged on Brandon National Guard Armory at the edge of campus. Tuscaloosa mayor Snow Hinton also made available the 35 officers normally working the day shift. The campus police force could muster 20 officers. All in all, 150 lawmen were available if needed.[21]

At six o'clock in the morning Dean Thomas and Morris Simon entered the Alabama Union, awakened Doug Newby and told him police were coming to remove demonstrators and suggested he urge those remaining to withdraw voluntarily. Newby, perhaps hoping that sympathetic students might flock to the Union, declined the suggestion. No throngs of sympathizers came forth. Half an hour later, campus police dispersed twenty people from the Union's steps and then entered the building to remove thirty more. Later that morning, President Mathews imposed a nine o'clock curfew and also canceled scheduled performances by the New York Brass Quintet and a rock group known as "Pirt."[22]

Otherwise, Thursday was calm. Students and faculty made their way to and from classes amid the presence of news media and beneath the watchful eyes of state, city, and campus police. Later that day, a delegation of students presented Mathews with nineteen demands. These included:

1. Do away with regulations specifically designed for females;
2. Change the food service and remove all mandatory food contracts;
3. Include students on all faculty and administration search committees;
4. Student funds must be used as students wish;
5. Accept the new SGA constitution;
6. Student strikes will be allowed and recognized by administrators;
7. No speaker ban;
8. Free the Panthers;
9. End the war in Vietnam;
10. Black demands will be met;
11. Amnesty will be given for all actions on campus;
12. No outside force will be brought to campus and campus police will no longer carry firearms;
13. Monthly meetings between Mathews and students;
14. Student presence on the Board of Trustees;
15. Right to collective bargaining for contract workers;
16. Women teachers will receive equal pay;
17. The president must be available to talk to students at all times;

18. No action against Experimental College for the Rubin incident;

19. Amnesty for coeds who stayed out all night on May 6.

On Friday, May 8, classes met without incident. In the early afternoon, the newly formed Student-Faculty Coalition (SFC) provided the administration with one hour's notice of a teach-in set for three o'clock. David Mathews, fearing a possible confrontation, asked that they call it off. When SFC did not respond, he alerted campus police and state troopers. Good as its word, SFC convened a teach-in at Denny Chimes. As soon as a contingent of troopers arrived, it dispersed only to reconvene at the same place at seven o'clock. Campus police, reenforced by state troopers, again rousted them, making several arrests.[23]

Meanwhile, SFC leaders handed Mathews the same list of demands presented on Thursday. He agreed to consider the list over the weekend and respond on Monday or Tuesday. The SFC and Mathews also agreed to make Saturday a "cooling-off period." On Saturday morning, Mathews warned that students arrested during campus disorders would be subject to university disciplinary proceedings. This answered the demand for amnesty.[24]

Sunday passed peacefully. Meanwhile, support for President Mathews remained high among students and the state's citizenry. Letters from alumni overwhelmingly supported the administration, many urging Mathews to deal more harshly with troublemakers. Several students wrote asking that he keep the university open and that their right to an education not be jeopardized.[25]

On Monday, May 11, Mathews and Thomas met with members of the Student-Faculty Coalition. Even though Mathews told them he felt it unreasonable for the university to respond to demands under duress, the SFC promised to work with the administration to deescalate tensions. Mathews commented only on demands affecting women and black students, stating that significant progress had been made in both areas. He promised to elaborate more fully on those two issues the following day.

In his elaboration, Mathews repeated in greater detail what he said on Monday. Regarding women's issues, he cited six significant changes made during his administration. As for African American students, he pointed to eight black staff members hired since the previous August. Mathews then underscored his determination not to be intimidated, "The cause of genuine reform has been seriously threatened. . . . Disruptions and threats of disturbances will be met with unequivocal condemnations."[26] Later that afternoon, after four nights of relative calm, the administration lifted the curfew.

That evening, following the president's response to their demands—or in the minds of some, his nonresponse—and with the curfew and ban on meetings lifted, the SFC gathered at the University Presbyterian Church on Eighth Street. When the crowd overwhelmed the small chapel's seating capacity, Bob Keever phoned Joab Thomas, who made Foster Auditorium available. University police shepherded the group as it ambled by Denny Stadium, flowed around houses on sorority row, and continued across parking lots until it congregated inside Foster, where five hundred to eight hundred dissidents stood on the floor of what used to be the basketball court.

Hank Hawkins, spokesman for the SFC, and John Bivens, representing the AAA, condemned President Mathews for not addressing—much less acceding to—all their demands. Hawkins accused Mathews of being disingenuous when he spoke of campus disorder, pointing out that there had been no major disruptions over the past two days. The crowd applauded and shouted their approval when Hawkins added, "We're winning!"

Hawkins, exerting control, announced a teach-in scheduled for noon the next day, Wednesday, May 13. When someone yelled for a march on the Union or a sit-in on the Quadrangle to test the university's willingness to accommodate assemblies, Hawkins urged restraint. "We've got the power now. Let's show them this generation of young people is going to use that power differently from the generation now in power."[27]

The crowd's diversity indicated dissent had expanded beyond student dissidents and faculty liberals. Fletcher Thornton, a Sigma Chi and president of the IFC, was present, as was Mark Mandell, vice president of SGA. They joined Hank Hawkins in urging students to abjure violence. The next day, the *Tuscaloosa News* account noted twenty state police cars clustered in the parking lot of Brandon Armory, less than a minute's drive from Foster. The article also stated campus police snapped photographs as students left the auditorium.[28]

Louie Crew, a doctoral student and instructor in English, often bicycled to and from his office in Morgan Hall. On May 13, Crew wrote Mathews castigating him for not responding to student demands. "Apathy here is at an all time low. Dissent has been well ordered." He accused the administration of "doing violence to the spirit of events" and closed with a plea, "Free us from the violence of administrative rhetoric. . . . Talk with us, not at us."[29] It was a gutsy letter for a doctoral student to write and presaged the career of a scholar who went on to teach English at Rutgers and become an advocate for gay and lesbian rights.

By midmorning, posters appeared calling for a noon rally at Denny Chimes to demand an end to ROTC and immediate withdrawal of US forces from

Vietnam. The teach-in, followed by singing of antiwar songs, took place without incident.

Members of the SFC met at six o'clock in the ballroom of the Alabama Union. Some urged taking over the building until the university met their demands. After that proposal failed, the coalition voted to march to the President's Mansion, serve David Mathews with a subpoena, and then put him on trial for "tampering in student affairs." Accordingly, 150 people, carried the "subpoena" to the mansion, doing so as police watched. After a couple of fruitless hours sitting on the lawn, they returned to the Union, settling on the steps. Police followed and asked that they disperse.[30]

As evening descended on the Capstone, students opposing the dissidents gathered across University Boulevard in front of Bibb Graves Hall. By ten fifteen, the opposing crowds had swelled into mingling factions. Forty years later, David Mathews recalled, "Somebody called the Tuscaloosa police without informing me. I had Alabama State Troopers, men trained in crowd control, standing by to keep order."[31] Within half an hour the Tuscaloosa police were on hand in force. A university official, either Chief Rayfield or Colonel Leigh, used a bullhorn to warn the crowd it had ten minutes to disperse. The fuse was lit.

Richard C. Winstead, a member of Delta Kappa Epsilon fraternity, and his date, having enjoyed dinner at the Cotton Patch Restaurant in nearby Eutaw, Alabama, arrived back on campus before ten o'clock. They stopped by the DKE house, located on University Boulevard within a stone's throw of the Alabama Union and Bibb Graves Hall. Inside, the brothers filled them in on what had transpired just up the street. A loud noise then drew everyone onto the front porch.

Richard and his date walked down the steps and onto the wide lawn to get a better look. Suddenly, the crowd began running onto DKE property from the direction of the Union and the Quadrangle. The couple stood there, holding hands as students rushed by. Then they turned to see a line of helmeted Tuscaloosa police wielding clubs and marching in lockstep toward them. When the phalanx numbering between thirty and fifty officers reached the fraternity house's lawn, it broke into a charge. Richard and his date raced for the porch. She fell. Richard looked back to see his date on the ground, one officer's boot planted on her back while another handcuffed her. When Richard protested that his date was not a demonstrator, they clubbed him to the ground, beat, and cuffed him. The police then marched the pair to a waiting bus. At half-past midnight, the bus, filled with students, some bloodied, was driven to jail where police armed with shotguns unloaded cuffed students by ones and twos. Richard and his date were charged with "failure to obey a police officer." Richard remained in the drunk-tank until a physician arrived to hear him complain of a gash on his forehead, bruised toe, and split thumbnail. Police officers without nametags and black tape obscuring their badge numbers escorted Richard and two other injured students to Druid City Hospital.

Later that morning, Richard, his date, and a fraternity brother arrested at the same time signed their own bail bonds and were released; their trial date set for May 18.[32] They were among fifty-seven students arrested on Wednesday night and Thursday morning. President Mathews declared an end to all campus assemblies and reimposed the nine o'clock curfew, this time indefinitely.[33]

Although a majority of letters received from alumni and citizens of Alabama continued to endorse Mathews' firmness, support from students weakened after Wednesday night's police rampage. One married male wrote, "Last Sunday my wife and I made a terrible mistake. We signed a petition supporting your actions. . . . I don't know how we could have been so wrong. I refer to the atrocities committed by so-called officers of the law last night. We are your students. Why betray us?"[34]

On the night of May 12, when Donna Brown, a freshman from Birmingham, heard the commotion on University Boulevard, her curiosity compelled her to investigate. She dressed in a skirt and short-sleeve shirt, to which she affixed her sorority pin, and then wandered outside. Short-cropped hair, conservative skirt, and Oxford shirt distinguished Donna from many of the female demonstrators. That may have saved her from arrest as she ambled around campus, observing from as safe a distance as possible. Whenever an officer told her to "keep moving," she smiled, coupled a nod to a polite "yes, sir," and kept walking.

Donna returned to her dorm after curfew and ruminated for three hours over things that disturbed her. Before daybreak, she used sorority stationery to write President Mathews. Donna described the beatings and brutality she had witnessed, wondering how he could have let such things happen. She concluded, "Please, please, get the city police off campus and replace them with state troopers. . . . The city police are using this as an opportunity to show us they can be tough."[35]

That same day SGA president Jim Zeigler along with John Bivens, AAA representative to the SFC, also wrote President Mathews. They told him they had contacted the three television networks to secure the widest possible media coverage of events on campus. The two also asked him to invite Charles Woods, a state political figure and sometimes-gubernatorial candidate, to mediate the crisis. At the bottom of their letter, in bold typeface, they wrote, "YOUR ANSWER WITH SIGNATURE."[36] The unanswered letter went straight to the files.

President Mathews spent Thursday afternoon visiting and speaking with students in residence halls and fraternity and sorority houses. On Friday, as a fragile calm settled over campus, he praised students for keeping things peaceful throughout the day. To help emotions subside, he also asked anyone who lived nearby to go home for the weekend.

Meanwhile, disorders continued on other campuses. Across the state line in Mississippi, in an angry confrontation, two students were killed at Jackson State.

On Friday evening, May 15, Governor Albert Brewer went on statewide television to warn that lawlessness would not be tolerated on Alabama's college campuses.[37] From the campaign stump, candidate Wallace issued similarly strong statements.

At four o'clock Saturday morning, arson destroyed a small maintenance shed at the edge of campus. That afternoon, SGA passed a resolution asking the administration to ban the Tuscaloosa police from campus and urging university police to put aside their nightsticks and stop wearing helmets. They also thanked Governor Brewer for sending state troopers and asked that a small contingent remain nearby in case they were needed. In a memorandum, SGA president Zeigler asked David Mathews to make final examinations optional.[38]

Late Sunday afternoon, May 17, President Mathews met with the Executive Committee of the board of trustees. He outlined the sequence of events and stated that his primary objectives had been to reduce tensions. Mathews promised an investigation to determine what charges might be filed against students involved in disorder. He told them a disciplinary committee comprised of faculty, administrators, and students would hear and consider the charges. The trustees unanimously adopted a resolution endorsing President Mathews' handling of the situation.[39]

On Monday, David Mathews authorized optional final examinations at the instructors' discretion. Students who declined finals would receive grades calculated on work completed. If, however, someone wanted to take a final, one had to be administered.[40] While the administration hoped this would clear the campus, the risk was that students bent on making trouble might opt out of finals and then stick around to raise hell.

Mathews also met with SGA leaders and SFC representatives who wanted to end the semester with a memorial service. An agreement reached with SGA specified the Union ballroom as a venue. SFC representatives, wanting an outdoor service, balked.

At six o'clock in the evening, a group of 150 to 200 demonstrators, escorted by university police and state troopers, walked from the Alabama Union to Denny Chimes to hold their memorial service on the Quadrangle. They carried signs, lighted candles, placed them on the low steps surrounding the cotillion, and then nestled onto the lawn. Police finally told them either to return to the Union ballroom, proceed to Foster Auditorium, or disperse. Most headed back to the Union, where they stood on the steps shouting, "Pigs! Pigs! Pigs!" until twenty-five Alabama State Troopers forced them to retreat into the building.

An hour later, students started trickling out of the front and side doors of the Alabama Union. As they did, troopers warned them to keep moving or face arrest. When a few gathered in front of the Union in defiance of the orders, the arrests began. Gina Twitty was one of the students in the ballroom. She left by a side door to retrieve her bicycle to ride back downtown to the room she rented in a house occupied by Doug Newby and his wife. Before she could pull away, a state trooper ordered her to leave the area, warning that if he saw her again, she would be arrested. Gina got on her bike, peddled to an alley, circled behind the Rose Administration Building, and then headed downtown on University Boulevard. When she reached the traffic light at the Union, she stopped for the red light. "I felt a tug on the bicycle seat. I turned around to see the same Alabama State Trooper hovering over me. 'I warned you. Now you're under arrest.'" He cuffed Gina and then walked her to a waiting bus. Forty-six students were arrested that night.[41]

Student support for Mathews plummeted following the arrests on May 18. Losing the support of sorority women like Donna Brown meant trouble for the administration. Letters like hers, and that of disgruntled English instructor Louie Crew, can help administrators gauge reactions. When criticism comes from a friend, it's personal. Morris Dees authored such a letter.

> Dear David:
>
> The Brutal vigilante justice Dickey Winstead received is a direct result of your lack of leadership. You are fully responsible.
>
> When I questioned you in the Hoffman case, I detected a very fearful, insecure person. You had to have ten lawyers around you to bolster you. Your answers were devious and not direct. I have questioned Dr.

Philpot, Ralph Adams, and Dr. Rose. These men did not beat around the bush. I respected them. I listened to your talk to the students during the Hoffman matter. You treated them like children. Your logic was faulty. They saw through you. Had you allowed Hoffman to speak; had you held a two-day moratorium for the Kent State students; had you gotten out from behind your lawyers and your big desk and become concerned about things that interest students, you would not have lost control. You effectively pushed the "small minority" you were concerned about in the Hoffman case into protesting. Then you stepped on them with Billy clubs. David, I was proud of you when you became President. I do hope you can brush aside the praise from your supporters long enough to see the real issue.

Sincerely,
Morris Dees.

David Mathews replied:

Dear Morris:

Perhaps there will come a time when you will feel justified in changing the views expressed in your recent letter. I hope so.

I don't mean to be pompous about the matter, but my position was described, far better than I can, by Mr. Lincoln: "If I were ever to try to read, much less answer, all the attacks made on me, this shop might well be closed for other business. I do the very best I know how—the very best I can; and I mean to keep doing so until the end. If the end brings me out all right, what is said about me won't amount to anything. If the end brings me out wrong, ten angels swearing I was right would make no difference."

With all good wishes to you and your family, I am

David Mathews
President

Four decades later, David Mathews reflected on the exchange. "Morris saw the University as a town square. My position was that we had a mandate to educate."[42]

At the behest of student leaders, including former SGA president Don Siegelman, New York congressman Allard K. Lowenstein, who spoke at Emphasis

'69, came to campus to investigate charges of police brutality. After meeting with students, Congressman Lowenstein discussed their arrests with university officials.

True to its Mandate

The campus remained calm on Tuesday, May 19, while students buckled down for the start of final examinations on Wednesday, which continued until the following Thursday, May 28. While some chose to forego all exams, most opted out in courses where they had good grades to focus on classes where they could do better. The faculty administered over thirty thousand exams; normally the number would have averaged around fifty-thousand. By Wednesday, May 27, most students had checked out of their dorms or fraternity or sorority houses and left campus. The following Sunday, because the university remained true to its mandate to educate, there was a commencement for those who earned it.

Twelve days after the last arrests, on May 30, President Mathews spoke at the annual Alumni Commencement Dinner. He expressed satisfaction that the university dealt with problems reasonably and without being "swept away by the forces of passion."[43] The following day, the university converted 2,300 former students into degree-holding alumni.

Before meeting with the trustees on May 30, David Mathews organized his thoughts into a handwritten note. His first point was that the primary objective had to be to minimize losses. Second, as a historian he wanted to place the turmoil at the Capstone in the context of a national climate of unrest. Third, he attributed student behavior to idealism mobilized by the "student power" movement and heightened by normal, youthful resistance to authority. Finally, Mathews detailed the elements of his approach: "Be open, always talking, knowing that it won't be enough. Be very firm on matters of discipline, never dealing with demands under duress."[44]

Over the summer, the university took to heart the disruptions of May, anxious to avoid future turmoil and, if faced with them, handle them better. Whether it was Colonel Leigh or Chief Rayfield who called the Tuscaloosa police on the night of May 13, both paid a price. Mathews replaced Beverly Leigh with Floyd Mann. Because of his years of service, Mathews retained Rayfield, although Mann's authority diminished the chief's responsibilities.

Meanwhile, George Wallace won the June Democratic primary. From September 1970 until the end of Brewer's term, Mann served the university as a part-time consultant on security. In January 1971, Mann moved into Leigh's old job as special assistant to the president for campus security. He subsequently developed a training program for law enforcement officers and made the campus police appear less threatening by accoutering them in blazers and slacks, their pistols and handcuffs hidden from view.[45]

The university flexed its alumni muscle in the legal and commercial communities to pressure Tuscaloosa into ameliorating the judicial harshness toward students. Accordingly, the city appointed two judges who took over most of Judge Joe Burns' caseload. Jack Drake and Ralph Knowles defended many of the students charged with "disorderly conduct" and "failure to obey a police officer." Gina Twitty Crosheck recalled Drake telling a judge his search of city, county, and state legal codes didn't turn up a single reference to "failure to obey a police officer." Most charges against students were dropped.[46]

While David Mathews refused to deal with student demands under duress, during the summer the university addressed many of their complaints. Unable to affect issues like "Free the Panthers" and "Stop the war in Vietnam," Mathews focused on accomplishing the doable. The administration replaced the contract food service with one used by three hundred other colleges and universities and stopped mandatory purchase of food contracts for female students. This concession met the expectations of many students, especially females limited in their off-campus living options and, therefore, compelled to sign food contracts.[47]

In June, the university established a Committee on Campus Unrest and Reconciliation composed of faculty, administrators, and students. Its thirty-eight members issued their eighty-three-page report in late August, one that faulted the administration, faculty, and students for their mutual lack of communication. In response, Mathews increased his availability to students and scheduled more news conferences. The university organized a cadre of student and faculty "marshals" to accompany campus police during times of campus unrest to act as observers and intermediaries. It also changed the academic calendar beginning with the 1971 fall semester by starting classes in late August to conclude with final exams before Christmas break.[48]

What the University of Alabama experienced in May 1970 was mild compared to what happened on many campuses. No one was killed, or for that matter, seriously injured. Property damage was light, the burning of Dressler Hall notwithstanding. The company that insured Dressler proposed a settlement of $60,000, even though the building was insured for $70,200. The university accepted the offer, hoping to avoid increased insurance rates and the cost of arbitration.[49]

Court hearings for students arrested in May started in September. George Dean, a lawyer affiliated with the ACLU, accused Charles Grimm, a former student, with setting the fire at Dressler. Dean further alleged that Grimm, who was an informant for the Tuscaloosa police and the FBI, acted as an agent provocateur during the disturbances.[50]

Grimm's student days were marred with problems. Recruited from California as a wrestler, the coaches booted him from the team over disciplinary issues. He also got in trouble for using lighter fluid to burn obscenities into the carpet in Paty Hall and was later placed on probation for breaking into a women's dorm. Additionally, at a meeting of the SFC at Jack and Carol Drake's house, Grimm offered to procure guns and dynamite.[51] The coalition rejected his offer, and Jack banned Grimm from future SFC meetings.

Grimm was arrested twice during the campus disorders. Campus police also apprehended his wife, who was siphoning gas from a car. The following day, when the couple fled to Minnesota, Grimm left the post office box number of Eric Wilson, a local FBI agent, as his forwarding address. In 1971, supposedly at the behest of FBI director J. Edgar Hoover, the Public Broadcasting System eliminated a fifteen-minute segment from a program titled *The Great American Dream Machine*, in which Grimm confessed to being a Tuscaloosa police and FBI informant. In the segment, he reportedly stated his handlers encouraged him to set fires so they could "crush those Communists on campus."[52]

Grimm was not charged with arson or any other crime associated with the May disorders. A Tuscaloosa police investigation turned up no evidence of arson in the Dressler Hall fire. After the university settled with the insurance company, the wreckage was hauled away. Groundbreaking for the new student center took place shortly thereafter.

Completed in 1973 and named for Hill Ferguson, a devoted alumnus and long-time trustee, the Ferguson Center—dubbed "the Ferg" by students—typifies the progress made at the University of Alabama since the 1960s. This modern complex contains a food court, dean of students' offices, a US Post Office, theater, SGA offices, a computer lab, a hair salon, game rooms, banquet and meeting rooms, an art gallery, an office for the Alabama Credit Union, an extensive books and souvenirs store, and several ATM machines.

The Ferg is located across the parking lot behind Woods Hall. Ironically, in 1965 and 1966, one of the first rumblings of student dissent involved the effort to save Woods Hall from demolition to make way for the proposed new student activities center. Like Woods Hall, built in the aftermath of the Civil War using materials salvaged from the first University of Alabama, the Ferguson Center shares the distinction of being built on the site of turmoil and strife.

The University of Alabama survived the tumultuous 1960s, as did other universities, many of which suffered much more. In the Capstone's case, once the energy focused on maintaining segregation was refocused to the pursuit of academic excellence, the university moved from what it was in 1963, a southern party school with an adequate if undistinguished academic reputation, toward becoming a nationally competitive research and teaching university. A determined process of reform took place between George Wallace's quixotic defense of the indefensible in June 1963 and the disorders of May 1970.

Frank Rose's vision, wrapped as it was around the "pursuit of excellence," became reality because student leaders, most of them as progressive as Rose, joined with the administration to resist the old order represented by George Wallace and his ardent supporters. Rose also placed people who shared his vision in key positions across the university and encouraged innovations like the New College. Frank Rose's political savvy kept potentially destructive forces at bay while also garnering financial support from beyond Alabama, especially from the Johnson administration. His contacts in the media depicted the university in a positive light, portraying it as an enlightened David heralding the New South while facing down a brutish Goliath, symbolic of an old order in decline. Additionally, Rose, like Denny, understood the role football played in the university's culture. As long as the Crimson Tide won championships, Alabama fans, whether in the stands or at home listening on the radio, along with members of the state legislature, remained supportive. Football provided cover while Rose turned the academic and cultural tide to move the university in a new and more progressive direction.

While the 1960s were the Capstone's "Rose Years," successors from David Mathews through Joab Thomas to E. Roger Sayers followed a similar pattern, providing the university nearly four decades of consistently focused leadership. President Robert E. Witt, after assuming office in 2003, embraced a similar approach. He built new classrooms and dormitories and recruited out-of-state students so that by the end of the first decade of the twentieth century, as enrollment climbed past thirty thousand, over a third of the student body hailed from outside Alabama. He also hired Nick Saban, one of the top football coaches in the country, to return the Crimson Tide to the glory days of Coach Bryant. In March 2012, President Witt accepted the chancellorship of the University of Alabama system. After serving about seven months as interim president, vice president and provost Judy Bonner was named president. The first woman to hold the post, President Bonner, with more than thirty years of service at the Capstone, most of it in administrative posts, will sustain the tradition of excellence propounded by Frank Rose and carried on by his successors. In the minds of hundreds of thousands of alumni and millions of supporters, as long as "the tradition continues," all is right with the University of Alabama.

The tide turned for the University of Alabama in the 1960s. Its turning was subtle and steady, as opposed to the riptide of change on some campuses, and for some progress came too slowly. Nevertheless, entering the last third of the century, the university was poised to move in a new direction. Frank Rose's successors perpetuated his vision, one with roots extending back to the presidency of Mike Denny, toward a future in which the Capstone might be truly worthy of the title, "Alabama's First University."

Notes

Introduction

1. "The University of Alabama: A History and Brief Academic Resume: 1963," Frank A. Rose Papers, Hoole Special Collections Library, University of Alabama (UA); hereafter cited as Rose Papers with file names following.

2. Marshal Frady, *Wallace* (New York: Random House, 1976), 78. George Wallace was on a five-year prelaw undergraduate program bypassing the bachelor's degree and leading to a law degree.

3. "Resolution by the Student Legislature, November 4, 1962," Rose Papers.

4. E. Culpepper Clark, *The Schoolhouse Door: Segregation's Last Stand at the University of Alabama* (New York: Oxford University Press, 1995), 157.

5. "Klan Leader Orders Forces for Barnett," *Birmingham Post-Herald*, October 1, 1962, 1.

6. Minutes of the University Faculty Meeting, November 14, 1962, Rose Papers, Hubert E. Mate Secretary, Faculty File, 1962.

7. "J. Jefferson Bennett Biographical Sketch," and "The Unitor" (weekly publication of the Tuscaloosa Exchange Club), October 17, 1964, Rose Papers, Jefferson Bennett File, 1962.

8. C. Vann Woodward, *The Burden of Southern History*, rev. ed. (Baton Rouge: Louisiana State University Press, 1968), 190.

9. "Learning from Oxford," *Tuscaloosa News*, October 7, 1962, 4.

10. Mark Stern, *Calculating Visions: Kennedy, Johnson, and Civil Rights* (New Brunswick, NJ: Rutgers University Press, 1992), 50–51.

Chapter 1

1. Suzanne Rau Wolfe, *The University of Alabama: A Pictorial History* (Tuscaloosa: University of Alabama Press, 1983), 51.

2. James B. Sellers, "History of the University of Alabama," vol. II, "1902–1957,"

W. Stanley Hoole, editor. This unpublished but bound and typed manuscript is available in the President's Office, University of Alabama. The first eight chapters have numbered pages while the remainder does not. See pages 22–56. References to Julia Tutwiler's role in opening the university to female students are found in Wolfe's *University of Alabama*, 97.

3. Sellers, "History of the University," unnumbered pages in chapter 30, "Reserve Officer Training."

4. Ibid., 74–75.

5. "Negro Attends Her First U of A Class," *Birmingham News*, February 3, 1956, 1. The best account of these events is in Clark, *The Schoolhouse Door*, 53–90.

6. Wolfe, *University of Alabama*, 200–202.

7. "Negro Student Barred from UA Campus to Halt Rioting," *Birmingham News*, February 7, 1956, 1.

8. F. David Mathews, interview by author, Dayton, Ohio, May 6, 2009.

9. "Resume for Autherine Lucy Case at the University of Alabama," Rose Papers, 1956 Desegregation File.

10. "What a Price for Peace," *Tuscaloosa News*, February 7, 1956, 1.

11. "Was the Klan Thinking of Violence?," *Crimson-White*, May 14, 1957, 1.

12. "Open Forum Meeting Undisturbed by KKK," *Crimson-White*, May 15, 1957, 2, and Clark, *The Schoolhouse Door*, 143.

13. Clark, *The Schoolhouse Door*, 140.

14. Frank A. Rose, interview by John L. Blackburn, tape recording, cassette 1, August 3, 1990, Hoole Special Collections Library, UA.

15. Paul "Bear" Bryant and John Underwood, *Bear: The Hard Life and Good Times of Alabama's Coach Bryant* (Chicago: Triumph Books, 2007), 144.

16. Allen Barra, *The Last Coach: A Life of Paul "Bear" Bryant* (New York: W. W. Norton, 2005), 214.

17. Ibid., 226.

18. Warren Trest, *Nobody but the People: The Life and Times of Alabama's Youngest Governor* (Montgomery, AL: New South Books, 2008), 279.

19. "State of the University, 1962," Rose Papers, Minutes of the Board of Trustees File, November 1962.

20. Ibid.

21. "A Bell Rang," *Crimson-White*, September 27, 1962, 4.

22. "Klan Leader Offers Force to Barnett," *Birmingham Post-Herald*, October 1, 1962, 1.

23. Robert E. Roberts, letter to author, June 15, 2010.

24. Frye Gaillard, *Cradle of Freedom: Alabama and the Movement That Changed America* (Tuscaloosa: University of Alabama Press, 2004), 165.

25. "Looking Back," *Mahout*, May 1963, 1, Hoole Special Collections Library, UA.

26. Letter, John L. Blackburn to Frank A. Rose, December 10, 1963, Rose Papers, Faculty Correspondence File R, 1962.

27. Letter, Frank A. Rose to Dr. John F. Ramsey, December 12, 1962, Rose Papers, Faculty Correspondence File R, 1962.

28. Letter, Frank A. Rose to Dean Eric Rogers, February 27, 1962, Rose Papers, Dean of Graduate School File, 1962. The university employed a three-hour/three-quality point system. Grades of "A-" to "A+" received three quality points despite gradations between 90 and 100 percent. All "Bs" received two, while "Cs" garnered a single quality point.

29. Wayne Flynt, *Alabama in the Twentieth Century* (Tuscaloosa: University of Alabama Press, 2004), 247–48; and University of Alabama Developments for the 1968–69 through 1972–73 at Its Main Campus in Tuscaloosa, draft attachment to memorandum, Raymond F. McLain to Frank A. Rose, November 3, 1967, Rose Papers, College of Arts and Sciences File, 1967.

30. Letter, Dean John L. Blackburn to Robert J. Miller, Executive Secretary Phi Delta Theta Fraternity, August 10, 1962, Rose Papers, Fraternity File, 1962–63.

31. "Wallace Says Reconstruction Is the Reason State Is Lagging," *Crimson-White*, May 2, 1963, 1.

32. "Past Won't Conquer the Race Problem—Stewart," *Crimson-White*, May 8, 1963, 1.

33. Barra, *The Last Coach*, 249–307.

34. George C. Wallace, *"Hear Me Out: This is Where I Stand"* (Anderson, SC: Droke House Publishers, 1968), 130.

35. Herbert Arnold, interview by author, Tuscaloosa, Alabama, December 19, 2010. Arnold, a local physician and a Meridian, Mississippi, high school classmate of Frank Rose, recalled conversations he had with Rose prior to accepting the presidency in which Rose expressed dismay at the virulence of racial animosity in Alabama.

36. "UA Dean Confirms Student Suspension," *Birmingham News*, August 12, 1963, 1.

37. "Court Says Dean Bound by Order," *Birmingham News*, May 17, 1963, 2.

38. Minutes of the Board of Trustees, May 19, 1963, Rose Papers, Board of Trustees File, 1963.

39. Rose interview, August 23, 1990, cassette 3, Hoole Special Collections Library, UA.

40. In the May 2009 interview, David Mathews recalled, "As president of the Baptist Student Union I, like most other students, was totally unprepared for what happed. Carmichael only contacted the presidents of SGA and AWS."

41. Email, James Wilder to David Mathews, subject: Frank Rose, dated January 19, 2003, in David Mathews Papers, Frank A. Rose File, Kettering Foundation, Dayton, Ohio.

Chapter 2

1. In the autumn of 2010, Alabama's student body had tripled to 30,232 students, 3,761 of them African Americans. Of that number, 3,065 came to the Capstone from

cities and towns across Alabama. University of Alabama, Office of Institutional Research and Assessment, "Ethnic Diversity 2010," *http://oria.ua.edu*, accessed May 5, 2011.

2. Flynt, *Alabama in the Twentieth Century*, 366.

3. "No Easy Life for Troopers on Campus," *Crimson-White*, June 13, 1963, 2.

4. "Curfew a Pain, but Needed," ibid., 1.

5. Clark, *The Schoolhouse Door*, 235.

6. Letter, Frank A. Rose to Oviatt Bowers, June 27, 1963, Rose Papers, General Correspondence File B, 1963.

7. "Needed More Students, Less Pickets," *Crimson-White*, June 27, 1963, 4.

8. Clark, *The Schoolhouse Door*, 241–42.

9. "Summer Usually Dull: Not This Time," *Crimson-White*, September 29, 1963, 10.

10. Letter, John L. Blackburn to James A. Hood, August 8, 1963, Dean of Students Records, Confidential File, 1963, Hoole Special Collections Library, UA.

11. Memorandum, Iredell Jenkins to Dean of Men, John L. Blackburn, August 7, 1963, Dean of Students Records, Confidential File, 1963, Hoole Special Collections Library, UA.

12. "Hood Quits U of A," *Birmingham News*, August 12, 1963, 1.

13. *Rebel Underground*, August 1963, vol. 4, 1.

14. Flynt, *Alabama in the Twentieth Century*, 354.

15. "Dean's Memo Curbs Drinking," *Crimson-White*, September 26, 1963, 1.

16. Ibid.

17. Carol Ann Self, personal interview, Tuscaloosa, Alabama, April 3, 2010.

18. Jack Drake, personal interview, Birmingham, Alabama, January 23, 2010.

19. "Senate Kills Resolution Commending Dr. Rose," *Crimson-White*, October 17, 1963.

20. "Senator Says Article on Rose Misleading," *Crimson-White*, October 24, 1963, 3.

21. "'Bomb?,'" *Crimson-White*, October 31, 1963, 4.

22. "A Cheerful Homecoming," *Tuscaloosa News*, November 2, 1963, 6.

23. "Proud Tide Fights Back to Nip State," *Tuscaloosa News*, November 3, 1963, 9.

24. "Bloodthirsty Bama Broads Bummed-up in Biting Brawl," *Crimson-White*, November 14, 1963, 1.

25. "Smothers Brothers to Appear Tuesday in Foster," *Crimson-White*, October 17, 1963, 1; "Julie London Foster Show Sold Out," *Crimson-White*, November 14 1963, 1; and "Joan Baez Plays for 'Subjects' at Stillman," *Crimson-White*, April 9, 1964, 8–9.

26. "Guard Release Affects 220 Here," *Tuscaloosa News*, November 6, 1963, 13.

27. "Blast Rocks Campus Area," *Tuscaloosa News*, November 16, 1963, 1; and "Bomber Hits Again, in Southside Section," *Tuscaloosa News*, November 17, 1963, 1.

28. "Students Urged to Stay Away from Future Bombings," *Crimson-White*, November 21, 1963, 1.

29. "Four Guardsmen Seized in Blasts," *Tuscaloosa News*, December 20, 1962, 1.

30. Dee Merrill, "While JFK Was a Crowd Pleaser, Johnson Is an Arm Twister," *Crimson-White*, December 6, 1963, 5.

31. "It Certainly Seems Strange," *Crimson-White*, October 10, 1963, 4.

32. "Main Library Extends Hours to Eleven," *Crimson-White*, February 6, 1964, 3.

33. "'Liberalism vs. Conservatism,' Alpha Lambda Delta Topic," *Crimson-White*, November 14, 1963, 1.

34. Letter, Dean Frederick W. Conner to Frank A. Rose, April 24, 1964, Rose Papers, Graduate School of Arts and Sciences File, 1964.

35. Report on New Sabbatical Policy, included in Minutes of the Board of Trustees, May 30, 1964, Rose Papers, Board of Trustees File, 1964.

36. Wolfe, *The University of Alabama*, 193 and 204; and President's Annual Report, Minutes of the Meeting of the Board of Trustees, May 30, 1964, Rose Papers, Board of Trustees File, 1964.

37. State of the University Report, in Minutes of the Board of Trustees, November 2, 1963, Rose Papers, Board of Trustees File, 1963.

38. Christopher Jencks and David Riesman, *The Academic Revolution* (New Brunswick, NJ: Transaction Publications, 2002), 119.

39. Minutes of the Board of Trustees, November 2, 1963, Rose Papers, Board of Trustees File.

40. Bryant and Underwood, *Bear*, appendix, 309 and 312.

41. Letter, Frank A. Rose to the Reverend Arno Gustin, President, Saint Johns University, April 27, 1963, Rose Papers, Personal Correspondence File R, 1963.

42. "Captain Yantis Wins Combat Award for Laos Action," *Crimson-White*, September 26, 1963, 2; and "'Havoc'Today on the Quad," *Crimson-White*, May 11, 1964, 1.

43. "Security Agency Tests Due Here in December," *Crimson-White*, September 26, 1963, 10.

44. "Huge Crowd Hears Porter in Arts Festival Feature," 1; and "'Waiting for Godot' Performed by UA Players," *Crimson-White*, February 13,1964, 1.

45. "'Hmmm' and 'Humdiddy' in Humdinger of a Show, April 2," *Crimson-White*, March 19,1964, 1; and "Ferrante & Teicher to Play at Foster Tuesday Night," *Crimson-White*, April 16, 1964, 1.

46. "Joan Baez Plays for 'Subjects' at Stillman," 8–9.

47. "Midnight Is Hour for Coeds Now on Friday Nights," *Crimson-White*, February 27, 1964, 1.

48. "'Miss Alabama' Elected at Concert Studio Presents Series," *Crimson-White*, May 7, 1964, 2.

49. "What Is Dex?," *Crimson-White*, January 9, 1964, 2.

50. Letter, George C. Wallace to Frank A. Rose, April 20, 1964, Rose Papers, American Studies File, 1964.

51. Carmichael's address quoted in "Conference on Deep South Brings Noted Leaders to University," *Crimson-White*, April 30, 1964, 2–3.

52. Brochure, Conference on the Social Sciences and the Development of the New South, April 23–25, 1964, Rose Papers, American Studies File, 1964.

53. "Unconfirmed Reports Say 3 Negroes In," *Crimson-White*, April 30, 1964; 1; and "Five Negroes Reportedly Accepted," *Crimson White*, June 18, 1964, 18.

54. "First African Baptist Church," Historic Places of the Civil Rights Movement, National Park Service, *https://www.nps.gov/nr/travel/civilrights/al1.htm*, accessed April 15, 2010.

55. "Theater Mixed Here; No Trouble," *Tuscaloosa News*, July 5, 1964, 1.

56. "Students, Faculty Harassed by Anti-Rights Act Pickets," *Crimson-White*, July 9, 1964, 1.

57. Ibid.

58. Mrs. James R. Jaquith, "Choice," letter to the editor, *Tuscaloosa News*, July 5, 1964, 4.

59. Buford Boone was physically smaller than my father, but he had the confidence of having been an FBI agent during World War II, a career he abandoned at the end of the war to return to journalism as publisher of the *Tuscaloosa News*.

60. "Ready for Mob Control?," *Tuscaloosa News*, July 7, 1964, 1.

61. Jim Boone, personal interview, February 2, 2009.

62. "Lullaby and Good Night," *Tuscaloosa News*, July 8, 1964, 1.

63. "Gas Used on Mob; City Orders Curfew," *Tuscaloosa News*, July 10, 1964, 1.

64. "Putting on the Squeeze," *Tuscaloosa News*, July 10, 1964, 1.

65. "No Penalty for Using Rights," *Crimson-White*, July 9, 1964, 1.

66. "Negro Group Here Calls off Boycott," *Tuscaloosa News*, July 14, 1964, 1.

Chapter 3

1. "Business As Usual," *Crimson-White*, June 18, 1964, 1.

2. "News Notes," *Crimson-White*, June 25, 1964, 2; and University of Alabama news release, October 21, 1964, J. Jefferson Bennett Papers, News Bureau File, 1964, Hoole Special Collections Library, UA.

3. *Alumni Bulletin*, Winter 1964, 1, Rose Papers, Alumni Association File, 1964–65.

4. Letter, Frank A. Rose to Jefferson L. Coleman, June 2, 1964, Rose Papers, Field House Committee File, 1964.

5. "Port Huron Statement of the Students for a Democratic Society," introduction, 1. https:coursea.matrix.msu.edu/whist306/documents/huron.html, accessed June 28, 2009.

6. Final Report on the Second Year of the Four-Year Fraternity Self-Evaluation Program, July 14, 1964, Rose Papers, Fraternity Evaluation File, 1964.

7. "Fraternities Are Called 'Irresponsible,'" *Crimson-White*, July 30, 1964, 1; and letter, John L. Blackburn to Frank A. Rose, July 31, 1964, Rose Papers, Fraternity Evaluation File, 1964.

8. "Fraternity Reforms Announced As IFC Prexy Answers Criticisms," *Crimson-White*, August 14, 1964, 1.

9. "New IFC Rush System Proposed: Parties Cut," *Crimson-White*, February 11, 1965, 1.

10. Letter, Thomas B. Alexander to Mayor George Van Tassel, July 13, 1964, J. Jefferson Bennett Papers, American Association of University Professors File, 1958–64, Hoole Special Collections Library, UA.

11. Students who studied, listened, and took notes found Dr. McElroy's classes enlightening. After the first class, he began every subsequent class in every course with, "Continuing our discussion. . . ." Discussions were rare. He spoke, students listened. For history majors, like the author, advanced courses like "Modern Europe" and "The Rise and Fall of the Third Reich," while demanding, were also fabulous. We also discovered David McElroy to be a wise and compassionate man. For some, David became a devoted mentor and lifelong friend.

12. "We Apologize," *Crimson-White*, November 12, 1964, 4.

13. "CAGE Is Theme for Homecoming," *Crimson-White*, October 8, 1964, 5.

14. Letters, Mrs. Joe Madden to Frank A. Rose, November 28, 1964; and Frank A. Rose to Mrs. Joe Madden, December 7, 1964, Rose Papers, Students Correspondence File, 1964.

15. Letter, Ellis B. Davis Jr. to Bill Renneker, December 9, 1964, Rose Papers, Students Correspondence File, 1964.

16. "'Satchmo' Was at Capstone Years Ago," *Crimson-White*, December 3, 1964, 1.

17. "Louis Armstrong Barred from Festival of Arts Here: Not the Right Time Says Administration Officials," *Crimson-White*, December 3, 1964, 1.

18. Flynt, *Alabama in the Twentieth Century*, 514–16; "Students Want Ban on Satchmo Lifted: Petitions Passed," *Crimson-White*, December 10, 1964, 1–2; letters, Michael Thompson to Frank A. Rose, December 6, 1964; and Frank A. Rose to Michael Thompson, December 14, 1964, Rose Papers, Louis Armstrong File, 1964.

19. "Students Want Ban on Satchmo Lifted," 1.

20. "Senate Backs Administration Viewpoint as Armstrong Issue Begins to Fade," *Crimson-White*, December 17, 1964, 1.

21. Letter, Theodore H. Fetter to J. Jefferson Bennett, December 14, 1964, Rose Papers, General Correspondence File F, 1964.

22. "Sloppy Handling," *Crimson-White*, December 17, 1964, 4.

23. Letter, Gessner T. McCorvey to Frank A. Rose, December 8, 1964, Rose Papers, Board of Trustees File, 1964.

24. Letter, Frank A. Rose to Gessner T. McCorvey, December 14, 1964, Rose Papers, Board of Trustees File, 1964.

25. Letter, Frank A. Rose to William E. Jones, December 18, 1964, Rose Papers, General Correspondence File J, 1964.

26. "Sororities Here Regulate Date Choices at Capstone," *Crimson-White*, Decem-

ber 17, 1964, 3. Several Alabama sorority alumna who read this manuscript disputed the existence of a point system, saying that their particular sorority didn't use it.

27. Memorandum, J. Jefferson Bennett to Frank A. Rose, March 8, 1965, Rose Papers, Integration General File, 1965.

28. Letters to writers critical of professor, Rose Papers, Integration, General Correspondence File, 1965.

29. Telegram, Margaret Chamber Rainey to Frank A. Rose, March 9, 1965; and letter, Frank A. Rose to Margaret Chamber Rainey, March 11, 1965, Rose Papers, General Correspondence File R, 1965.

30. "Reeb Widow Fund Begun," *Tuscaloosa News*, March 12, 1965, 2.

31. "Seven Negroes Turned Away from Church," *Tuscaloosa News*, February 12, 1962, 1.

32. Letter, Edward J. May, Clerk of the Session, First Presbyterian Church to Reverend Howard Lawson, Chairman, Council on Campus Christian Life, Synod of Alabama, April 12, 1962, Session Records, 1961–65, First Presbyterian Church, Tuscaloosa, Alabama.

33. "University Minister Resigns Due to Racial Discord," *Crimson-White*, July 5, 1962, 1.

34. Robert Keever, telephone interview, June 29, 2009.

35. Ibid.; and "Sympathy Parade Planned Here," *Tuscaloosa News*, March 11, 1965, 1.

36. "All Is Quiet during March," *Tuscaloosa News*, March 13, 1965, 1.

37. "University of Alabama Students in Sympathy Demonstration Here," *Crimson-White*, March 18, 1965, 3.

38. Ibid.

39. "Rogers Speaks to Over 100 at UA Civil Rights Meeting," *Crimson-White*, March 25, 1965, 1.

40. "Senate Defeats Civil Rights Group Charter by One Vote," *Crimson-White*, April 1, 1965, 1.

41. "Rights Group Reorganized after Senate Denies Charter," *Crimson-White*, April 7, 1965, 1.

42. "Human Rights Forum Passes SGA House," *Crimson-White*, September 30, 1965, 1.

43. Nancy Zaroulis and Gerald Sullivan, *Who Spoke Up?: American Protests against the War in Vietnam, 1963–1975* (New York: Holt, Rinehart, and Winston, 1978), 37.

44. "Senators Agree on Viet Negotiations, but Differ on Right Time and Methods," *Crimson-White*, April 4, 1965, 3.

45. "Million More Men Needed to Win in Vietnam, Fall Says Here," *Crimson-White*, April 8, 1965, 3.

46. Letters, Cadet Major Ronald E. Clary to Frank A. Rose, May 12, 1965; and Frank A. Rose to Bob Hope, May 13, 1965, Rose Papers, General Correspondence File H, 1965.

47. "Graham Sermon Cancelled by Rain," *Crimson-White*, April 29, 1965, 1; and letter, Frank A. Rose to Dr. Billy Graham, April 30, 1965, Rose Papers, General Correspondence File G, 1965.

48. Sherwood Wirt, "God's Radiance in Alabama," *Decision*, August 1965, 8–9.

49. "Serious Book-Loving Students to Relax at Bama Day, April 9," *Crimson-White*, April 1, 1965, 1.

50. "Wallace Presents Citations, Speaks Here at Governor's Day," *Crimson-White*, April 29, 1965, 2.

51. Flynt, *Alabama in the Twentieth Century*, 241.

52. Jim Murray, "Stars Rise on Alabama," *Los Angeles Times*, January 5, 1965, CC 1.

53. Melvin Durslag, "Wanted Tackles for 'Bama,'" *Los Angeles Times*, undated clipping attached to a letter, Eugene B. Ethridge to Frank A. Rose, April 29, 1965, Rose Papers, General Correspondence File E, 1965.

54. Letter, Frank A. Rose to David Nevin, February 4, 1965, Rose Papers, General Correspondence File N, 1965.

55. Letter, Frank A. Rose to Lyndon B. Johnson, October 18, 1964, Rose Papers, General Correspondence File J, 1964–65.

56. "UA Trains 1,700 Teachers for Project Head Start Here," *Crimson-White*, July 1, 1965, 1.

57. Letter, Frank A. Rose to David Nevin, June 22, 1965, Rose Papers, ABC Scope File, 1965.

58. "Civil Rights: She Came Through," *Newsweek*, June 14, 1965, 17–38.

59. Gay Talese, "Presence of Negro Students Brings Quiet Changes to University of Alabama Campus," *New York Times*, May 11, 1965, C 22, Amelia Gayle Gorgas Library, University of Alabama.

60. Letter, Thomas W. Moore to Frank A. Rose, May 3, 1965, Rose Papers, Personal Correspondence File M, 1965.

61. Commencement Address, Thomas W. Moore, May 30, 1965, Rose Papers, Commencement File, 1965.

62. Letters, Lawrence E. McGinty to Frank A. Rose, June 10, 1965; and Frank A. Rose to Lawrence E. McGinty, June 16, 1965, Rose Papers, ABC Scope File, 1965.

Chapter 4

1. "UA Administrator, Civic Leader, Dies," *Tuscaloosa News*, July 4, 2009, 1 and 7A. Also, Blackburn, in his interview with Frank Rose in 1990, reminisced about arriving at the Capstone and seeing Klansmen marching at the edge of campus.

2. Letter, John L. Blackburn to C. T. Sharpton, January 19, 1965, Rose Papers, Dean of Men's Files, 1965–66.

3. Forrest David Mathews, "Eulogy for John Blackburn," First Presbyterian Church, Tuscaloosa, Alabama, July 7, 2009.

4. David Mathews, personal interview, February 2, 2009.

5. Letter, Frank A. Rose to David Nevin, June 22, 1965, Rose Papers, ABC Scope File, 1965.

6. "Progress and Growth at U of A," *Crimson-White*, June 17, 1965, 4. In addition to the main campus in Tuscaloosa, there were extension centers in Birmingham, Gadsden, Dothan, Huntsville, and one in Montgomery soon to be turned over to Auburn.

7. "Sharpton Plays Major Role in UA Expansion Program," *Crimson-White*, June 24, 1965, 3; and letter, Alex G. Pow to Raymond F. McLain, December 19, 1965, Rose Papers, Correspondence File Mc, 1965.

8. Letter, Frank A. Rose to Ralph W. Adams, June 11, 1965, Rose Papers, Commencement File, 1965.

9. Zaroulis and Sullivan, *Who Spoke Up?*, 39–41.

10. "Unique Boundary for UA Summer," *Crimson-White*, September 23, 1965, 7.

11. Letter, Frank A. Rose to Susie Mosley, Secretary, Committee on Speech Policy, University of Arkansas, January 7, 1965, Rose Papers, General Correspondence File M, 1965.

12. "Marchers Carry Viet Protests to Capitol Hill," *Birmingham News*, August 10, 1965, 1.

13. Letters, R. B. Jones to George C. Wallace, August 9, 1965; Frank A. Rose to R. B. Jones, August 11, 1965; and Raymond D. Hurlbert to Frank A. Rose, August 11, 1965, Rose Papers, Alabama Educational Television File.

14. "Rose Outlines New Programs at Student Leaders Retreat," *Crimson-White*, September 23, 1965, 1.

15. "Collegiate Reformers: 1965," speech by David Mathews, reprinted in *Crimson-White*, September 23, 1965, 5.

16. Ibid.

17. Ralph Knowles, quoted in "Emphasis '66 Seeks Focus by Issues," *Crimson-White*, September 23, 1965, 1.

18. "Board Bill Passes SGA Senate, 16–3," *Crimson-White*, November 18, 1965, 1.

19. *Corolla*, 1966, Coleman Lollar, ed. (Tuscaloosa: University of Alabama, 1966), "Board of Publications" photograph and caption, 182.

20. *The Alabama COED*, University of Alabama, 1964, 1.

21. "Coed Rules Called Faulty," *Crimson-White*, October 1, 1965, 1.

22. "Rose Issues Restatement of UA COED Drinking Rules," *Crimson-White*, October 1, 1965, 1.

23. "Death of the Greeks," *Crimson-White*, July 22, 1965. 4.

24. Letter, Mrs. Darnell R. Nordwall, National President, Alpha Chi Omega, to Frank A. Rose, August 25, 1965, Rose Papers, Fraternity File, 1965.

25. "Death of the Greeks," 4.

26. Memorandum, David Mathews to J. Jefferson Bennett, August 11, 1965; memorandum, J. Jefferson Bennett to Frank A. Rose, August 16, 1965, J. Jefferson Bennett

Papers, Frank A. Rose Correspondence File, Hoole Special Collections Library, UA; and "Screaming James Brown Here Tuesday for Cotillion Club Show," *Crimson-White*, September 30, 1965, 1.

27. Personal remembrance. I was among the students in the audience.

28. "Shelton Still Mum on Klan Doings," *Tuscaloosa News*, October 20, 1965, 1.

29. "KKK Killing Alabama's Image," *Crimson-White*, October 28, 1965, 4.

30. "Plans Completed for Homecoming," *Crimson-White*, October 14, 1965, 1.

31. "Pete Fountain to Play Bama into Homecoming," *Crimson-White*, October 22, 1965, 1.

32. "Happiness Is No. 1!" *Crimson-White*, January 13, 1965, 4.

33. Letter, Herbert J. Matlack to Frank A. Rose, January 2, 1966, Rose Papers, Orange Bowl, January 1, 1965, File.

34. Letter, G. C. Garrett, chapter manager, American Red Cross, to Frank A. Rose, December 10, 1965, Rose Papers, General Correspondence File G, 1965; and "Students to Donate Blood to Aid U.S. Troops in Viet Nam," *Crimson-White*, November 4, 1965, 1.

35. Letter, PFC Dale E. Easterling to Frank A. Rose, December 9, 1965, Rose Papers, General Correspondence File E, 1965.

36. "NAACP Head Here Tuesday," *Crimson-White*, December 9, 1965, 13.

37. Letter, Frank A. Rose to Jack W. Hines, November 2, 1965, Rose Papers, General Correspondence File H, 1965.

38. "Viet Nam Effort Supported by UA Petition Signers," *Crimson-White*, January 13, 1966, 15.

39. "SGA Survey Claims 'Most All Coeds Do!'" *Crimson-White*, February 21, 1966, 4.

40. "UA Welcome Mat Down for Visitor," *Tuscaloosa News*, February 23, 1966, 1.

41. "Mrs. Johnson Impresses Women at Conference," *Tuscaloosa News*, February 26, 1966, 1.

42. "Democracy Needs College Students Says Senator Morton," *Crimson-White*, March 22, 1966, 1.

43. "RFK Urges New System for Health Education," *Tuscaloosa News*, March 19, 1966, 1.

44. "RFK Makes Appeal for National Unity," *Crimson-White*, March 22, 1966, 1.

45. "Dissent and Freedom Now Altered—Editor," *Crimson-White*, March 22, 1965, 1.

46. Letter, Nathan Glazer to Frank A. Rose, March 21, 1966, Rose Papers, General Correspondence File G, 1966.

47. "George Hits Papers at Courthouse Rally," *Crimson-White*, March 22, 1966, 5.

48. "Wallace Hits Pres, RFK," *Tuscaloosa News*, March 20, 1966, 1.

49. Letter, Frank A. Rose to David H. Griffin, March 23, 1966, Rose Papers, Correspondence File G, 1964–66.

50. "Speaker Decision in Proper Hands," *Crimson-White*, March 29, 1966, 1.

51. "Wallace Protest," *Crimson-White*, April 21, 1966, 1.

52. "Police Here Break Up Protests," *Tuscaloosa News*, April 19, 1966, 1; and "Two Pickets Free on Bond after University Arrest," *Tuscaloosa News*, April 20, 1966, 1.

53. Jack Drake, interviewed by author, tape recording, Birmingham, Alabama, January 23, 2010; and "UA Asks Charges Be Dropped," *Crimson-White*, April 25, 1966, 1.

54. "University and Stillman Students Considering Court Action," *Crimson-White*, April 28, 1966, 1.

55. "George's Day—It Was a Real Comedy," *Crimson-White*, April 25, 1966, 4.

56. "AU Band Plays at AF Ball," *Crimson-White*, March 24, 1966, 1.

57. "Bama Day, 1966, Cotton Candy Plus," *Crimson-White*, March 29, 1966, 1.

58. "Sweethearts One and All," *Crimson-White*, May 2, 1966, 1.

59. "Defense Tops Offense in Bama Scrimmage," *Crimson-White*, May 9, 1966, 5.

60. "A Night with the Black Berets: They Said It Was a Game," *Crimson-White*, May 9, 1966, 1.

61. "Be 'Gay, High,' Says Pamphlet on How to Beat the Draft," *Crimson-White*, May 12, 1966, 1.

62. "Million Dollar Miss," *Crimson-White*, May 12, 1966, 3.

63. "Rose Stricken, Undergoes Surgery," *Tuscaloosa News*, May 23, 1966, 1; and letter, Frank A. Rose to Albert B. Moore, June 6, 1966, Rose Papers, Letters and Flowers during Illness in Washington, 6/21/66 File.

64. "All's Well—Bear's Back," *Crimson-White*, July 2, 1966; and Barra, *The Last Coach*, 332.

65. Mathews interview, May 6, 2009.

66. "Atmosphere Important Says Last Year's Dean," *Crimson-White*, June 23, 1966, 1.

Chapter 5

1. "State of the University Address, 1966," in *Corolla*, 1967, 138.

2. Letter, David Mathews to Bert S. Nettles, June 20, 1966, David Mathews Papers, Box 171, Personal Correspondence File, 1966–67, Hoole Special Collections Library, UA; and Mathews interview, May 6, 2009.

3. "Atmosphere Important Says Last Year's Dean," *Crimson-White*, June 23, 1966, 1.

4. Carl Davidson, "Towards Student Syndicalism," typescript copy 3, in F. David Mathews Papers, Box 174, Students for a Democratic Society File, Hoole Special Collections Library, UA.

5. Ibid., 4–7.

6. An excellent analysis of who served and who did not can be found in Thomas C. Thayer, *War without Fronts: The American Experience in Vietnam* (Boulder, CO: Westview Special Military Studies, 1986), 109–23.

7. John F. Guilmartin, *America in Vietnam: The Fifteen Year War* (New York: Ran-

dom House, 1991) 84–87; and George C. Herring Jr. *America's Longest War: The United States and Vietnam, 1950–1975*, 2nd ed. (New York: McGraw-Hill, 1995), 166.

8. Letter, Frank A. Rose to H. E. Williams, July 13, 1966, Rose Papers, Correspondence File W, 1966.

9. Letters, Frank A. Rose to Vice President J. Jefferson Bennett; and Frank A. Rose to F. David Mathews, both dated September 9, 1966, Rose Papers, Faculty General Salaries File, 1967.

10. Letter, Alex S. Pow, Vice President for Academic Affairs, to F. David Mathews, July 1, 1966, F. David Mathews Papers, Box 167, General Administration File, Hoole Special Collections Library, UA.

11. "Chicago, Indiana Scholars on Loan," *Crimson-White*, September 15, 1966, 1.

12. "Board Blames Delay on Cowden," *Crimson-White*, October 10, 1966, 1.

13. "First Negro Rushee Found It Exciting," *Crimson-White*, September 22, 1966, 1.

14. Glenda Guyton, personal interview, January 14, 2011.

15. Letter, Herman B. Wells to Frank A. Rose, November 3, 1966, Rose Papers, General Correspondence File W, 1966.

16. Letter, Frank A. Rose to Herman B. Wells, November 17, 1966, Rose Papers, General Correspondence File W, 1966.

17. "Sigma Chi Discriminates at Colorado: Booted," *Crimson-White*, September 26, 1966.

18. "Greek System Exists, for Better or Worse," *Crimson-White*, February 1, 1967, 1.

19. "Polls Say Bear to Win Third Crown," and "Playboy Names Bear Coach of the Year," *Crimson-White*, September 12, 1966, 1.

20. "LA Tech First Victim," *Crimson-White*, September 26, 1966, 1.

21. *Corolla*, 1967, 230–31.

22. Memorandum, John L. Blackburn to Frank A. Rose, October 10, 1966, David Mathews Papers, C-W Endorsement File, 1967, Hoole Special Collections Library, UA.

23. "Undeniably Sparkman," Billie Blair, *Crimson-White*, October 13, 1966, 4.

24. Norman R. Blaylock, "Board of Publications Index," unpublished paper summarizing major decisions of the Board of Publications, F. David Mathews Papers, Box 168, Board of Publication File, 1966–67; and letter, Frank A. Rose to Frank M. Johnson Jr., October 15, 1966, Rose Papers, Personal Correspondence File J, 1966.

25. "C-W Controversy Goes to Board," *Crimson-White*, October 17, 1966, 1.

26. "SGA Senate Resolution #3," Rose Papers, Student Government Association File, 1966; and "The Crimson-White Issue," *Birmingham Post Herald*, October 28, 1966, 4.

27. "Billie Blair's Statement before the Board of Publications," transcript in F. David Mathews Papers, Box 168, C-W Endorsements File, 1966, Hoole Special Collections Library, UA.

28. "Board Undecided—Wants Outside Study," *Crimson-White*, November 7, 1966, 1.

29. "U.A. Paper Endorses Don Collins," *Montgomery Advertiser*, October 20, 1966, 3.

30. "And Now, the Governor," Billie Blair, *Crimson-White*, November 7, 1966, 4.

31. Voices from within Alabama did not cry alone in the wilderness. In an editorial supporting the Tide's case for the national championship, *Sports Illustrated* chided, "Now be honest, Notre Dame and Michigan State, would you really want to play Alabama?," quoted in the *Corolla*, 1967, 228.

32. Ibid., 229.

33. Keith Dunnavant, *The Missing Ring: How Bear Bryant and the 1966 Alabama Crimson Tide Were Denied College Football's Most Elusive Prize* (New York: St. Martin's Press, 2007), 206.

34. President's Report to the Board of Trustees, November 12, 1966, F. David Mathews Papers, Box 170, Homecoming File, 1966, Hoole Special Collections Library, UA.

35. Ibid., 3–4; and "First Lady Sits In on Trustee Meeting," *Crimson-White*, November 14, 1966, 1.

36. Memorandum, David Mathews to Frank A. Rose, September 22, 1966, Rose Papers, David Mathews File, 1966; and, "Apartment Visitation Ban Lifted: Parents Can Decide, Closing Hours Kept," *Crimson-White*, February 6, 1967, 1. As a matter of safety, most young women provided the required information. Many, however, visited men's apartments whenever they pleased, constrained only by the established curfew hours.

37. "Ex UA Student LSD High Chief," *Crimson-White*, September 19, 1966, 8.

38. "Reports of Drugs Here 'Shock' Students," *Crimson-White*, March 16, 1967, 6.

39. Edward O'Brien, "Far Leftist Plan Disruptions on College Campuses," *Birmingham News*, February 14, 1967, 24.

40. Gertude Samuels, "Four Years after Governor Wallace Stood in the Door," *New York Times Sunday Magazine*, May 14, 1967, 22.

41. Ibid.

42. "Black Students Face Recreational Dilemma at UA," *Crimson-White*, February 26, 1968, 1.

43. News release, August 5, 1966, Austin R. Meadows, State Superintendent of Education, Rose Papers, State Legislature File, 1966.

44. "Sweeping School Mix Ruled," *Birmingham News*, March 22, 1967, 1.

45. Memorandum, David Mathews to Frank A. Rose, February 17, 1967, F. David Mathews Papers, Box 169, Emphasis '67 File, Hoole Special Collections Library, UA.

46. Memorandum, David Mathews to Frank A. Rose, March 3, 1967, F. David Mathews Papers, Box 169, Emphasis '67 File, Hoole Special Collections Library, UA.

47. Schedule of Events, Emphasis '67 Program, Rose Papers, Emphasis '67 File; and James B. Reston, "Tuscaloosa: Report from the University of Alabama," *New York Times*, Sunday, March 19, 1967, E14.

48. Photograph of the Emphasis demonstrators, *Corolla*, 1968, 22 (since the 1967

Corolla had already gone to press, the Emphasis '67 program was covered in the next year's annual.)

49. "Protests Sounds Help Hippies Keep in Mood," *Crimson-White*, March 20, 1967, 1.

50. "Four War Protestors Arrested at UA: Pickets Booked for Trespassing; Trial Date Set," *Crimson-White*, March 20, 1967, 1; and "Four Arrested Protestors Released," *Birmingham News*, March 18, 1967, 2.

51. "Higgins Petitions Rusk," *Crimson-White*, March 20, 1967, 1.

52. Reston, "Report from the University of Alabama," E14.

53. "Wallace Bares Plan to Defy Integration Order," *Birmingham News*, March 28, 1967, 1; and letter, Frank A. Rose to William S. Farmer Jr., April 4, 1967, Rose Papers, Personal Correspondence File F, 1967.

54. "Rose-Wallace Tiff Now in the Open," *Birmingham News*, April 6, 1967, 1.

55. "SGA Denounces Gov. Wallace: Joint Session Decries Action," *Crimson-White*, April 3, 1967, 1.

56. "University Program Blasted," and "College Speaker Ban Bill Introduced: UA Magazine Prompts Move," *Birmingham News*, April 5, 1966, 1.

57. House Resolution 68, April 5, 1967, Rose Papers, State Legislature File, 1967.

58. "Angry Rose Backs UA Policy: Threatens to Resign," *Birmingham News*, April 5, 1967, 1.

59. "Fed Up with Legislature, Most Students Support Rose," *Crimson-White*, April 13, 1967, 1.

60. Telegram, E. B. Bailey, Citizens Council of Tarrant, to Frank A. Rose, April 7, 1967; and letter, R. L. Flowers to Frank A. Rose, April 10, 1967, Rose Papers, Crank Letters File, 1967.

61. Letter, Shelby H. Batson to Frank A. Rose, April 5, 1967, Rose Papers, Crank Letters File, 1967.

62. "Troy Asks for Freedom of Press after Censorship," *Crimson-White*, April 17, 1967, 2.

63. "C-W Can Endorse—Board," *Crimson-White*, April 17, 1967, 1.

64. "Lurleen Warns of Collision," *Crimson-White*, May 1, 1967, 1.

65. Ibid.

66. "Bryant Suspends Stabler," *Crimson-White*, April 24, 1967, 5.

67. Barra, *The Last Coach*, 346.

68. John David Briley, *Career in Crisis: Paul "Bear" Bryant and the 1971 Season of Change* (Macon, GA: Mercer University Press, 2006), 23–25; and Dunnavant, *The Missing Ring*, 275–77.

69. "UP Endorses Siegelman over Geren for SGA Head," *Crimson-White*, March 9, 1967, 1.

70. "Colleges Join, Support Rose, Hit Lurleen, Adams," *Crimson-White*, April 17, 1967, 1.

71. "Why Make Films?," *Crimson-White*, April 24, 1967, 5.

72. "Kicks, Costumes and Derby: Five Sororities to Battle," *Crimson-White*, April 27, 1968, 2.

73. D. Michael Van De Veer, "Manifesto of the Alabama Democratic Students Organization," copy in F. David Mathews Papers, Box 171, Dean of Men's Files, 1967, Hoole Special Collections Library, UA.

74. Memorandum, Thomas A. McLeod, Director of Men's Activities, to John L. Blackburn, May 15, 1967, Rose Papers, Dean of Student Development/John L. Blackburn File, 1967.

75. "High Rise Dorm Given Go-Ahead," *Tuscaloosa News*, January 22, 1967, 2.

76. Memorandum, Frank A. Rose to C. T. Sharpton and J. Jefferson Bennett, April 12, 1967, Rose Papers, Physical Planning File, 1967.

77. Col. Willard V. Brown Papers, Commencement File, 1967, Hoole Special Collections Library, UA.

Chapter 6

1. Letter, J. Jefferson Bennett to Hugh Merrill, Chairman, House Judiciary Committee, July 6, 1967, Rose Papers, Legislature File, 1967.

2. Letter, Frank A. Rose to McGeorge Bundy, September 26, 1967, Rose Papers, General Correspondence File B, 1967.

3. Letter, David Mathews to Clarence C. Mondale, May 5, 1967, F. David Mathews Papers, Box 171, Personal Correspondence File, 1966–67, Hoole Special Collections Library, UA.

4. "Dr. Rose Said," *Crimson-White*, August 7, 1967, 1.

5. "Speaker Ban Again," *Crimson-White*, July 7, 1967, 2.

6. "'Speaker Ban' Finds Rough Road: State Bar and APA Oppose Childs' Bill," *Crimson-White*, August 7, 1967, 1.

7. Memorandum, David Mathews to Frank A. Rose, July 17, 1967, Rose Papers, State Legislature File, 1967.

8. "Speaker Ban Hits a Snag," *Tuscaloosa News*, August 2, 1967, 1.

9. "Speaker Ban Bill Falls to Senate Ax," *Montgomery Advertiser*, August 2, 1967, 1.

10. Memorandum, David Mathews to Frank A. Rose, July 17, 1967, Rose Papers, State Legislature File, 1967.

11. "Projections for Education: 15-Minute Report for College and University Trustees," October 16, 1967, Baltimore, Maryland, in Frank M. Rose Papers, Correspondence with the Board of Trustees File, 1967.

12. Letter, Frank A. Rose to State Senator William D. Sellers Jr., September 7, 1967, Rose Papers, State Legislature File, 1967.

13. Zaroulis and Sullivan, *Who Spoke Up?*, 116.

14. Todd Gitlin, *The Sixties: Years of Hope, Days of Rage* (New York: Bantam Books, 1989), 261–62.

15. "Bama's Sylvia Named Miss Universe," *Crimson-White*, July 17, 1967, 1.

16. "Whose Got the Eggs? Tide or Seminoles," *Tuscaloosa News*, September 18, 1967, 4.

17. "Heap Big Bama Defense? Seminoles Say 'Ugh!,'" *Tuscaloosa News*, September 24, 1967, 11; and "Bear: Lucky to Tie," *Crimson-White*, September 27, 1967, 5.

18. "UA Faculty Called Key to Excellence," *Tuscaloosa News*, October 19, 1967, 3.

19. "University-SGA Relations," position paper by Dean John L. Blackburn, September 25, 1967, David Mathews Papers, Box 171, Dean of Men's File, Hoole Special Collections, Library UA.

20. "SGA President Wants Changes," *Crimson-White*, October 9, 1967, 1.

21. Letter, Frank M. Johnson Jr. to Frank A. Rose, September 8, 1967, and attached court order, Gary Dickey v. Alabama State Board of Education, Governor Lurleen B. Wallace, Ralph W. Adams, et al., September 8, 1967, Rose Papers, Speaker Ban Bill File, 1967.

22. "SGA Seeks Court Ruling on Student Rights Issue," *Crimson-White*, October 16, 1967, 1.

23. Letter, Frank A. Rose to Don Siegelman, November 9, 1967, Rose Papers, Student Government Association File, 1966–67.

24. Letter, Don Siegelman to Frank A. Rose, November 9, 1967, Rose Papers, Student Government Association File, 1966–67.

25. Letter, Frank A. Rose to Don Siegelman, November 10, 1967, Rose Papers, Student Government Association File, 1966–67.

26. Zaroulis and Sullivan, *Who Spoke Up?*, 134–37.

27. Ibid.; and "Pentagon Invasion Blocked, Hippies, Pot Make Scene," *Tuscaloosa News*, October 22, 1967, 1.

28. "Sylvia's Just a Football Fan," *Tuscaloosa News*, October 20, 1967, 1.

29. "Cotillion Club Presents First of Season," *Crimson-White*, September 25, 1967, 1.

30. "*Farrago* Due in November," *Crimson-White*, October 16, 1967, 1.

31. "Defense Carries Tide to 13–0 Win," *Crimson-White*, November 6, 1967, 5.

32. Jim Dent, *The Junction Boys: How Ten Days in Hell with Bear Bryant Forged a Championship Team* (New York: Saint Martin's Press, 1999), 143.

33. "Peace with Freedom: A Volunteer Committee of American Citizens Dedicated to Peace with Freedom in Vietnam"; and letter, Paul H. Douglas to Frank A. Rose, January 3, 1968, Rose Papers, Peace in Vietnam Committee File, 1967.

34. "Lynne's a Beauty; Charles a Genius," *Crimson-White*, November 16, 1967, 1.

35. Zaroulis and Sullivan, *Who Spoke Up?*, 126–27.

36. Ibid., 147.

37. "Kennedy's in the Running," *Tuscaloosa News*, March 16, 1968, 1; and Larry Ber-

man, *Lyndon Johnson's War: The Road to Stalemate in Vietnam* (New York: W. W. Norton, 1989), 186.

38. Townsend Hoopes, *The Limits of Intervention: An Inside Account of How the Johnson Policy of Escalation in Vietnam Was Reversed* (New York: David McKay, 1969), 204–5, and Earl H. Tilford, *Crosswinds: The Air Force's Setup in Vietnam* (College Station: Texas A&M University Press, 1993), 100.

39. "Under Cold Steel," *Crimson-White*, March 4, 1968, 2.

40. "Says Hershey, No Graduate Draft Deferment," *Crimson-White*, March 4, 1968, 1.

41. "Friday Peace Vigil Is 'Just the First of Many,'" *Crimson-White*, March 18, 1968, 1.

42. Directions: American Society at the Crossroads: Emphasis '68, program for Emphasis, 3, Rose Papers, Emphasis '68 File.

43. Undated draft staff memorandum, David Mathews Papers, Box 169, Emphasis '68 File, Hoole Special Collections Library, UA.

44. "Rose Nixes Emphasis Speaker," *Crimson-White*, February 19, 1968, 1; and "Rev Coffin Affair 'Typical,'" *Crimson-White*, April 2, 1968, 4.

45. Telephone interview, author with Redding Pitt, January 21, 2010.

46. Emphasis program, 5–6, Rose Papers, Emphasis '68 File.

47. "Kennedy Sparks Emphasis Week" and "RFK Draws 10,000," *Crimson-White*, March 25, 1968, 1.

48. "Emphasis Shows Student Apathy," *Crimson-White*, March 25, 1968, 4.

49. "Dr. Klitzke Leaving UA," *Tuscaloosa News*, March 24, 1968, 1.

50. Letter, Frank A. Rose to David Mathews, October 25, 1967, F. David Mathews Papers, Box 167, Academic Liaison Committee File, Hoole Special Collections Library, UA.

51. Memorandum, David Mathews, Chairman, Academic Liaison Committee, to Dean Robert E. Bills, Dean Raymond F. McLain, and Dean W. Edward Lear, February 9, 1968, David Mathews Papers, Box 167, Hoole Special Collections Library, UA.

52. "Joe Espy Announces for SGA Presidency," *Crimson-White*, February 29, 1968, 1.

53. "Ed Still Announced SGA Candidacy," *Crimson-White*, February 15, 1968, 1.

54. "Still: An Underdog, Poll Indicates," *Crimson-White*, February 18, 1968, 4.

55. "Roots of the Machine Seen in Outlawed TNE," *Crimson-White*, March 28, 1968, 1.

56. Jo Anne Singley-Sharlach, personal interview, January 16, 2010; and "Discrediting Our University: The Campus Machine," *Crimson-White*, March 22, 1961, 1, reprinted in *Crimson-White*, March 28, 1968, 4.

57. "Secret Group Exposed," *Crimson-White*, March 28, 1968, 1.

58. Ibid. and interview with a female student who attended such a dinner but who prefers to remain anonymous.

59. "Discrediting Our University," 4.

60. "Joe Espy Wins Top SGA Post in Landslide," *Crimson-White*, April 9, 1968, 1.

61. "Association to Present Rose List," *Crimson-White*, April 9, 1968, 1.

62. "Silvis: He Always Felt He Was 'Bound to Get It,'" *Tuscaloosa News*, October 20, 1968, 1.

63. Personal recollection. Bud Silvis and I were fellow AFROTC cadets for three years. He was in the same seminar with me during the spring of 1967.

64. "Pete Pours in 59 as LSU Tops Tide," *Crimson-White*, February 19, 1968, 5; and "Riley Resigns: Newton Named New Coach," *Crimson-White*, March 7, 1968, 5.

65. Letter, C. M. Newton to Frank A. Rose, November 7, 1967, Rose Papers, General Correspondence File N, 1967.

66. C. M. Newton, personal interview, March 21, 2010.

67. "Full Text of Knowles' Blast against UA, SGA Leaders," *Crimson-White*, May 2, 1968, 4.

68. "UA, SGA Leaders Blasted by Knowles," *Crimson-White*, May 2, 1968, 1.

69. "Open Your Eyes," *Crimson-White*, May 2, 1968, 1.

70. Stephen Lesher, *George Wallace, American Populist* (Reading, PA: Addison-Wesley Publishing, 1993), 384–86.

71. Letter, Frank A. Rose to all Administrative Officials, Deans, and Department Heads, April 29, 1968, Rose Papers, University Reorganization File.

72. Summary of Revised Organization for the Main Campus, April 29, 1968, Rose Papers, Reorganization File.

73. Letter, David Mathews to J. W. Marsh III, July 16, 1968, F. David Mathews Papers, Box 172, Personal Correspondence File, Hoole Special Collections Library, UA.

74. Letter, Frank A. Rose to James B. Antell, President of the United States Jaycees, July 10, 1968, Rose Papers, Executive Vice President's File, 1968.

75. Statement of Trust: Responsible, Intellectual, Dedication to Excellence, Alabama Alumni News, May–June 1968, 3, Rose Papers, Alumni Association File, 1967–69.

76. A-STRIDE, program for the University of Alabama Convocation, May 10, 1968, Col. W. V. Brown Papers, Convocation, May 10, 1968, File, Hoole Special Collections Library, UA; and "STRIDE Program: UA Tells Plan Friday Night," *Crimson-White*, May 6, 1968, 1.

77. Procedures for Graduation Exercises on Sunday, May 26, 1968, F. David Mathews Papers, Box 168, Commencement File, Hoole Special Collections Library, UA.

Chapter 7

1. Jeffrey A. Turner, *Sitting In and Speaking Out: Student Movements in the American South, 1960–1970* (Athens: University of Georgia Press, 2010), 269–70.

2. "History of SDA Recounted," *Crimson-White*, December 17, 1968, 1; and Zaroulis and Sullivan, *Who Spoke Up?*, 167.

3. Robert Hessen, "'Campus Battleground,' Columbia Is a Warning to All American Universities," originally printed in the May 1968 issue of *Barron's* and reprinted

as an advertisement in the *National Observer*, May 27, 1968, 11, David Mathews, personal papers, Kettering Foundation, Dayton, Ohio.

4. "Tactics for Handling Campus Disturbances," *College and Business Magazine*, July 1968, 57.

5. "Southern Student Organizing Committee Handbook," spring 1968, 8, in Carol Ann Self, personal papers, Mandeville, Louisiana.

6. "Dr. Rose: No Easy Solution to Drive by Protesting Students," *Birmingham News*, June 28, 1968, 2.

7. Letter, Frank A. Rose to D. G. McKenzie, July 22, 1968, Rose Papers, General Correspondence MC File, 1968–69.

8. Memorandum, Richard Thigpen, Director of Men's Activities, to Dean John L. Blackburn, September 11, 1967, in F. David Mathews Papers, Student Government Association File, 1967, Hoole Special Collections Library, UA.

9. Letter, David Mathews to Joffre T. Whisenton, June 26, 1968, Rose Papers, Executive Vice President David Mathews File.

10. "Rose Relates Extent of Federal Straight," *Crimson-White*, August 12, 1968, 1.

11. "Departing Provost Talks about Past 25 Years," *Crimson-White*, July 22, 1968, 1.

12. University of Alabama Fact Sheet, September 1968, 1–4, Rose Papers, L. T. McGehee, Executive Assistant to the President File, 1968–69.

13. "Experimental College Lures 500 with Unconventional Curricula," *Crimson-White*, September 24, 1968, 2.

14. A New College for the University, draft, F. David Mathews Papers, New College, 1968–69 File, Hoole Special Collections Library, UA.

15. Letter, Raymond F. McLain to David Mathews, November 5, 1968, F. David Mathews Personal Papers, New College File, Kettering Foundation, Dayton, Ohio.

16. *Corolla*, 1966, 57.

17. Letter, John L. Blackburn to Johnny Johnson, April 2, 1968, J. Jefferson Bennett Papers, Dean for Student Development File, 1968, Hoole Special Collections Library, UA.

18. "Radical Speakers Invited to UA in 'Freedom Test,'" *Tuscaloosa News*, Friday, October 11, 1968, 2.

19. Transcript, Student Life and Learning Committee Meeting, October 3, 1968, 1, Rose Papers, Student Life Committee File, 1968.

20. "Pair Arrested on LSD Charge Following Raid," *Tuscaloosa News*, October 5, 1968, 1.

21. "Rebels Snap 58-Year Tide Streak," *Crimson-White*, October 12, 1968, 5.

22. "Rose Rules Out Talk by Radicals," *Tuscaloosa News*, October 13, 1968, 1–2.

23. Letter, E. Roger Sayers to Frank A. Rose, October 11, 1968, attached to A Report on Speaker Policy at the University of Alabama by the Ad Hoc Committee on the Role of the Student at the University, F. David Mathews Papers, Student Speakers Controversy File, 1966 and 1968, Hoole Special Collections Library, UA.

24. Letter, Howard B. Wilson Jr. to Frank A. Rose, October 15, 1968, Rose Pa-

pers, Personal Letters of Support on Speaker Stand File, 1968; and telegram, Leland Childs to Frank A. Rose, October 15, 1968, Rose Papers, Democratic Students Organization File, 1968.

25. "News Group Backs Dr. Rose in Stand," *Tuscaloosa News*, October 16, 1968, 14.

26. "Suit against Rose, UA Filed Today," *Crimson-White*, November 5, 1968, 1; and Turner, *Sitting In and Speaking Out*, 150.

27. "Indicted Student Kills Self," *Tuscaloosa News*, October 19, 1968, 1; and "Bud Silvis" *Tuscaloosa News*, 1–2.

28. "Trammel Honored," *Tuscaloosa News*, October 13, 1968, 1.

29. Letter: Robert Keever to Frank A. Rose, October 28, 1968, Rose Papers, Personal Correspondence File K, 1968.

30. Letter, John Blackburn to Michael Stambaugh, October 9, 1968, John L. Blackburn Papers, DSO 1968 File, Hoole Special Collections Library, UA; and "Small Group Stirs Disorder at 'Bama,'" *Atlanta Journal*, October 30, 1968, C-2.

31. "Two Arrested Here Following Rally," *Tuscaloosa News*, October 22, 1968, 5.

32. "Impressions," October 29, 1968, F. David Mathews Papers, Democratic Students Organization File, 1968, Hoole Special Collections Library, UA.

33. "Last DSO Protest Stirs 100 to Steps," *Crimson-White*, November 5, 1968, 1.

34. "Burns Blasts Bains, Phillips: Hearing Moved to Nov. 18," *Crimson-White*, November 7, 1968, 1.

35. "AWS Resolutions, April 1968," J. Jefferson Bennett Papers, Associated Women Students File, Hoole Special Collections Library, UA.

36. "Lois Cobb Means Action," *Crimson-White*, February 11, 1969, 7.

37. "Students Take Opposing Stands on Women's Rights Controversy," *Crimson-White*, August 12, 1968, 5.

38. Joint Resolution #2, Student Government Legislature, 1968–69, Rose Papers, Student Government Association File, 1968–69

39. Memorandum, Richard Thigpen to J. Jefferson Bennett, March 29, 1968, J. Jefferson Bennett Papers, Student Government Association File; letter, Frank A. Rose to C. E. Hornsby Jr., April 10, 1968, Rose Papers, African American Association File, 1968.

40. "Afro Demands Met: Black History Course Planned for Fall Term," *Crimson-White*, July 1, 1968, 1.

41. Letter, John L. Blackburn to Frank A. Rose, July 24, 1968, Rose Papers, Dean of Student Development File, 1968.

42. "Afros Reiterate Demands," *Crimson-White*, August 5, 1968, 1.

43. Memorandum, Willard F. Gray to David Mathews, August 19, 1968, F. David Mathews Papers, Afro-American Association File, 1968, Hoole Special Collections Library, UA.

44. Schedule of Events, Black Students Conference, December 6–8, 1968, David Mathews Papers, Student Organizations: Afro-American Association File, 1968–69, Hoole Special Collections Library, UA.

45. "Missouri Stuns Tide 34 to 10," *Tuscaloosa News,* January 1, 1969, C-1.

46. Carol Ann Self, telephone interview, May 30, 2010.

47. Letter, Henry J. Richardson Jr. to Frank A. Rose, September 16, 1968; and letter, Frank A. Rose to Henry J. Richardson Jr., September 19, 1968, Rose Papers, General Correspondence File R, 1968–69.

48. "Campus Heads Quit Indiana, Wisconsin, and Georgia Tech," *Chronicle of Higher Education,* July 22, 1968, 1.

49. Letter, Frank A. Rose to Governor Albert P. Brewer and Justice Thomas A. Lawson, January 27, 1969, Rose Papers, General Correspondence File B, 1969.

50. Ibid.

51. "Rose Leaving University," *Tuscaloosa News,* January 29, 1969, 1–3.

52. "Crowd Offers Mixed Reaction," *Crimson-White,* February 20, 1969, 1–2.

53. "Espy Will Not Call Referendum of UA Petition Presented," *Crimson-White,* March 5, 1969, 1.

54. Jack Drake, personal interview, January 23, 2010.

55. News release, March 27, 1969, University of Alabama News Bureau, Rose Papers, News Bureau—News Clippings File, 1967–69.

56. "Herlong Wins Top Post in Student Government," *Crimson-White,* April 14, 1969, 1.

57. Blackburn mentioned how he enjoyed living in Denver during the 1990 interview he conducted with Frank Rose.

58. Letter, Frank A. Rose to Alex A. Daugherty, April 8, 1969, Rose Papers, General Correspondence File, 1968–69.

59. Letter, Frank A. Rose to Robert R. Jones, May 16, 1969, Rose Papers, Correspondence File J, 1969.

60. Procedure for Graduation Exercises, Sunday, June 1, 1969, Rose Papers, Commencement File, 1966–69.

Chapter 8

1. Letter, David Mathews to J. Ralph Murray, President, Elmira College, December 18, 1967, Rose Papers, F. David Mathews File; and Minutes of the Recessed Meeting of the Board of Trustees, June 5, 1969, F. David Mathews Papers, Board of Trustees File, March–August 1969, Hoole Special Collections Library, UA.

2. "Mathews Named U of A president: Volker to UAB," *Birmingham News,* June 16, 1969, 1.

3. "A Special Report to Alumni," *Alabama Alumni Bulletin,* vol. XXIII, no. 1, Summer 1969, F. David Mathews Papers, Alumni Affairs, January–April 1970 File, Hoole Special Collections Library, UA.

4. Myra Crawford Johnson, "Youth Is Not Wasted on the Young Dr. Mathews," *Southern Living,* January 1970, 38.

5. "Where We Stand," *Alabama Alumni Bulletin*, vol. XXIII, no. 1, Summer 1969, 2–4, F. David Mathews Papers, Alumni Affairs, January–April 1970 File, Hoole Special Collections Library, UA.

6. Ibid.

7. University of Alabama News Bureau release, September 30, 1969, Rose Papers, Student Enrollment File, 1964–69.

8. Briley, *Career in Crisis*, 27–29.

9. Wilmina M. Rowland, "Gifts South for Scholarship Program," *Presbyterian Life*, July 15, 1969, 25.

10. Letter, Willard F. Gray to Robert J. Cadigan, September 3, 1969, F. David Mathews Papers, Athletic Committee File, 1968–73, Hoole Special Collections Library, UA.

11. Coach C. M. Newton, personal interview, January 21, 2010; and "Negro Athlete Is Signed: First for UA Sports," *Crimson-White*, April 2, 1969, 1.

12. Memorandum, Richard Thigpen to David Mathews, October 3, 1969, F. David Mathews Papers, Student Organizations, Afro-American Association File, 1969–70, Hoole Special Collections Library, UA.

13. Report to the President of the Afro-American Grievance Committee, August 19, 1970, 14–15, in F. David Mathews Papers, Student Organizations, Afro-American Association File, January–June 1970, Hoole Special Collections Library, UA.

14. "A Storm Is Coming," *Crimson-White*, September 22, 1969, 1.

15. Handwritten note titled, "Evaluation of Critical Steps in the Curfew Crisis," F. David Mathews Papers, Women's Issues, Curfew Hours File, 1969, Hoole Special Collections Library, UA.

16. "Curfew Rules Ended for Some UA Coeds," *Crimson-White*, September 17, 1969, 1; and "Curfew Rule Is Unsatisfactory," Ibid., 4.

17. Memorandum, Glenn W. Stillion to F. David Mathews, November 3, 1969, F. David Mathews Papers, Student Affairs, Women's Rules File, August–December 1969, Hoole Special Collections Library, UA.

18. "Coeds Vote to End Curfew," *Crimson-White*, October 30, 1969, 1; and "Midnight Curfew Approved for Women," *Crimson-White*, December 18, 1969, 2.

19. *Report of the Federal Bureau of Investigation on Campus Unrest*, US Bureau of Justice, January 2, 1970, 1–6, F. David Mathews Papers, Student Demonstrations 1970, Correspondence File, January–April 1970, Hoole Special Collections Library, UA.

20. "Dr. Mathews Asked to Call Off Classes," *Crimson-White*, October 6, 1969, 1.

21. "More on Moratorium from Students," *Crimson-White*, October 13, 1969, 1.

22. "Moratorium Movement Gaining Strength: Senate Delays Passage of Moratorium Resolution," *Crimson-White*, October 2, 1969, 1.

23. "Sen. Tydings, Jim Martin Scheduled for Moratorium," *Crimson-White*, October 13, 1969, 1.

24. "Student Leaders Hear Mathews," *Crimson-White*, September 15, 1969, 1.

25. Johnson "Youth Is Not Wasted," 41.

26. Letter, Raymond F. McLain to David Mathews, October 21, 1969 (note marginalia in Mathews' handwriting), F. David Mathews Papers, New College File, Kettering Foundation, Dayton, Ohio; and "A New College for You," pamphlet in F. David Mathews Papers, New College File, September–December 1970, Hoole Special Collections Library, UA.

27. *Corolla*, 1970, 229–325.

28. "The Machine," *Crimson-White*, April 16, 1970, 4.

29. Briley, *Career in Crisis*, 4–5; Bryant and Underwood, *Bear*, appendix, 310; and *Corolla*, 1970, 174–95.

30. Bryant and Underwood, *Bear*, 275.

31. Barra, *The Last Coach*, 361; and "Bryant to Stay at Bama," *Tuscaloosa News*, January 8, 1970, 1.

32. "Bonfire, Beauties Spark Activities," *Crimson-White*, November 13, 1969, 1.

33. "Student Power: A Forked Road," UA News Bureau, September 15, 1969, F. David Mathews Papers, SGA File, 1969–70, Hoole Special Collections Library, UA.

34. "Petition Protesting the Selection of Thomas," F. David Mathews Papers, Student Development File, 1970–71, Hoole Special Collections Library, UA; "Thomas Appointment Outrageous," *Crimson-White*, December 11, 1969, 4; and Glenda Guyton, personal interview, January 14, 2011.

35. "Experimental College Making Noises at U of A; But No One Claims It," *Birmingham News*, November 2, 1969, A-2.

36. Memorandum, Richard Thigpen to Larry McGehee, October 10, 1969, F. David Mathews Papers, Office of Student Development File, 1969, Hoole Special Collections Library, UA.

37. "Officials Pull Plug, but Quad Goes On," *Crimson-White*, October 26, 1969, 1.

38. "Won't Be Intimidated, Says UA's Mathews after Protests," *Tuscaloosa News*, October 28, 1970, 1–2.

39. Tape transcript, Dr. Mathews Conversation with Students over Quadrangle Issue, October 28, 1969, available in the Hoole Special Collections Library, UA.

40. Letter, Mayor C. Snow Hinton to David Mathews, October 29, 1969, in David Mathews Papers, Student Demonstrations File, September–October 1969, Hoole Special Collections Library, UA.

41. Resolution of Support and Appreciation for Dr. Mathews, November 4, 1969, Tuscaloosa Rotary Club; and letter, Buford Boone to F. David Mathews, November 12, 1969, F. David Mathews Papers, Student Demonstrations File, November–December 1969, Hoole Special Collections Library, UA.

42. Faculty Senate Resolution of Support, October 29, 1969, Student Demonstrations File, September–October 1969; and letter, Iredell Jenkins to David Mathews, November 3, 1969, F. David Mathews Papers, College of Arts and Sciences File, 1969–70, Hoole Special Collections Library, UA.

43. Letter, Patricia Goubil, Mary Bess Kirksey, and Lucie Underwood to David Mathews, October 28, 1969, in F. David Mathews Papers, Student Demonstrations File, September–October 1969, Hoole Special Collections Library, UA.

44. Letter, Thomas R. Tradup to Dr. F. David Mathews, October 30, 1969, in F. David Mathews Papers, Student Demonstrations File, September–October 1969, Hoole Special Collections Library, UA.

45. Report on the Special Press Conference, University Police, October 30, 1969, in F. David Mathews Papers, Student Demonstrations File, September–October 1969, Hoole Special Collections Library, UA.

46. "Campus Peace Declared," *Tuscaloosa News*, October 30, 1969, 22.

47. Letter, Iredell Jenkins to David Mathews, November 3, 1969, F. David Mathews Papers, College of Arts and Sciences File, 1969, Hoole Special Collections Library, UA.

48. Eviction Notice, F. David Mathews Papers, Student Demonstrations File, September–October 1969, Hoole Special Collections Library, UA.

49. Memorandum, Larry T. McGehee to Academic Deans and Department Heads, December 1, 1969, F. David Mathews Papers, Student Demonstrations File, November–December 1969, Hoole Special Collections Library, UA.

50. UA News Bureau Announcement, November 25, 1969, in F. David Mathews Papers, Office of Student Development File, 1969, Hoole Special Collections Library, UA.

51. "Black Panel Gives Study in Contrasts," *Crimson-White*, October 23, 1969, 1.

52. "Joplin Threatened with Arrest, Puts On Good Show," *Crimson-White*, December 8, 1969, 1.

53. "Sequence of Events Told in Hoffman Dispute," *Crimson-White*, March 5, 1970, 1.

54. Memorandum, Col. Beverly M. Leigh Jr. to David Mathews, February 10, 1970, Subject: Alabama vs. LSU Basketball Game, February 7, 1970, in F. David Mathews Papers, Athletes File, January–April 1970, Hoole Special Collections Library, UA.

55. "Students to Choose Leaders," *Crimson-White*, March 12, 1970, 1; and "Campus Sexually Segregated," *Crimson-White*, February 23, 1970, 1.

56. Letter, J. Rufus Beale to the Board of Trustees, March 9, 1970, F. David Mathews Papers, Gordon v. Brewer (Abbie Hoffman) File, 1970, Hoole Special Collections Library, UA.

57. "Mathews Nixes Hoffman: Emphasis Goes to Court," *Crimson-White*, March 5, 1970, 1.

58. "Court Suit Slated in Hoffman Controversy," *Tuscaloosa News*, March 5, 1970, 1.

59. Telegram, 3:10 p. m., March 6, 1970, F. David Mathews Papers, Abbie Hoffman File, 1970, Hoole Special Collections Library, UA.

60. "Public Opinion Affected Decision," *Crimson-White*, March 9, 1970, 1.

61. Ibid.; and "Mathews Addresses Students in Abbie Hoffman Case," *Crimson-*

White, March 6, 1970; and tape recording, David Mathews Addresses Students, March 6, 1970, in Hoole Special Collections Library, UA.

62. "Faculty Senate and Student Legislature Support Speaker Suit," *Crimson White*, March 9, 1970, 1; and "Resolution of the Campus Affairs Committee of the Graduate Students Association," F. David Mathews Papers, Abbie Hoffman File, 1970, Hoole Special Collections Library, UA.

63. "Montgomery Court Rejects Hoffman Ban Suit," *Crimson-White*, March 17, 1970, 2.

64. "Wallace Heckled at Emphasis," *Tuscaloosa News*, March 17, 1970, 1.

65. "UA Police to Probe Arrests: Two Carried from ROTC Field," *Crimson-White*, April 27, 19701, 1

Chapter 9

1. "Rubin Speaks at University," *Birmingham Post-Herald*, May 4, 1970, 1; and university news release, May 3, 1970, F. David Mathews Papers, Experimental College File, 1969–70, Hoole Special Collections Library, UA.

2. "Chicago Seven Yippie Leader Rubin Speaks at UA Rock Concert," *Tuscaloosa News*, May 4, 1970, 1–2.

3. Ibid.

4. "Rubin Speaks; Probe Promised," *Crimson-White*, May 4, 1970, 1–2.

5. Ibid., 2.

6. "Rubin and the Rules," *Crimson-White*, May 4, 1970, 1.

7. Zaroulis and Sullivan, *Who Spoke Up?*, 319.

8. Michael Richards, "Kent State University," in *Encyclopedia of the Vietnam War: A Political and Military History*, vol. I, ed. Spencer C. Tucker (Santa Barbara, CA: ABC-CLIO, 1998), 335–36.

9. Carol Ann Self, email message to author, June 28, 2010.

10. Statement by Morris Simon, undated report in David Mathews Papers, Student Demonstrations/Arrests File, May 1970; and Gina Twitty Crosheck, telephone interview, July 3, 2010. Gina Crosheck wrote her own speech. She later married Michael McGee and the two of them enjoyed long academic careers at the University of Iowa until Michael passed away in 2003.

11. "Disorder for Thirteen Days," *University of Alabama Bulletin*, summer, 1970, 2.

12. Ibid., 4–5.

13. The Wednesday Report, May 6, 1970, statement by Dr. Mathews, F. David Mathews Papers, Student Demonstrations, Memoranda and Reports File, May 1970, Hoole Special Collections Library, UA.

14. Captain Gray quoted in Major Colin Williams, "A Damn Interesting Story: The University of Alabama's 1970 Spring Uprisings" (paper for a graduate course in

history, University of Alabama, provided by Major Williams to the author, summer of 2007), 1.

15. Carol Self, personal interview, April 3, 2010.

16. David Mathews, personal interview, May 9, 2009.

17. "Disorder for Thirteen Days," 2; and Jenny Osterman, telephone interview, March 17, 2010; and Fletcher Thornton, email message to author, February 27, 2012.

18. Self interview, April 3, 2010.

19. Statement by Morris Simon, 10.

20. "Governor Brewer Warns UA Protestors Violence Will Not Be Tolerated," *Birmingham News*, May 7, 1970, 1.

21. "Troopers Called In As Safety Measure," *Tuscaloosa News*, May 7, 1970, 1.

22. "Disorder for Thirteen Days," 2; Statement by Morris Simon, 10; and memorandum, David Mathews to Members of the University Community, May 7, 1970, David Mathews Papers, Internal Memoranda and Reports File, May 1970, Hoole Special Collections Library, UA.

23. "Disorder for Thirteen Days," 2.

24. University news release, May 9, 1970, F. David Mathews Papers, Student Demonstrations File, Internal Memoranda and Reports File, May 1970, Hoole Special Collections Library, UA; and "Students Gather at UA after Curfew Is Imposed," *Birmingham News*, May 8, 1970, 3.

25. Letters in David Mathews Papers, Student Demonstrations File, General Correspondence, 1970, Hoole Special Collections Library, UA.

26. "Won't Be Pressured, UA's Mathews Says," *Tuscaloosa News*, May 13, 1970, 1.

27. "Reply Is Unacceptable, UA Dissidents Report," *Tuscaloosa News* May 13, 1970, 1.

28. Ibid.

29. Letter, Louis Crew to F. David Mathews, May 13, 1970, F. David Mathews Papers, Student Demonstrations File, General Correspondence, May 1970, Hoole Special Collections Library, UA.

30. "UA Curfew Imposed after Clash," *Tuscaloosa News*, May 14, 1970, 1–2.

31. David Mathews, personal interview, September 13, 2010.

32. Undated affidavit by Richard C. Winstead, in F. David Mathews Papers, Student Demonstrations File, Student Arrests, 1970, Hoole Special Collections Library, UA.

33. "UA Curfew Imposed after Clash," *Tuscaloosa News*, May 14, 1970, 2.

34. Letter, David C. Patterson to David Mathews, May 14, 1970, David Mathews Papers, Student Demonstrations File, 1970, Hoole Special Collections Library, UA.

35. Letter, Donna Brown to President Mathews, May 14, 1970, David Mathews Papers, Student Demonstrations File, General Correspondence, May 16–29, 1970, Hoole Special Collections Library, UA.

36. Letter, Jim Zeigler and John D. Bivens to F. David Mathews, May 14, 1970,

F. David Mathews Papers, Student Demonstrations File, May 1970, Hoole Special Collections Library, UA.

37. Herring, *America's Longest War*, 262, and "Disorder for Thirteen Days," 3.

38. Memorandum, SGA President Jim Zeigler to F. David Mathews, May 16, 1970, F. David Mathews Papers, Student Demonstrations File, Internal Memoranda and Reports, May 1970, Hoole Special Collections Library, UA.

39. Minutes of the Meeting of the Executive Committee of the Board of Trustees, May 17, 1970, F. David Mathews Papers, Student Demonstrations File, May 1970, Hoole Special Collections Library, UA.

40. Memorandum to Deans of Schools and Colleges and All Teaching Personnel, Subject: Final Examination Options Available to Faculty, May 18, 1970, F. David Mathews Papers, Student Demonstrations File, Internal Memoranda and Reports File, 1970, Hoole Special Collections Library, UA.

41. Crosheck, telephone interview, July 3, 2010; and The University Report, May 19, 1970, University News Bureau, F. David Mathews Papers, Student Demonstrations File, Internal Memoranda and Reports, May 1970, Hoole Special Collections Library, UA.

42. Letter, Morris Dees to David Mathews, May 18, 1970; letter, David Mathews to Morris Dees, May 21, 1970, F. David Mathews Papers, Student Demonstrations File, General Correspondence, May 16–29, 1970, Hoole Special Collections Library, UA; and Mathews interview, September 13, 2010.

43. Mathews quoted in "Disorder for Thirteen Days," 1.

44. Handwritten note in F. David Mathews Papers, Board of Trustees File, 1970, folder 2, Hoole Special Collections Library, UA.

45. David Mathews, personal interview, May 9 2009.

46. "Summer 1970," *Crimson-White*, May 14, 1970, 28; Gina Twitty Crosheck, email message to author, July 2, 2010.

47. "Summer of 1970," 28.

48. "In Prevention of Another May," *Crimson-White*, September 14, 1970, 28.

49. Memorandum, Richard Thigpen to David Mathews, October 7, 1970, F. David Mathews Papers, Dressler Hall Fire, 1970, Hoole Special Collections Library, UA.

50. "Grimm Is Pawn of FBI, ACLU Attorney Says," *Crimson-White*, September 14, 1970, 8.

51. Ibid.

52. Courtney Haden, "When the World Itself Seemed Afire," *Birmingham Weekly*, http://www.bhamweeklyyu.com, accessed May 5, 2010, 3.

Sources

Books

Barra, Allen. *The Last Coach: A Life of Paul "Bear" Bryant.* New York: W. W. Norton, 2005.

Berman, Larry. *Lyndon Johnson's War: The Road to Stalemate in Vietnam.* New York: W.W. Norton, 1989.

Briley, John David. *Career in Crisis: Paul "Bear" Bryant and the 1971 Season of Change.* Macon, GA: Mercer University Press, 2006.

Bryant, Paul W., and John Underwood. *Bear: The Hard Life and Good Times of Alabama's Coach Bryant.* Chicago: Triumph Books, 2007.

Clark, E. Culpepper. *The Schoolhouse Door: Segregation's Last Stand at the University of Alabama.* New York: Oxford University Press, 1995.

Dent, Jim. *The Junction Boys: How Ten Days in Hell with Bear Bryant Forged a Championship Team.* New York: Saint Martin's Press, 1999.

Dunnavant, Keith. *The Missing Ring: How Bear Bryant and the 1966 Alabama Crimson Tide Were Denied College Football's Most Illusive Prize.* New York: Saint Martin's Press, 2007.

Flynt, Wayne. *Alabama in the Twentieth Century.* Tuscaloosa: University of Alabama Press, 2004.

Frady, Marshal. *Wallace.* New York: Random House, 1976.

Gaillard, Frey. *Cradle of Freedom: Alabama and the Movement That Changed America.* Tuscaloosa: University of Alabama Press, 2004.

Gitlin, Todd. *The Sixties: Years of Hope, Days of Rage.* New York: Bantam Books, 1989.

Guilmartin, John F. *America in Vietnam: The Fifteen Year War.* New York: Random House, 1991.

Herring, George C., Jr. *America's Longest War: The United States and Vietnam, 1950–1975.* 2nd ed. New York: McGraw Hill, 1995.

Hoopes, Townsend. *The Limits of Intervention: An Inside Account of How the Johnson Policy of Escalation in Vietnam Was Reversed.* New York: David Mackay, 1969.

Jencks, Christopher, and David Riesman. *The Academic Revolution.* New Brunswick, NJ: Transaction Publications, 2002.

Lesher, Stephen. *George Wallace, American Populist.* Reading, PA: Addison-Wesley Publishing, 1993.

Richards, Michael. "Kent State University." In *Encyclopedia of the Vietnam War: A Political and Military History.* Vol. I. Edited by Spencer C. Tucker. Santa Barbara, CA: ABC-CLIO, 1998.

Sellers, James B. "History of the University of Alabama." Vol. II, "1902–1957." Edited by W. Stanley Hoole. Unpublished manuscript, President's Office, University of Alabama, Tuscaloosa.

Stern, Mark. *Calculating Visions: Kennedy, Johnson, and Civil Rights.* New Brunswick, NJ: Rutgers University Press, 1992.

Thayer, Thomas C. *War without Fronts: The American Experience in Vietnam.* Boulder, CO: Westview Special Military Studies, 1986.

Tilford, Earl H. *Crosswinds: The Air Force's Setup in Vietnam.* College Station: Texas A&M University Press, 1993.

Trest, Warren. *Nobody but the People: The Life and Times of Alabama's Youngest Governor.* Montgomery, AL: New South Books, 2008.

Turner, Jeffery A. *Sitting In and Speaking Out: Student Movements in the American South, 1960–1970.* Athens: University of Georgia Press, 2010.

Wallace, George C. *"Hear Me Out: This Is Where I Stand."* Anderson, SC: Droke House Publishers, 1968.

Wolfe, Suzanne Rau. *The University of Alabama: A Pictorial History.* Tuscaloosa: University of Alabama Press, 1983.

Woodward, C. Vann. *The Burden of Southern History.* Rev. ed. Baton Rouge: Louisiana State University Press, 1968.

Zaroulis, Nancy, and Gerald Sullivan. *Who Spoke Up?: American Protests against the War in Vietnam, 1963–1975.* New York: Holt, Rinehart and Winston, 1978.

Research in Primary Sources

Research among primary sources took place exclusively in the Hoole Special Collections Library at the University of Alabama and the library at the Kettering Foundation in Dayton, Ohio. The papers of Frank A. Rose, J. Jefferson Bennett, John L. Blackburn, and F. David Mathews constituted most of the primary documentation. The papers of former presidents Rose and Mathews are the most extensive and significant. In the Rose papers, letters between Frank Rose and his friends reveal an increasing antipathy between him and Governor George Wallace. After the desegregation crisis passed with the peaceful admission of Vivian Malone in June 1963, Rose began preparing the university for his eventual departure. That took six years.

Letters also show how Rose related to the handful of progressive faculty members. Correspondence between Rose and philosophy professor Iredell Jenkins and the History Department's Professor John F. Ramsey reveal a president committed to bringing about change. He also defended both men, but particularly the more out-spoken and liberal Ramsey, when responding to letters attacking these men, some accusing them of being Communist or Socialists.

While Rose rarely corresponded with perennial faculty dissident, Art Department chair Theodore Klitzke, the way he responded to letters of complaint, especially from people who wanted Klitzke disciplined for his participation in the Selma demonstrations in February 1965, show how adept Rose became at handling complaints. He assured one writer that FBI investigations of Klitzke turned up nothing—but added, "We're watching." No records of such investigations were found. Rose told another that Klitzke was an "unimposing," even "meek looking" man who, while liberal, refrained from imposing his political views on students.

His relationship with Klitzke notwithstanding, Rose also took personal and professional risks to fend off encroachments on academic freedom, especially in the aftermath of Emphasis '67. The following year, however, responding to a letter from an alumnus in the state legislature warning against a repeat of the controversy over Emphasis '67, Rose pressured the Emphasis '68 committee into rescinding the invitation to Yale chaplain and antiwar activist William Sloane Coffin, an invitation Rose had extended as required by university policy on speakers.

Documents in the David Mathews papers reveal the rapid rise of a man generally considered one of the South's most promising young educators. While Mathews clearly loved the classroom and was a gifted as well as challenging teacher, his correspondence with Frank Rose while working on his doctorate at Columbia University indicated Mathews would be returning to Alabama in an administrative position. Between 1966 and 1969, Mathews received and turned down a number of offers from other universities for higher administrative positions with better salaries. By 1968, it was clear Frank Rose was grooming Mathews as his successor.

The positions President Mathews took on a variety of issues during his first year perplexed and angered some—but not all—students and faculty. Sources reveal two reasons for these stands. First, David Mathews truly believed the university was a place for intellectual inquiry and learning and not a public forum for expressing opinions. Second, his experience as a student observing the behavior of mobs out to lynch Autherine Lucy in February 1956 deeply affected Mathews. He was determined to keep the university open and, to the extent possible, safe from violence. While students were responsible for the disorders of May 1970, the Tuscaloosa police initiated most of the violence.

In the Mathews papers one finds articles about student unrest on other campuses and an FBI report on growing violence in the student antiwar movement. Mathews circulated these among appropriate administrators, including John Blackburn and his successor in the Office of Student Affairs, Joab Thomas. While Mathews thought Alabama might be susceptible to the violence extant on other campuses, the Rose files indicate he viewed student discontent as limited to a "handful of troublemakers."

The papers of J. Jefferson Bennett and John L. Blackburn are more limited. Bennett's sudden departure from Alabama in June 1968, after being elevated to provost for the Tuscaloosa, Birmingham, and Huntsville campuses, may have resulted from frustrations over the appointment of Mathews as executive vice president. In early 1969, during the presidential search, Bennett wrote President Rose asking if his application was receiving serious consideration. Rose answered that while the committee considered him among the top candidates, he was remaining neutral. Rose was disingenuous since he strongly supported Mathews' candidacy.

While John Blackburn's papers are far less extensive, they reveal his commitment to progressive change, especially concerning racial matters. Blackburn worked with student dissidents, even if he sometimes thwarted some of their initiatives when he believed doing so was in the university's best interest. He also prevented promising young dissidents like Ralph Knowles, Jack Drake, and Don Siegelman from making mistakes with potential consequences for their futures, which turned out to be significant.

In addition to correspondence, the Rose and Mathews papers include other administrative documents like board of trustee minutes, university self-assessment studies, salary scales, committee reports on reforming fraternity behavior, memoranda on revising in loco parentis rules attendant to coeds visiting in men's apartments and women's dress codes, tightening tenure requirements, raising academic standards, and studies on how to attract higher quality students and faculty. The Mathews papers are split between the Hoole Special Collections and boxes maintained at the Kettering Foundation; those tending to be more personal and general in nature.

Newspapers and Magazines

The University of Alabama's student paper, the *Crimson-White*, provided a rich source of information. Both microfilm and hard copies are available in the Hoole Special Collections Library at the University of Alabama. Editors, starting with Jo Anne Singley in 1961 and continuing with Billie Blair in 1967 on through 1970, were committed to academic freedom and asserting the independence of the paper. Indeed, editorials occasionally drew the ire of Alabama's more conservative alumni, including some on the board of trustees. In addition to reflecting student perspective on issues from desegregation and civil rights to state politics associated with the governor's races in 1958, 1962, and 1966 and increasing unrest over the war in Vietnam, the *Crimson-White* also provides insight into Capstone culture with articles attendant to beauty contests, fraternity and sorority events, dress code struggles, and visiting entertainers.

Each year, in April or May, Alabama students awaited the publication of the *Corolla*, the school yearbook, with great anticipation. The Hoole Special Collections Library maintains copies of every *Corolla* published from the late nineteenth century to the last edition published in 2010. These are available in hard copies and online. Like the *Crimson-White*, *Corollas* provide insight into student culture. A word of caution is in order. The quality of copyediting in both publications is uneven. Spelling of names, even of administration officials is serendipitous. For instance, student copyeditors at *Corolla* and *Crimson-White* often spelled David Mathews' last name using two "t's" rather than one. Don Siegelman's name also proved troubling. Modern researchers must be wary of pre–spell check copyediting.

During the 1960s, the University of Alabama had two student magazines of note: *Mahout* and *Farrago*. First published in 1956, through eleven years of existence *Mahout* gained a reputation as one of the more edgy publications in the collegiate humor magazine genre. *Mahout* often poked fun at the straight-laced culture that pervaded the Bible Belt. Its brand of ribald humor, particularly on matters attendant to race and sex, drew several warnings from the Publication Review Board (PRB) before the university shut down *Mahout* in 1967. There are, however, gems of cultural insight to be found in its pages, expressions that seem somehow refreshingly out of place on one of the South's most traditional campuses. One observer likened it to finding marijuana hidden in your grandmother's chest of drawers.

In November 1967, *Farrago*, edited by Ed Still, opened with an article by Russian history professor Hugh Ragsdale celebrating the fiftieth anniversary of the Bolshevik takeover in Petrograd. Coming a semester after the controversy over Emphasis '67, it was a bold move, one that must have been approved by the PRB. *Farrago* continued publication into the 1970s, its articles more serious and contemplative than those found in *Mahout*. *Farrago* reflected the turning of Capstone culture during the late 1960s. Hoole Special Collections possesses a complete set of *Mahout* and *Farrago*. *Mahout* also is available through the University of Alabama Libraries online using the "Acumen" search engine.

Articles in the *Tuscaloosa News*, *Birmingham Post-Herald*, *Birmingham News*, and the *Montgomery Advertiser* were important in moving the story throughout a decade of change. Occasional articles cut from the pages of papers like the *Los Angeles Times* and *New York Times* were found in the letters of Frank Rose and David Mathews, often accompanying correspondence.

The *Tuscaloosa News*, available in microfilm at the Tuscaloosa City Library, was by far the most important newsprint media source explored for *Turning the Tide*. Pulitzer Prize–winning publisher Buford Boone's crusade against the Ku Klux Klan, dating from 1949 through the mid-1960s and beyond, provided the tenor for the *Tuscaloosa News* reporting during the civil rights era. Microfilm copies of the *Birmingham Post-Herald*, *Birmingham News*, and *Montgomery Advertiser*, as well as the *Los Angeles Times*, *New York Times*, and *Washington Post* are available in the Amelia Gayle Gorgas Library.

Research for *Turning the Tide* included articles published in the following newspapers:

Atlanta Journal
Birmingham News
Birmingham Post-Herald
Chronicle of Higher Education
Crimson-White
Los Angeles Times
Montgomery Advertiser
New York Times
Tuscaloosa News
Washington Post

Interviews

Interviews provided insights from the perspectives of former students, student leaders, faculty, and members of the administration. The author conducted all interviews either in person or over the telephone with the exception of a tape-recorded interview of Frank Rose conducted by John Blackburn in August 1990 and shared with the author by former University of Alabama president E. Roger Sayers. That interview is now available in the Hoole Special Collections Library.

Persons interviewed included:

Arnold, Herbert. Interviewed by author, December 19, 2010, Tuscaloosa, AL.

Boone, Jim. Interviewed by author, February 2, 2009, Tuscaloosa, AL.

Crosheck, Gina Twitty. Telephone interview by author, July 3, 2010.

Drake, Jack. Interviewed by author, January 23, 2010, Birmingham, AL.

Guyton, Glenda. Interviewed by author, January 14, 2011, Tuscaloosa, AL.

Keever, Robert. Telephone interview by author, June 29, 2009.

Mathews, F. David. Interviewed by author, 2009–11, Dayton, OH.

Newton, C. M. Interviewed by author, March 21, 2010, Tuscaloosa, AL

Osterman, Jenny. Telephone interview by author, March 17, 2010.

Pitt, Redding. Telephone interview by author, January 21, 2010.

Rose, Frank A. Interview by John L. Blackburn, August 3, 1990, Washington, DC.
    Tape recording available in Hoole Special Collections Library.

Self, Carol A. Interviewed by author, April 3, 2010, Tuscaloosa, AL.

Singley-Sharlach, Jo Anne. Telephone interview by author, January 16, 2010.

Final Thoughts

There remains plenty of opportunity for future research into the history of the University of Alabama. Only one history detailing the history of the university in the nineteenth century exists, James B. Sellers, *History of the University of Alabama*, vol. I, *1818–1902* published in 1953. Sellers had just begun a second volume before his death; the typed manuscript remains in the office of the president. Suzanne Rau Wolfe's *The University of Alabama: A Pictorial History*, published by the University of Alabama Press in 1983, takes the story to that point, albeit in a form limited by its pictorial format. E. Culpepper Clark's *The Schoolhouse Door* remains the authoritative account of attempted desegregation in 1956 and the successful breaching of the racial barrier in 1963. This author is indebted to Clark's seminal work as inspiration for *Turning the Tide*. What's needed is a history of the development of the university from 1970 to the present, one that explores the Capstone's growth as the "Third University of Alabama."

Index